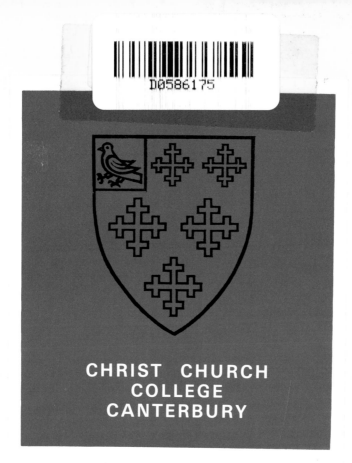

CHRIST CHURCH
COLLEGE
CANTERBURY

TWENTIETH CENTURY VIEWS

The aim of this series is to present the best in
contemporary critical opinion on major authors,
providing a twentieth century perspective on
their changing status in an era of profound
revaluation.

Maynard Mack, *Series Editor*
Yale University

MARLOWE

A COLLECTION OF CRITICAL ESSAYS

Edited by
Clifford Leech

A SPECTRUM BOOK

Prentice-Hall, Inc. *Englewood Cliffs, New Jersey*

Current printing (last digit):

11   10   9   8   7

Table of Contents

Introduction

by Clifford Leech

There is wide enough agreement that Marlowe is one of the major figures in English dramatic writing. That he was the most important of Shakespeare's predecessors—though born in the same year—is not disputed, nor is the poetic excellence of what Ben Jonson, in the Shakespeare Folio of 1623, called Marlowe's "mighty line." But beyond that the area of agreement is limited. There is uncertainty, or at least difference of opinion, concerning the kind of drama Marlowe wrote. And there is doubt concerning the stageworthiness of his plays. Certainly *Doctor Faustus* is revived from time to time, but it is a fortunate person who manages to see any other Marlowe play. *Tamburlaine* was revived at the Old Vic in 1951, and in Toronto and New York in 1956. Many have rightly praised the Marlowe Society production of *Edward II* that during a few weeks in the summer of 1958 was given at Cambridge, Stratford-upon-Avon, and London. Few people indeed have seen *The Jew of Malta,* and as far as I know there have been no performances of *The Massacre at Paris* and *Dido* since the sixteenth century. The theatre, it appears, has felt little confidence in Marlowe during the centuries since his death.

This is understandable in view of the state of the texts that have come down to us. *Tamburlaine* was printed in 1590, the printer admitting in an address to the reader that he had left out certain "fond and frivolous" things that he had found in the manuscript: whether these were Marlowe's own or another man's interpolations we cannot know. In general, the text of this play seems reliable, but it is a two-part play putting a considerable demand on the theatre's resources. The performances in London, Toronto, and New York were of a condensed version. *Doctor Faustus* exists in two texts, published in 1604 and 1616—that is, eleven and twenty-three years after the playwright's death. Neither version is reliable: in W. W. Greg's view, the earlier is a "bad quarto," based on a reconstruction from memory by a group of actors for provincial playing, and the later is dependent partly on the earlier version and partly on a manuscript (probably a first draft which Marlowe later revised).[1] Our modern texts of the play are generally based on the 1616 version, but it is clear that

---

[1] *Marlowe's Doctor Faustus 1604-1616: Parallel Texts,* ed. W. W. Greg (Oxford, 1950), pp. 60, 65, 80-81.

we can put no firm trust in its fidelity to Marlowe. *The Massacre at Paris* exists in a "bad quarto" too: it runs to just over 1200 lines, and must represent a drastically cut version of Marlowe's work. *The Jew of Malta* was not published until 1633, after it had been revived at the Cockpit Theatre and at court. For these performances the dramatist Thomas Heywood wrote special prologues and epilogues, and we cannot be entirely sure that he did not make some modifications in the text of the play. Only the texts of *Edward II* and *Dido,* both published in 1594, do not arouse suspicion.

Marlowe's career in the theatre lasted for approximately six years, and —if we count *Tamburlaine* as two—we have seven plays from his pen, three of them existing in particularly dubious shape. Moreover, though we can place *Tamburlaine* at the beginning of this short career (only *Dido* conceivably being earlier), we have no real clue to the order of composition of the other plays. It used to be generally believed that *Faustus* was written immediately after *Tamburlaine,* both being concerned with the aspiring mind, the respective heroes working through military conquest and the acquisition of knowledge. In recent years, however, a substantial number of scholars—probably a majority—have come to see *Faustus* as written in the last year of Marlowe's life, their case being supported by W. W. Greg's bibliographical argument that the 1592 edition of *The Damnable Life and Deserved Death of Doctor John Faustus* was certainly the first edition: this was an English version of the German *Faustbuch,* published in 1587, and Marlowe was evidently dependent to some extent on the translation.[2] Greg's case is perhaps not compelling, but it has not been formally disputed.

The contrast with Shakespeare is extreme. Not only has Shakespeare left us a much larger body of work spread over more than twenty years, but most of his plays have come down to us in tolerably good versions: except for *Pericles,* there is no play where we are wholly dependent on a "bad quarto." Moreover, there is general agreement about chronology. Some scholars will put certain plays a few years earlier than majority opinion suggests, but the order of composition is hardly in dispute except for one or two of the earliest writings and for *Timon of Athens.* It is not surprising that Marlowe is difficult to grasp, that the theatre responds to him with some uncertainty.

A man who died in 1593 belongs to the earliest phase of Elizabethan dramatic writing. It was a phase in which formal rhetoric was the staple medium of high utterance, when the long set speech was cultivated as a matter of course, when departures into informality stood out in sharp and simple contrast. A very few years after Marlowe's death, we can find Shakespeare and others using a much freer manner of writing, in which the tension could slacken unobtrusively. When Marlowe makes grotesque

[2] *Ibid.,* pp. 1-7.

fun in *Tamburlaine* by giving mocking prose-speeches to Calyphas, the hero's unruly son, or allows the high sentence of the play to slide suddenly into the formless baiting of Bajazeth in his cage, the effect is brusque and startling. Shakespeare in *Henry IV* or *Julius Caesar* can slip from formality to informality with ease, because—except in some cases of manifestly public utterance—the speech is never rigid, but is shot through with a sense of the casual, the improvised. Shakespeare is at his most Marlovian in *Richard III*, but the humor with which he endows Richard goes along with the sense of improvization that already in some measure comes into the picture. Tamburlaine and Faustus can laugh at an enemy's humiliation, never at their own prowess. To bring Marlowe to the stage today requires a mode of stylized acting which we lack, and an ability to harmonize the general formality with the occasional, but highly functional, use of sharp contrast.[3]

The fact that the twentieth century has hardly responded to the challenge has made the task of the critic much more difficult. If we cannot see the plays acted, we are inevitably making a guess when we discuss either their stageworthiness or the kind of effect they would have in the theatre. (Of course, even if they were revived more often, we should still need to relate what we saw on our stage to an imagining of what they were like when Edward Alleyn and his Admiral's Men were performing them.) However, the wide differences in the interpretation of Marlowe are comparatively new. The view current until some forty years ago, and in some quarters more recently than that, can be illustrated from Emile Legouis's comments on Marlowe in the *History of English Literature* that he wrote with Louis Cazamian.[4] The dramatist is described as "dazzled" by the idea of Tamburlaine, who "seemed to him a superior being, a superman to whom the petty rules of morality did not apply," who "is in the right" because he is "the conqueror of the world." This play is "simply Tamburlaine's life divided into scenes": "Nothing could be less dramatic or more monotonous." *Edward II,* though "better constructed than Marlowe's other plays," "shows the author's dramatic weakness the more clearly because of its very merits": it lacks "lucidity," "variety," and "dramatic progression." Marlowe was a "madcap" who "added nothing to dramatic technique saving that he determined the victory of blank verse." His heroes "were no more than his mouthpieces, voicing his extravagant dreams."

If we ask what has changed since Legouis was able to express these ideas as commonplaces of literary history, we can, I think, suggest three ways in which Marlowe criticism has taken new directions. The first matter we

[3] Marlowe's handling of the formal set speech is the subject of the extract here reprinted from Wolfgang Clemen's *Die Tragödie vor Shakespeare* (Heidelberg, 1955; English translation, London, 1961).
[4] The French edition first appeared in Paris in 1924; the passages referred to are in the 1934 edition of the English translation on pp. 413-21.

should note is that, however critics may differ in their total interpretations, most would now recognize in Marlowe's writing an intellectual quality of which we have hardly a glimpse in Legouis. In her essay on "Marlowe's Map," first published in 1924 and here reprinted, Miss Ethel Seaton showed how carefully Marlowe prepared for the writing of *Tamburlaine* by mastering the geographical complexities of Tamburlaine's world. Though he is not likely to have travelled further than France, he saw to it that he knew where places were in relation to one another, as far as current information could serve him. Moreover, his use of source material for this play was extensive, shown most fully in Roy W. Battenhouse's *Marlowe's Tamburlaine* (1941), from which an extract is here reprinted. For most popular English writers of the sixteenth century, "Mahomet" was simply a bogy-word, a suitable invocation for a morality Vice figure. Marlowe alone among Elizabethan dramatists could see the fittingness of a Moslem doing honor to Christ, a major prophet in the world of Islam. And Paul H. Kocher in his book *Christopher Marlowe: A Study of his Thought, Learning and Character* (1946) and in a number of articles in learned journals has emphasized that the blasphemies reported of Marlowe by the informer Richard Baines and Marlowe's fellow dramatist Thomas Kyd were the result of some substantial theological study. One of Kocher's articles, here reprinted, attempts to reconstruct the "atheist lecture" that, according to Richard Chomley, Marlowe had read in Raleigh's presence. The playwright's learning is further demonstrated in another article in this volume, Greg's "The Damnation of Faustus," first published in 1946, where Marlowe is shown as fascinated by the medieval notion of "demoniality" and as using Faustus's practice of this vice as marking his definitive adherence to the forces of hell. More recently, Eugene M. Waith in *The Herculean Hero* (1962) has studied *Tamburlaine* as a variant on the Hercules myth which the Renaissance had inherited from antiquity. Although Waith, unlike Battenhouse, sees Tamburlaine as predominantly demanding the audience's admiration, his view is by no means that Marlowe is an adolescent actualizing his dreams: rather, he is a writer conscious of the tradition, molding and extending it.

Most of the scholars who have thus made us aware of the intellectual stature of Marlowe have been indebted to the six-volume edition of his works published in the years 1930-1933 under the general editorship of R. H. Case. The indication of sources alone, amply documented in this edition, annihilates the idea of Marlowe as an intoxicated undergraduate seizing on any opportunity to identify himself with an aspiring mind, and as a man merely fated to transform the nature of English blank verse.

The second way in which the picture has been changed is in the growth of an awareness that the nature of Marlowe's writing is as complex as that of most major Elizabethans and Jacobeans. It would be manifestly wrong to see *Faustus* and *Macbeth,* or *Edward II* and *Henry IV,* as equally complex, but we can find in Marlowe that degree of complexity which we associate with Jonson or Webster or perhaps even Chapman. This idea may have been first suggested in T. S. Eliot's well-known essay of 1918, which is put first in this volume, not merely because of its date but because in its brief compass it ran counter to the previously current view. Eliot raises the question whether Marlowe was, in temperament and outlook, a tragic writer, and suggests that *The Jew of Malta* at least has a strain of dark humor anticipatory of *Volpone.* It has become a commonplace to echo this, but there is as yet no sufficient recognition of the important place of the comic in the fabric of all Marlowe's writing. Even in *Hero and Leander,* C. S. Lewis could protest that humor had to be, and was, kept rigorously at bay.[5] But the beginning of a perception of the comic element—that is, of Marlowe's recognition of the puniness of human ambition, the ludicrous gap between aspiration and any possible fulfillment, the basic oneness between the grandest, most self-absorbed figure and the slightest of crushable pygmies—goes along with a generally subtler interpretation of the plays. The damnation of Faustus, as seen in the short extract here reprinted from Una Ellis-Fermor's *The Frontiers of Drama* (1945), carries with it, though covertly expressed, a total repudiation of the Christian scheme. Harry Levin in *The Overreacher* (1954), of which the concluding section is given in this volume, talks of *Faustus* in terms of a Blake paradox, seeing the playwright in the end as closer to Mephostophilis than to Faustus: "Through his agency Marlowe succeeds in setting the parable of intelligence and experience within a Christian framework, even while hinting that the framework is arbitrary and occasionally glancing beyond it." Similarly, in a passage from his *Marlowe: Dr. Faustus* (1962) here reprinted, J. P. Brockbank has invoked the authority of D. H. Lawrence, relating to Marlowe's play the novelist's assertion that a work of art "must contain the essential criticism of the morality to which it adheres." Both Levin and Brockbank, though with differing degrees of stress, see the play as hovering between morality-play statement and tragic implication. So, too, does Nicholas Brooke in his article "The Moral Tragedy of Doctor Faustus." [6] Miss Helen Gardner has argued for a special irony in Part II of *Tamburlaine,* seeing it as by no means an attempt to reproduce the effect of Part I or merely to carry on the story to the hero's death.[7] And, of *Tamburlaine* as a whole, G. I. Duthie has urged that we should recognize its firm structure.[8] He presents

[5] *English Literature in the Sixteenth Century excluding Drama* (Oxford, 1954), p. 487.
[6] "The Moral Tragedy of Doctor Faustus," *Cambridge Journal,* V (August 1952), 662-87.
[7] "The Second Part of 'Tamburlaine the Great,'" *Modern Language Review,* xxxvii (January 1942), 18-24.
[8] The Dramatic Structure of Marlowe's 'Tamburlaine the Great,' Parts I and II," *English Studies 1948* (London, 1948), pp. 101-26.

Part I as a conflict between Honor and Beauty, with a resolution when Tamburlaine spares Zenocrate's father at her entreaty, thus modifying his previous course of destruction, and Part II as a conflict between Honor and Death, similarly resolved when Tamburlaine becomes willing to die, yet insures the continuation of his empire through the succession of his eldest son. We may feel that this account of the matter makes the plays altogether too neat, and in particular that Duthie misses an important irony in the ending of Part II, but the contrast between this conception of *Tamburlaine* and the older view that it was merely a succession of similar scenes, arbitrarily dramatizing episodes from the hero's life, is indeed extreme. Though the subject needs further study, we can nevertheless recognize in Duthie's article an important moment in Marlowe criticism, surely a point of no return. We are unlikely to go back to the notion of Marlowe as a dramatist who merely looked for occasions of verbal and visual display. The difference in tone is noticeable between the old view and that expressed by Tyrone Guthrie in his preface to the cut text prepared by him and Donald Wolfit (1951):[9] although Guthrie's conception does not suggest conflict and resolution in Duthie's way, we no longer hear of "Tamburlaine's life divided into scenes," but of "a sort of ritual dance" and "a kind of savage Oratorio." Both terms suggest that the playwright has ordered his material.

Critical recognition of the complexity of Marlowe's work has inevitably induced a wider range of interpretation. This can be broadly characterized as extending from Christian to agnostic views of the plays. For some, Marlowe the dramatist, whatever the opinions of Marlowe the man or whatever impatiently blasphemous remarks he may have let fall (and did let fall if we credit Kyd and Baines), is always a Christian writer. *Faustus* is a morality play ending in damnation, the final chorus enunciating the lesson in the way of a morality epilogue. That does not mean that we are not invited to feel the horror and the pity of damnation: the closer we are brought to the hero's plight, it is argued, the more terrible is the picture of Divine Wrath, the more precious the Divine Mercy which Faustus rejected. This is the view put forward by Douglas Cole in his *Suffering and Evil in the Plays of Christopher Marlowe* (1962) and by John D. Jump in his Revels Plays edition of *Faustus* (1962). It is at the opposite extreme to the view of Una Ellis-Fermor and Paul H. Kocher, in their books already referred to, where Marlowe is seen as taking the opportunity offered by this story to express, in a necessarily oblique fashion, his quarrel with the Christian notion of the universe. Roy W. Battenhouse's book on *Tamburlaine* has been mentioned above for its account of Marlowe's learning: it is important, too, for its thesis that the play is written as a warning to Elizabethans of the destruction that the ambitious man and the tyrant bring on themselves as well as on others. Al-

---

[9] *Tamburlaine the Great: An Acting Version prepared and introduced by Tyrone Guthrie and Donald Wolfit* (London, 1951).

though Battenhouse does perhaps recognize a higher degree of ambivalence in the play than he fully admits—noting with pleasure that the
binding of his book has the colors red, black and gold that meant much to
the dramatist—his interpretation would put *Tamburlaine* within the
same category (though of course of a far different order of excellence) as
Preston's *Cambises,* which did indeed show that tyrants must expect to be
confronted with an exhaustion of God's patience. Not many critics have
accepted this view as a whole, but Battenhouse's book has had a noticeable effect on subsequent writings on the play. Eugene M. Waith—though
seeing *Tamburlaine* as one of a group of plays where, under the influence
of classical epic or myth, the writer chooses for his hero a man who struggles to extend the limits of human sovereignty, who arouses admiration
through his challenge of destiny—nevertheless brings out the antitheses in
the character's presentation. Waith's account is subtler than Battenhouse's, but it is partly because of Battenhouse's work that no critic today
is likely to talk of the play as merely a glad story of conquest.

Our interpretation of *Tamburlaine,* however, may also partly depend
on what we have learned about conquest through living in the twentieth
century. Indeed Marlowe profits, with Shakespeare and Webster, from
the deeper understanding that has come to us through the intimate awareness of cruelty and insanity that we have been unable to avoid. The
plucking out of Gloucester's eyes, the mental torment imposed on the
Duchess of Malfi, the physical dreadfulness of Edward II's death, of
Bajazeth's exposure in his cage, of the king-drawn chariot—these can no
longer be seen as things merely contrived to please the groundlings or as
relics of a barbarous past. We are more likely now to see that Shakespeare
and Webster and Marlowe were making their audiences contemplate
actuality, and an actuality placed within a context of evaluation. The
dreadfulness is always underlined, whether by semi-choral comment (as
with Cornwall's servants in *Lear* or with Bosola's and Ferdinand's remorse
in *The Duchess of Malfi*) or by a minuteness of documentation, even of the
tormentors' and executioners' glee, which exposes the spectacle as an
abortive attempt to give pleasure to those who within the play contrive it.
Of course there was horror enough in the nineteenth century, when
scholars and critics could see these things in drama as extravagance, but it
was not so often a horror that scholars and critics had to live with as they
read. Here the change in the general aspect of things has supplemented
the fruits of academic research to clarify our notion of what these playwrights were doing.

The third notable movement in Marlowe criticism has done little more
than show its beginnings. This is the consideration of Marlowe's relation
to the stage in the few years of his working career. C. F. Tucker Brooke,
in his *Life of Marlowe* included in the Case edition, suggested that Part I
of *Tamburlaine* was written for an innyard theatre in which the dramatist
had little more than a bare platform and simple doors on stage level to

make use of, while Part II shows that a more elaborate stage was envisaged, with "relatively more detailed stage devices." [10] That perhaps is not the only explanation of the freer disposition of the incidents in Part II, but the difference from Part I does at least suggest that Marlowe was more conscious of the full resources of the Elizabethan stage than he had been. An attempt to reconstruct how *Tamburlaine* or *Faustus* was originally put on the stage is, with our limited knowledge of the Elizabethan playhouse, necessarily hazardous. Yet, if we are to see Marlowe's work with any degree of adequacy, we must in reading it be always concerned with its relation to the theatrical conditions within which he worked. We know that in scene xix of *Faustus*[11] the heavenly throne that was intended for the protagonist descends from above, and that somehow *"Hell is discovered"*—effectively if this is done by the opening of a trap with smoke rising from it, in polar opposition to the heavenly descent. At the beginning of this scene (which is in the 1616 text only) Lucifer, Beelzebub, and Mephostophilis enter: since Boas's edition in the Case Marlowe (1932), it has been usual to insert *"above"* in the stage direction. The infernal trinity remain on stage until Faustus is carried away by devils after his soliloquy. We cannot prove the *"above,"* but it would obviously be most convenient to have them there. If that is how Marlowe saw it, we have here a remarkable inversion of the universe's normal order. It is the infernal trinity who preside over, and look down on, the action: they oversee the heavenly throne, the burning chair awaiting Faustus in hell, and the Good and Bad Angels who must appear on the main stage. The visual effect, indeed, reinforces the ambivalence that Levin and Brockbank and others have noted in the text itself. So daring is the device that at this point the extreme view of Una Ellis-Fermor becomes harder to refute. And it is achieved, if the conjectures about staging are right, through Marlowe's employment of the Elizabethan theatre's resources. Another example of the way in which the visual effect carries a powerful implication is seen at the end of Part I of *Tamburlaine,* when the dead bodies of Bajazeth, Zabena, and the King of Arabia are still on the stage when Zenocrate is crowned, when she is betrothed to Tamburlaine, when the hero makes "truce with all the world." Here, indeed, Marlowe reinforces the visual effect by making Tamburlaine refer to the bodies: otherwise they might not be sufficiently noticeable when the hero is speaking his words of triumph. Nevertheless, their presence charges his words with irony: we are reminded of what the triumph is costing, the question of its worth is raised. Similarly in *Edward II,* IV, vi, when Edward and Spencer and Baldock have taken refuge in the Abbey of Neath, the emissaries of Mortimer are led to the king by "a Mower." This figure

---

[10] *The Life of Marlowe and The Tragedy of Dido Queen of Carthage,* ed. C. F. Tucker Brooke (London, 1930), pp. 64-65.
[11] I am here using the scene numbering in John D. Jump's Revels edition.

speaks only twice: "Upon my life, those be the men ye seek" on his entry
and "Your worship, I trust, will remember me?" when the king has been
led away and the informer seeks payment. The text describes this man before his entry simply as "A gloomy fellow in a mead below," but the
stage direction, which a reader may not sufficiently attend to, suggests that
he comes with his scythe. The presence of this almost silent figure on the
stage at the time of Edward's capture has a manifestly powerful effect.[12]
Examples such as these demonstrate that Marlowe thought not merely in
terms of lavish spectacle, that he had a dramatist's eye for that kind of
dumb eloquence that can reside in a purely visual device, that the total
effect of a scene in his plays may depend on an interrelation of the aural
and visual properties of the theatre. More work seems to be required in
this kind of exploration of his text.

Meanwhile David M. Bevington's *From Mankind to Marlowe* (1962)
has related Marlowe's plays to the moralities that provided the staple en-
tertainment of the popular stage through the greater part of the sixteenth
century. This book, from which a passage is here reprinted, strengthens
our idea of Marlowe's dramatic and theatrical inheritance, bringing closer
to us the nature of the theatre that he found waiting for him in London.

If, however, we seem to be near the beginning of things here, that is
perhaps not uncharacteristic of the state of Marlowe criticism. Certainly
enormous steps forward have been taken since the early years of this
century, and the distinction of some recent writing is beyond question.
Yet the nature of Marlowe's drama remains a thing that most readers are
still groping after. Partly, of course, this is due to the theatre's neglect;
partly, too, it arises from his difference from Shakespeare, his use of characters that are drawn in the broad outlines that he inherited from his
predecessors, with little of the detailed verisimilitude that marks the later
Shakespeare; and partly it is the result of his kind of verse. Everyone
praises his eloquence. It is an eloquence in which the drive is straight-
forward, in which the terms do not constitute a paradox, as they frequently do in early seventeenth-century drama. The ambivalences of
Marlowe are on the large scale, depending sometimes on the clash of
aural and visual effects, sometimes quite simply, but deliberately, on over-
assertion.

We need, too, a fuller study of his less-known plays. Little has been
written about *The Massacre at Paris* or *Dido Queen of Carthage;* yet both
these plays could contribute powerfully to an understanding of Marlowe's
work. That one exists only in a "bad quarto" and that the other may
perhaps be, as its title-page asserts, a collaboration should not deter
Marlowe's readers from finding clues here, both to his double view of the
aspiring mind and perhaps to his notion of the irresponsibility with which

[12] Cf. the editor's article, "Marlowe's 'Edward II': Power and Suffering," *Critical Quarterly*, I (Autumn 1959), 181-96.

the universe functions. And we need to remember, too, that Marlowe is also the author of *Hero and Leander,* that magnificent and widely influential epyllion[13] in which he shows a supreme and mocking disrespect for the universe's governors and at the same time sees his human beings as beautiful and fragile and capable of joy. He was author, too, of translations of Ovid's *Elegies* and of the first book of Lucan—the poetry of love and the poetry of disastrous war.

There is a large-mindedness in Marlowe that could not easily have been imagined by those who called him "madcap" not so long ago. He had a profound sense of the Christian scheme: no one has written better in English of the beatific vision and the wrath of God. He could resent man's subjection to the divine will. He could express, too, a sense of horror at the very aspiration that was part of his own being. He had learning, diligence, and a growing sense of theatrical possibility. He could write about cruelty, and show the dreadfulness of it; about ambition, and see as clearly as anyone that its goal is by its nature unreachable. He could make a dramatic character abjure and defy his god, and see the comedy of the assertiveness. He could communicate an understanding of the processes of love, heterosexual or homosexual—no one has put these things better than in the simple exchange between Mortimer and Edward:

> *Mor. jun.* Why should you love him whom the world hates so?
> *K. Edw.* Because he loves me more than all the world.

—and yet see that Faustus's love for the appearance of Helen, or Dido's love for Aeneas, or Edward's love for Gaveston, could mean death and destruction. He had not much interest in the welfare of kingdoms, making *Edward II* a more personal play than any of Shakespeare's histories and *The Massacre at Paris* a pageant of human inadequacy rather than a chronicle of national suffering. He was not much conscious of change or development in character, but perhaps Shakespeare too was less interested in that than is commonly believed. He wrote tragedy because he was aware that man's aspirations made his destruction more poignant. His tragedy had always an undercurrent of comedy because he had a sense of the absurdity of man's trying. He knew what virtue means, as shown in the Olympia of Part II of *Tamburlaine* and in the Abigail of *The Jew of Malta,* and he knew that its existence rebukes the aspiring mind. And he could understand remorse, as in Faustus and in the Sigismund of Part II of *Tamburlaine.* He could laugh at politics, as in *The Massacre at Paris,* and yet see the evil that political intrigue led to. He could suggest a world

---

[13] Its influence has been fully demonstrated by Miss Elizabeth Story Donno in her *Elizabethan Minor Epics* (London, 1963).

in which men kept faith with one another, as they do not do in *Tamburlaine, The Jew of Malta, The Massacre, Edward II,* but he knew better than to dramatize that world directly. Insofar as power was a dream he shared, it was one that he looked at with astonishingly clear eyes, admiring the man who fully and remorselessly exercised that power, yet knowing his term was limited, his ambition never satisfied, his self-regard comic.

We come back to our need of the theatre. *Faustus* must be done in a way that is not a pious exercise, that does not shirk its disturbing quality. *Tamburlaine,* for all its difficulty, must be with us more often, as must *Edward II* and the smaller plays. Yet, though the scholar has much to learn from the theatre—needs the theatre in order properly to understand the plays that were written for it—the people of the theatre need the scholar's help when undertaking to put Marlowe on the stage. His inheritance was a complicated one, from the medieval church drama and from the classical drama rediscovered, from Christian and from pagan ethic. His playhouse was near the beginning of its development into the superb instrument it became from 1594, when Shakespeare's company, the Lord Chamberlain's Men, was formed after Marlowe's death. His plays, as we have seen, depend on an interrelation of visual and verbal properties. Though *Tamburlaine* is carefully constructed, it has the epic manner. Though *Faustus* is "modern" in thought, it has the guise of a morality play. Though *Edward II* is an intimate study of human relations in high places, it is emergent from the broad-canvased pageant of the *Henry VI* plays. An uninformed production of a Marlowe play might do more harm than good. With all the plays of Shakespeare's time, including Shakespeare's own, we need in the future a closer collaboration than in the past between scholar and director and actor. But with Marlowe the need is extreme. When Bertolt Brecht and Lion Feuchtwanger made a German adaptation of *Edward II* in 1924, they rationalized the ill-treatment of Edward by having him refuse to abdicate, they made his killing a mere suffocation, they missed entirely the large ambulation of the kingdom that Marlowe insisted on (for Brecht and Feuchtwanger, Tynemouth was a place easily within reach of London), they diluted both the sense of gratuitous, but profoundly intelligible, horror and the sense of Edward's dispersed wanderings. And doubtless many of us have seen *Faustus* presented in a fashion that accommodated the play to the simplest Christian's notion of decorum.

Even so, the beginnings of Marlowe criticism are with us. In the remaining years of this century we may yet have on our stages, and in the minds of scholars, a fuller realization of the way in which eloquence and irony, word and visual effect, the comic and the tragic, are fused in his plays. And this despite the condition in which several of the texts have come down to us, despite his belonging to the earliest phase of the major Elizabethan theatre.

Christopher Marlowe

by T. S. Eliot

Swinburne observes of Marlowe that "the father of English tragedy and the creator of English blank verse was therefore also the teacher and the guide of Shakespeare." In this sentence there are two misleading assumptions and two misleading conclusions. Kyd has as good a title to the first honour as Marlowe; Surrey has a better title to the second; and Shakespeare was not taught or guided by one of his predecessors or contemporaries alone. The less questionable judgment is that Marlowe exercised a strong influence over later drama, though not himself as great a dramatist as Kyd; that he introduced several new tones into blank verse and commenced the dissociative process which drew it further and further away from the rhythms of rhymed verse; and that when Shakespeare borrowed from him, which was pretty often at the beginning, Shakespeare either made something inferior or something different.

The comparative study of English versification at various periods is a large tract of unwritten history. To make a study of blank verse alone would be to elicit some curious conclusions. It would show, I believe, that blank verse within Shakespeare's lifetime was more highly developed, that it became the vehicle of more varied and more intense feeling than it has ever conveyed since; and that after the erection of the Chinese Wall of Milton blank verse has suffered not only arrest but retrogression. That the blank verse of Tennyson, for example, a consummate master of this form in certain applications, is cruder (*not* "rougher" or less perfect in technique) than that of half a dozen contemporaries of Shakespeare; cruder, because less capable of expressing complicated, subtle, and surprising emotions.

Every writer who has written any blank verse worth saving has produced particular tones which his verse and no other's is capable of rendering; and we should keep this in mind when we talk about "influences" and "indebtedness." Shakespeare is "universal" because he has more of these tones than anyone else; but they are all out of the one man; one man cannot be more than one man; there might have been six Shakespeares at once without conflicting frontiers; and to say that Shakespeare expressed nearly all human emotions, implying that he left very little for anyone else, is a radical misunderstanding of art and the artist—a misunderstanding which, even when explicitly rejected, may lead to our neglecting the effort of attention necessary to discover the specific properties of the verse of Shakespeare's contemporaries. The development of blank verse may be likened to the analysis of that astonishing industrial product coal-tar. Marlowe's verse is one of the earlier derivatives, but it possesses properties which are not repeated in any of the analytic or synthetic blank verses discovered somewhat later.

The "vices of style" of Marlowe's and Shakespeare's age is a convenient name for a number of vices, no one of which, perhaps, was shared by all of the writers. It is pertinent, at least, to remark that Marlowe's "rhetoric" is not, or not characteristically, Shakespeare's rhetoric; that Marlowe's rhetoric consists in a pretty simple huffe-snuffe bombast while Shakespeare's is more exactly a vice of style, a tortured perverse ingenuity of images which dissipates instead of concentrating the imagination, and which may be due in part to influences by which Marlowe was untouched. Next, we find that Marlowe's vice is one which he was gradually attenuating, and even, what is more miraculous, turning into a virtue. And we find that this poet of torrential imagination recognized many of his best bits (and those of one or two others), saved them, and reproduced them more than once, almost invariably improving them in the process.

It is worth while noticing a few of these versions because they indicate, somewhat contrary to usual opinion, that Marlowe was a deliberate and conscious workman. Mr. J. M. Robertson has spotted an interesting theft of Marlowe's from Spenser. Here is Spenser (*Faery Queen,* i. vii. 32):

> Like to an almond tree y-mounted high
>> On top of green Selinis all alone,
> With blossoms brave bedeckèd daintily;
>> Whose tender locks do tremble every one
> At every little breath that under heaven is blown.

And here Marlowe (*Tamburlaine,* Part II. Act iv. Sc. iii):

> Like to an almond tree ymounted high
> Upon the lofty and celestial mount
> Of evergreen Selinus, quaintly decked
> With blooms more white than Herycina's brows,
> Whose tender blossoms tremble every one
> At every little breath that thorough heaven is blown.

This is interesting, not only as showing that Marlowe's talent, like that of most poets, was partly synthetic, but also because it seems to give a clue to some particularly "lyric" effects found in *Tamburlaine,* not in Marlowe's other plays, and not, I believe, anywhere else. For example, the praise of Zenocrate in Part II. Act II. Sc. iv:

> Now walk the angels on the walls of heaven,
> As sentinels to warn th' immortal souls
> To entertain divine Zenocrate.

This is not Spenser's movement, but the influence of Spenser must be present. There had been no great blank verse before Marlowe; but there was the powerful presence of this great master of melody immediately precedent; and the combination produced results which could not be repeated. I do not think that it can be claimed that Peele had any influence here.

The passage quoted from Spenser has a further interest. It will be noted that the fourth line:

> With blooms more white than Herycina's brows,

is Marlowe's contribution. Compare this with these other lines of Marlowe:

> So looks my love, shadowing in her brows
>
> *(Tamburlaine)*
>
> Like to the shadows of Pyramides
>
> *(Tamburlaine)*

and the final and best version:

> Shadowing more beauty in their airy brows
> Than have the white breasts of the queen of love
>
> *(Doctor Faustus)*

and compare the whole set with Spenser again *(F. Q.)*:

> Upon her eyelids many graces sate
> Under the shadow of her even brows,

a passage which Mr. Robertson says Spenser himself used in three other places.

This economy is frequent in Marlowe. Within *Tamburlaine* it occurs in the form of monotony, especially in the facile use of resonant names (*e.g.* the recurrence of "Caspia" or "Caspian" with the same tone effect), a practice in which Marlowe was followed by Milton, but which Marlowe himself outgrew. Again,

> Zenocrate, lovelier than the love of Jove,
> Brighter than is the silver Rhodope,

is paralleled later by

> Zenocrate, the loveliest maid alive,
> Fairer than rocks of pearl and precious stone.

One line Marlowe remodels with triumphant success:

> And set black streamers in the firmament
>
> (*Tamburlaine*)

becomes

> See, see, where Christ's blood streams in the firmament!
>
> (*Doctor Faustus*)

The verse accomplishments of *Tamburlaine* are notably two: Marlowe gets into blank verse the melody of Spenser, and he gets a new driving power by reinforcing the sentence period against the line period. The rapid long sentence, running line into line, as in the famous soliloquies "Nature compounded of four elements" and "What is beauty, saith my sufferings, then?", marks the certain escape of blank verse from the rhymed couplet, and from the elegiac or rather pastoral note of Surrey to which Tennyson returned. If you contrast these two soliloquies with the verse of Marlowe's greatest contemporary, Kyd—by no means a despicable versifier—you see the importance of the innovation:

> The one took sanctuary, and, being sent for out,
> Was murdered in Southwark as he passed
> To Greenwich, where the Lord Protector lay.
> Black Will was burned in Flushing on a stage;
> Green was hanged at Osbridge in Kent . . .

which is not really inferior to:

> So these four abode
> Within one house together; and as years
> Went forward, Mary took another mate;
> But Dora lived unmarried till her death.
>
> (Tennyson, *Dora*)

In *Faustus* Marlowe went further: he broke up the line, to a gain in intensity, in the last soliloquy; and he developed a new and important conversational tone in the dialogues of *Faustus* with the devil. *Edward II* has never lacked consideration: it is more desirable, in brief space, to remark upon two plays, one of which has been misunderstood and the other underrated. These are the *Jew of Malta* and *Dido Queen of Carthage*. Of the first of these it has always been said that the end, even the last two acts, are unworthy of the first three. If one takes the *Jew of Malta* not as a tragedy, or as a "tragedy of blood," but as a farce, the concluding act becomes intelligible; and if we attend with a careful ear to the versification, we find that Marlowe develops a tone to suit this farce, and even perhaps that this tone is his most powerful and mature tone. I say farce, but with the enfeebled humour of our times the word is a misnomer; it is the farce of the old English humour, the terribly serious even savage comic humour, the humour which spent its last breath in the decadent genius of Dickens. It has nothing in common with J. M. Barrie, Captain Bairnsfather, or *Punch*. It is the humour of that very serious (but very different) play, *Volpone*.

> First, be thou void of these affections,
> Compassion, love, vain hope, and heartless fear,
> Be mov'd at nothing, see thou pity none . . .
> As for myself, I walk abroad a nights,
> And kill sick people groaning under walls:
> Sometimes I go about and poison wells . . .

and the last words of Barabas complete this prodigious caricature:

> But now begins the extremity of heat
> To pinch me with intolerable pangs:
> Die, life! fly, soul! tongue, curse thy fill, and die!

It is something which Shakespeare could not do, and which he did not want to do.

Dido appears to be a hurried play, perhaps done to order with the *Æneid* in front of him. But even here there is progress. The account of the sack of Troy is in this newer style of Marlowe's, this style which secures its emphasis by always hesitating on the edge of caricature at the right moment:

> The Grecian soldiers, tir'd with ten years' war,
> Began to cry, "Let us unto our ships,
> Troy is invincible, why stay we here?" . . .

> By this, the camp was come unto the walls,
> And through the breach did march into the streets,
> Where, meeting with the rest, "Kill, kill!" they cried. . . .

> And after him, his band of Myrmidons,
> With balls of wild-fire in their murdering paws . . .

> At last, the soldiers pull'd her by the heels,
> And swung her howling in the empty air. . . .

> We saw Cassandra sprawling in the streets . . .

This is not Virgil, or Shakespeare; it is pure Marlowe. By comparing the whole speech with Clarence's dream in *Richard III,* one acquires a little insight into the difference between Marlowe and Shakespeare:

> What scourge for perjury
> Can this dark monarchy afford false Clarence?

There, on the other hand, is what Marlowe's style could not do; the phrase has a concision which is almost classical, certainly Dantesque. Again, as often with the Elizabethan dramatists, there are lines in Marlowe, besides the many lines that Shakespeare adapted, that might have been written by either:

> If thou wilt stay,
> Leap in mine arms; mine arms are open wide;
> If not, turn from me, and I'll turn from thee;
> For though thou hast the heart to say farewell,
> I have not power to stay thee.

But the direction in which Marlowe's verse might have moved, had he not "dyed swearing," is quite un-Shakespearian, is toward this intense and serious and indubitably great poetry, which, like some great painting and sculpture, attains its effects by something not unlike caricature.

The Dead Shepherd

by Harry Levin

John Lyly had been the innovator in comedy, as Marlowe was in tragedy. When Lyly switched from Euphuistic prose to blank verse in his latest play, *The Woman in the Moon,* his passionate shepherds could but adopt the Marlovian speech of persuasion:

I'le giue thee streames whose pibble shalbe pearle . . .

(V, i, 104)

Robert Greene had balked at the adoption of blank verse as the idiom of tragedy. Yet Greene was never the man to resist a fashion; and, with the triumph of *Tamburlaine,* he tried to out-brave the Marlovian speech of intimidation.

I clap vp *Fortune* in a cage of gold,

boasts *Alphonsus* (1481); but the royal canopy of Aragon makes a feeble showing after the Scythian chariot drawn by kings. *Selimus,* the most abjectly imitative of these camp-following tragedies of ambition, verbally reckons with "millions of Diadems" (1620). But the imitation multiplies the compliment to Marlowe's originality, and the multiplication quickly attains the point of diminishing returns. Marlowe had endowed the purposes of Elizabethan drama with words and gestures, both persuasive and intimidating, which were repeated until they exhausted their impact. After a decade of Tamburlaine and his followers, their speeches were tagged as "fustian"—the sort of cheap material that wears badly, and that looks better on the stage than anywhere else. Fustian had its inveterate admirers but they too were disreputable, notably Ancient Pistol in the second part of *Henry IV.* Even Pistol's befuddled echo rings hollow, and redounds to the disadvantage of Tamburlaine's pomp:

"The Dead Shepherd." From *The Overreacher: A Study of Christopher Marlowe* by Harry Levin. Copyright 1952 by the President and Fellows of Harvard College. Reprinted by permission of the author, Harvard University Press, and Faber and Faber, Ltd. The pages reprinted here are part of the chapter entitled "The Dead Shepherd."

These be good Humors indeede. Shall Pack-Horses,
And hollow-pamper'd Iades of Asia,
Which cannot goe but thirtie miles a day,
Compare with *Caesar,* and with Caniballs,
And Troian Greekes? . . .
> Shall we fall foule for Toyes?

> (II, iv, 177-83)

By the turn of the century, *Tamburlaine* was synonymous with that brash theatricality which the English theatre had now outgrown. The role that Alleyn had created was truly a part to tear a cat in, to split the ears of the groundlings and make Hamlet grit his teeth; while Hamlet's creator Burbage, and other more sophisticated actors soon to be patronized by King James I, developed with the developing Shakespearean repertory at the new Globe Theatre. Meanwhile Shakespeare had rounded out the cycle of histories with *Henry V,* which coincided chronologically with the highest point in the fortunes of the Earl of Essex. The last few years of Elizabeth's reign heralded the Stuarts with a waning of political hopes and a tightening of economic opportunities. Literature reversed its heroic trend; satire flourished; poets waxed introspective; tragic heroes were, typically, disinherited princes rather than self-enthroning conquerors.

Attempts have been made to enlarge the restricted canon of Marlowe's plays by ascribing to him the authorship of several Shakespearean histories, with presumptive revision and collaboration in varying degrees from the other University Wits and from the upstart crow himself. The most recent and rigorous bibliographical studies, however, render unto Shakespeare the substantial integrity of his text. To think of him rather as an emulator than as a collaborator is sounder in every respect and enables us to watch him assimilating and bettering his instructions. It was enough for Marlowe, with his other achievements, to have written *Edward II.* Shakespeare's journeywork is full of unassimilated Marlowe and smells no less of the classics than it would if he too had gone to the university. But it was Shakespeare's mastery of the English chronicle that gave the drama a local habitation and gradually eliminated its artificial colouring.

Not *Amurath,* an *Amurath* succeeds,
But *Harry, Harry,*

in the second part of *Henry IV* (V, ii, 48-9). Hotspur, in the first part, is not so much a Marlovian character as a characterization of the Marlovian attitude in all its intransigence, truculence, and grandiloquence. But Hotspur is the champion of a losing cause; and for his practical rival, Prince Henry, the sweetness of a crown is hedged with cares and responsibilities.

For Macbeth it is much more complex; and ambition is revenged by conscience long before Macduff has whetted his sword. Yet, whenever Shakespeare's heroes stand with their backs to the wall defying the world, they
betray a wild trick of their Marlovian ancestors: Othello in his valedic-
tory, Coriolanus at the gates of Rome, Antony flinging the absolute
alternative: "Let Rome in Tyber melt . . ." (I, i, 33). Hyperbole pre-
supposes exalted occasions; if the time is unpropitious, the result is bathos
—or, at any rate, belittlement. When Marlowe's tropes were pirated for
The Taming of a Shrew, making the domestication of Kate sound like the
tenth labour of Hercules, they covered the short distance between the
sublime and the ridiculous. When Thomas Nashe deliberately squinted
through the wrong end of the telescope, he improvised a hyperbolic prose
which was hailed as the English counterpart of Aretino's invective. Somehow the fine madness, the *furor poeticus,* was becoming a stranger and re-
moter phenomenon. Such pedestrian forms as domestic drama asked for a
less elevated tone: *Arden of Feversham* was least convincing in its
"Ouidlike" embellishments of middle-class adultery (I, i, 60). Such a play
as Dekker's *Old Fortunatus* marks a transition by skilfully alternating between a Marlovian sphere of wish-fulfilment and the prosaic realism of
every day.

The daring-dash-and-grandiosity, to sum up Marlowe's style in a Goe-
thean phrase, was no longer attuned to the epoch. Shakespeare had
glanced in passing at the new spirit, the increasingly social and psychological observation of playwrights, when he permitted Pistol to speak of
humours. This was the slogan for Jonsonian comedy; and Jonson's *Dis-
coveries* would look back, with neo-classical asperity, at "the *Tamerlanes,*
and *Tamer-Chams* of the late Age, which had nothing in them but the
scenicall strutting and furious vociferation, to warrant them to the ignorant gapers" (777-9). But, even with Ben Jonson, the gap is wide between critical theory and theatrical practice; and in the theatre, as T. S.
Eliot has shown, "Jonson is the legitimate heir of Marlowe." That pat-
rimony was equivocal, like the will that defrauds the heirs in *Volpone*
while enticements are dangling under their very noses. Jonson unques-
tionably inherited Marlowe's rhetoric of enticement; but, whereas most
of Marlowe's characters take the proffered jewels and delicacies at their
face value, Jonson's cheaters employ them as Barabas did—to ensnare and
delude. Jonson never lets us forget how selfishly and how unnaturally
they deviate from the norms of morality, as when Volpone promises Celia:

> . . . could we get the phoenix
> (Though nature lost her kind) shee were our dish.
>
> (III, vii, 204-5)

The luxuries of *Volpone,* though tainted, are perfectly tangible; those
of *The Alchemist* do not really exist, but are conjured up by such puis-

sant and mighty talk as that of Sir Epicure Mammon; and the alchemy itself is no magical art but a coney-catching swindle devised by Subtle, "the FAUSTUS, / That . . . cures / Plague, piles, and poxe" (IV, vi, 46-8). Here again, poetry and life are at odds; what is concrete with Marlowe is insubstantial with Jonson; the imaginative fabric is exploited to mask a sordid scene. Jonson's locale is ordinarily what Marlowe's was fitfully at Malta and Paris, the city and especially the underworld. In the Rome of *Sejanus,* neutralized by the pressures of opportunism, "Mens fortune there is vertue" (III, 740). As he loses his public Jonson escapes from the commercial sharpness of his subject matter—from Volpone's "fine delusive sleights" (I, ii, 95)—into the illusory realm of the court masque: for example, in *Love's Triumph through Callipolis.* His unfinished pastoral, *The Sad Shepherd,* is not less poignant than *Hero and Leander* as a record of discontinuity, with its nostalgia for Elizabethan May-games and its protest against the rampant Puritanism that would soon be closing the playhouses. The sad shepherd and the dead shepherd—*Arcades ambo.*

The succession is more explicit with George Chapman, whom Marlowe had known through Sir Walter Raleigh's circle. A laying on of hands takes place in the third Sestiad of *Hero and Leander,* when Chapman invokes the "most strangely-intellectuall fire" of Marlowe's muse (III, 183). If that incandescence does not inform Chapman's Sestiads, it is breathed by some of the protagonists that he went on to portray. Most of his tragedies are located on the terrain of contemporary French politics that Marlowe had signalized in *The Massacre at Paris.* But Chapman's heroes have less scope than their predecessors, for they are contemporaries of Jacobean courtiers rather than of Elizabethan adventurers; they are not conquerors followed by kings but followers of kings. Bussy d'Ambois displays his prowess and policy in duels and amours; as a soldier of fortune he is deservedly its victim; and fortune, for Chapman, is the sternest necessity. Virtue, in its eternal opposition, is by no means the Machiavellian *virtù;* it is once more the Stoic and Christian concept. Thus the wheel of Marlovian ethics comes full circle, precisely as it did for Mortimer. Bussy, the corrupted man of action, is balanced by his contemplative brother, Clermont d'Ambois, the "Senecal man" who rises above the world through his contempt for it, the Hamlet-like revenger who hesitates and—having done his duty—commits suicide. Marlowe's heroes might have lived by the maxim of *Bussy d'Ambois:*

> Who to himselfe is law, no law doth neede,
> Offends no Law, and is a King indeede.
>
> (II, i, 203-4)

But kingship is no longer a problem of expansion and domination; it becomes, as its sphere contracts, a problem of self-control. The individual manifests his will, not by actively controlling his fortunes, but by exerting the more passive virtues of resignation and fortitude in the face of events beyond his control. In *The Conspiracy of Byron* the protagonist combines the prowess of Tamburlaine with the policy of the Guise, and his stormy eloquence would do credit to either or both:

> There is no danger to a man, that knowes,
> What life and death is: there's not any law,
> Exceeds his knowledge.
>
> (III, iii, 140-2)

But in the sequel, *The Tragedy of Byron*, self-assertion is confounded by royal authority. True knowledge is self-knowledge, Byron finally realizes, just as the higher law is an inner law. "Talk of knowledge," he concludes resignedly. "It serues for inward vse" (V, iv, 50-1).

Marlowe's influence through the later Jacobean and Caroline drama is sporadic and diffused. Yet in some measure every dramatist felt it directly or indirectly. The popularity of *The Jew of Malta* prompted many revivals, and stimulated the newer writers then coming to grips with the tragedy of revenge. Among them, John Marston reveals the closest affinities, stylistic and temperamental, though the decade between the two may spell the difference between his eccentricity and Marlowe's centrality. John Webster, who yields only to Shakespeare and Marlowe among the English tragic dramatists, owes most to Shakespeare; to Marlowe he owes very little in detail, but something perhaps in the posture of his characters, his splendid sinners and grim ironists, and the palatial ruins in which they dwell. Cyril Tourneur may have found an exemplar, if not a model, for his *Atheist's Tragedy* in Marlowe. A generation after his death, unexpectedly but appropriately, Marlowe's rhetorical intonation flavours the speeches of the mortgage-holding villain, Sir Giles Overreach, in Philip Massinger's melodramatic comedy, *A New Way to Pay Old Debts*. Marlowe might have been but was not forgotten by the new school of courtly playwrights centring on John Fletcher. Fletcher's collaborator, Francis Beaumont, satirizing the middle class in *The Knight of the Burning Pestle,* has his merchant sack an apprentice by sending him out "to discover / New masters yet unknown" (I, ii, 7). When the title character rants, in *Philaster,*

> Place me, some god, upon a *Piramis,*
> Higher than hills of earth, and lend a voice
> Loud as your thunder to me,
>
> (IV, iv, 91-3)

it might almost be said that his prayer is forthwith answered, and he is filled with Marlovian afflatus. Indeed it could be said that, through the continuing vogue of Beaumont and Fletcher, Marlowe's astounding terms were transmitted to the Almanzors and Drawcansirs of the Restoration heroic play. Fletcher's well-made plays were skilfully contrived to please the ladies, and his versification was as different from Marlowe's as it could be while remaining within the bounds of blank verse. But when Fletcher tried his experiment in pastoral tragicomedy, *The Faithful Shepherdess,* reminiscence from Marlowe was inescapable. When the river-god woos the nymph, he is predestined to fall into the familiar melody of "The Passionate Shepherd to His Love":

> And if thou wilt go with me,
> Leaving mortal companie,
> In the cool streams shalt thou lye,
> Free from harm as well as I.
>
> (III, i, 408-11)

This is the measure that Keats employs to evoke the "souls of poets dead and gone" who frequented the Mermaid Tavern. It is not quite the metre of "The Passionate Shepherd"; it is that which Shakespeare uses for fairies' spells and witches' incantations; and it differs from Marlowe's iambic tetrameter by dropping the first foot and thereby shifting to a trochaic beat. Milton demonstrates the trochaic rhythm in *L'Allegro:*

> These delights if thou canst give,
> Mirth with thee I mean to live.
>
> (151-2)

Which is syncopated against the iambic couplet of *Il Penseroso:*

> These pleasures *Melancholy* give,
> And I with thee will choose to live.
>
> (175-6)

Although both couplets reverberate to Marlowe's bucolic refrain, Milton characteristically proposes a choice. The aesthetic choice becomes ethical in *Comus*—the perfect foil for *Doctor Faustus*—and is sharpened and deepened by Milton's succeeding poems. Mephostophilis has adumbrated some of the darker aspects of *Paradise Lost;* and Pandemonium is a Marlovian apocalypse; but there is likewise Eden, and Milton out-Marlowes Marlowe when he blazons it forth in comparisons and superlatives. When Milton's dramatis personae transcend their classical prototypes, as they invariably do, it is not vainglory but an act of piety. The very notion of a Christian epic is founded upon the conviction that this argument is

Not less but more Heroic than the wrauth
Of stern *Achilles.*

(IX, 14-5)

But, of course, it is Milton's humanistic commitment that makes such choices difficult, weighty, and tense; that makes his great renunciation of Greece, in *Paradise Regained,* a secular crucifixion. The Marlovian dialectic of temptation is given monumental treatment by Milton, who—for better or worse—resists where Marlowe succumbs. Yet we have noted a prophetic strain in Marlowe, a Hebraism which sometimes comes to the surface as concretely as Milton's Hellenic feeling. It may be more pertinent to envision each of them wrestling with his particular angel than to relegate either to the devil's party. *Samson Agonistes* is a belated epilogue to Elizabethan tragedy, completing the cycle initiated by *Tamburlaine,* as well as a Puritan commentary upon the Restoration. The shackled agonist is a divine avenger who starts from humbled pride and proceeds toward moral victory. The pedestal that self-consciously raises his prowess to this isolated stature is more Æschylean than Marlovian. Milton's personal spokesman could not be Marlowe's; it is their common medium that registers the largest indebtedness and the nearest kinship. How Milton reanimated blank verse, by variously drawing out the sense, hardly needs to be illustrated. How he extended the geographical and astronomical flight of Marlowe's imagery is salient enough in Satan's interplanetary journey, or the hemispheric vistas that Michael exhibits to Adam.

During the eighteenth century Marlowe, the embodiment of all the proscribed excesses, practically ceased to occupy a place in English literature. Seldom reprinted, little discussed, and never performed, his works dropped into the limbo of subliterature, from which the gradual forays of antiquarianism and the enthusiasm of certain romanticists were to rescue him in the nineteenth century. Since unique books have unusual fates which are often interconnected, we are not as amazed as we otherwise might be at the return of *Doctor Faustus* to Germany, its survival through a puppet show, and its resurgence via Lessing in Goethe. In England, Marlowe's later fame has been that of a poet's poet. His tutelage must have aided Keats, in *Endymion,* to cultivate "ravishments more keen / Than Hermes' pipe" (II, 875-6). But the shock of recognition is a stimulus only when it encounters reciprocal talent. When Robert Bridges cites Marlowe in *The Testament of Beauty,* the touchstone shows up the tired flaccidity of his own verse and the tame eclecticism of his thought. Marlowe, despite his premature eclipse, was fortunate in working within an exciting context of fertile idioms and usable notions, which fellow-poets could bandy back and forth with enhancements and innovations at every stage. A slight but significant instance is his "Passionate Shepherd." This lyric was itself the distillation of a mood which thematically recurs, as we have frequently seen. It was also a provocation to rejoinders and sequels on the part of Marlowe's friends and successors, who are perspicuously mirrored in their responses. Robert Herrick, in "To Phyllis, to Love and Live with Him," welcomed the occasion to revel in those rustic amenities which he obviously enjoyed so much more than Marlowe. John Donne, in "The Bait," turned the pastoral into a piscatory where—with the expected twist of Donne's unexpectedness— the fisherman is caught by the fish.

But the truest counterpart was Raleigh's answer, printed with "The Passionate Shepherd" in *England's Helicon,* "The Nymph's Reply to the Shepherd." Marlowe's poem was sung when his works went unread; Sir Hugh Evans sang it to keep up his waning courage in *The Merry Wives of Windsor;* in *The Compleat Angler* Izaak Walton hears it from a milk-maid and hears the rejoinder from the milkmaid's mother. The mirth and melancholy of the two songs are proper to the ages of the singers; the nymph replies with sobering commonplaces which are no less Eliza-bethan than the ebullient promises of the shepherd; time passes, beauty fades, and men are false.

> If all the world and loue were young,
> And truth in euery Sheepheards tongue,
> These pretty pleasures might me moue,
> To liue with thee, and be thy loue.

The debate was not confined to Raleigh and Marlowe. It was a strongly marked tendency of Italian literature during the Cinquecento, which— according to Francesco de Sanctis—oscillated between idyll and carnival, between a bucolic and a satirical outlook. It was exemplified in Thomas Nashe's "Scholler-like Shepheard," Robert Greene, who longed for the countryside from the stews of London, oscillating between Arcadian romances and pamphlets exposing the chicaneries of coney-catchers. It was a phase of that primitivistic longing for ease and happiness and sim-plicity which is a sentimental revelation of crowded cities, complicated lives, and mellow civilizations. In the Christmas play, *The Return from Parnassus,* the Cambridge scholars end by becoming shepherds, having run through other trades and thrived by none; but, alas, their sheepcote is the Isle of Dogs, a garbage-dump in the middle of the Thames. Such was the end of scholarism for Marlowe: after the seductions of the metrop-olis, the cohabitation of learning and poverty. It is easy to understand why Thomas Dekker, who spent so much of his life in a debtors' prison, dramatized the fable of Fortunatus and his wishing-purse. Essentially Marlowe did likewise, somewhat more subtly, when—for a few pounds from Philip Henslowe—he imagined Barabas counting his gold. That was stage money, and the magic of Faustus was sleight of hand; but the art that conjured with them was genuine, the power of the studious artisan to create a world of profit and delight, the evocative power of the mighty line and the hyperbolic image.

Any man was free to wish for such powers as life had not granted him: to be a magician, a merchant-prince, a king. To be a poet was not so much to make one's own wishes come true as to grant a vicarious realization—to play Mephostophilis, as it were—to the wishes of other men. All of us are gratified and soothed by the appealing wish-dream of the passionate shepherd. Would it were true, we say with the sceptical nymph. But Sir Walter Raleigh was not the first, and Sigmund Freud is not the last, to observe that the pleasure principle must be tempered by the sense of reality. That sense is not instinctive; it has to be learned; and, proverbially, there is only one teacher. *Experientia docet.* "And your experience makes you sad," says Rosalind to the melancholy Jaques in *As You Like It* (IV, i, 27). Whatever Marlowe's experience may have been, it changed his mind, as Faustus was warned by Mephostophilis; it must have been purchased with grief, as was Abigail's experience. Marlowe must have felt a hell of grief, like Edward, like Mephostophilis himself; and, unlike Faustus, he ran no risk of confounding hell with Elysium. The nightmare of the hell-mouth is at least as real as the day-dream of Helen of Troy.

> Yet both exist side by side in the human intellect; as it were, the battle with its fury and its bloody swords, together with the harp-playing, the drinking from golden cups, and the kisses of fair women in the tents. And it is in these two forms that all poetry has been composed, lyric beauty and epic power. Which is the greater? [This is Liàm O'Flaherty, as it happens, writing of Joseph Conrad.] To me the battle and the blood, the terrible Genghiz, with his camel herds, his hosts of horsemen and his jewelled concubines, the storming of Troy, the war for the great bull of Cuailgne, all the terrible madnesses of men and women crashing their bodies and their minds against the boundary walls of human knowledge.

Fantasy may be an escape from anxieties; and Marlowe may dally in that golden world where, as Sir Philip Sidney well understood, poetry improves upon nature. There, if not elsewhere, the words "live" and "love" are synonymous. "Live with me" is also Tamburlaine's suit to Zenocrate, who is persuaded to live and die with him; while Edward poses for himself the alternative of either living or dying with Gaveston. The scholarly career from which Faustus strays, guided by fallen angels who live with Lucifer, was to "liue and die in *Aristotles* workes" (33). But that would have been a cloistered state of unworldly isolation; whereas the individual is dependent upon a society; and the individualistic Barabas can neither live with others nor without them. Loving only himself, trusting neither Christians nor Turks, he vainly undertakes to "live with" both; and the island of Malta is an embattled citadel of self-interest—even as the gulf between two individuals is crossed when Leander swims from Abydos to Sestos.

The heroine of *Hero and Leander,* whose name increases a pre-existing confusion, diverges somewhat from the heroines of Marlowe's plays: the embalmed Zenocrate, the evanescent Helen, the rejected Dido, the neglected Isabell, the unfaithful Duchess of Guise. Hero's foredoomed love is happily consummated, where Abigail enters a convent and dies a virgin; while the characteristic Olympia, in the Second Part of *Tamburlaine,* is wooed but not won; she tricks her unwary suitor into cutting her throat. The passionate shepherd's lyric is a monologue, and the nymph's response—if we heed it—is a rejection. Moving from Venus to Mars, from love to strife, Marlowe effected his militant entrance into the theatre; leaving the meadows of pastoralism for the fields of conflict, he armed himself with the Machiavellian dictum that it is better to be feared than loved. Since drama is the most social of the arts, and monodrama is a contradiction in terms, he resolved it through the dramatization of masterful personalities overpowered by contradictory circumstances—the immovable object, the irresistible force. Love and majesty do not agree with each other; affection, seemingly thwarted, gives way to aggression; yet Marlowe's threatening oratory is disarmingly prone to lapse into amorous cajolery. Unloved, the Marlovian protagonist desiderates a companion, a minion, a deuteragonist; and here the exception that proves the rule is the Uranian Eros of Edward and Gaveston. More ideally, with Faustus and Mephostophilis, the second self becomes a projection of the ego, a *daimon*. "One is no number" for Leander and Hero (I, 255), but Marlowe's dramatic heroes stand alone in their singularity and single-mindedness. Conscious at every moment of their identity, they are supremely self-conscious at the moment of death. From what we know of Marlowe's own character, we may fairly suppose that he threw a good deal of himself into these monomaniac exponents of the first person: egoists, exhibitionists, infidels, outsiders.

As Marlowe progresses from Tamburlaine and Barabas to Edward and Faustus, the mask seems to fit more closely; the viewpoint is more sympathetic, and fear is mellowed by pity. After his imaginary flights through the realms of higher policy, he comes back with Faustus to the scholar's study. He has pursued ambition, the wish to outsoar one's fellow men, as well as revenge, the animus against them. Between the active voice of Tamburlaine and the passive voice of Edward, between the scourge of sadism and the self-torture of masochism, Barabas is the equivocating figure who unwittingly contrives his own punishment. The triumph symbolized by the chariot is easy and unrealistic; but there is poetic justice in the caldron; and Marlowe's deepened concern with suffering propounds its final symbol in the hell-mouth. Among the reiterated images that carry his peculiar impetus through his various writings, probably the most typical recurrence is the constellation of "topless towers" and "quenchless fires." Both of these complementary phrases impose concreteness on the idea of infinity: unlimited construction, ambition, pride; unlimited destruction, purgation, suffering. The underlying antagonism between civilization and nature has its *locus classicus* in Faustus' vision of the Trojan holocaust, and again in the frescoes that adorn Hero's temple:

> Loue kindling fire, to burne such townes as *Troy*.
>
> (I, 153)

Fire is so standard a trope for love that Racine's lovers speak casually of *nos feux*. Doubtless its primitive symbolism was phallic. However, the taming of fire was the crucial step toward human culture, as prefigured in the myth of Prometheus, the fire-bringer. Freud finds an analogy for this in the curbing of the sexual instinct, and asserts that the findings of psychoanalysis "testify to the close connection between the ideas of ambition, fire, and urethral erotism." In *The Tragedy of Dido,* where the fiery imagery culminates in an actual funeral pyre, the Promethean theft is associated with all-consuming and unrequited passion, when the Queen begs Æneas to "quench these flames." But in *The Massacre at Paris* it is the ambitious thoughts of the Guise which are flames, and they can only be quenched with blood; and it is the same with Tamburlaine's thirst for sovereignty. Red was, at all events, Marlowe's favourite colour.

Tamburlaine, who burned the town where Zenocrate died, who shed so much blood freely and callously, felt no pain when he stabbed himself as a lesson to his sons. When Faustus stabbed himself as a preliminary to signing the devil's contract, his blood did not flow. This was an unheeded omen of his damnation, when the drop of Christ's blood that would save his soul is denied him; and it seems to betoken what is conspicuously lacking in Marlowe's heroes, the motives of altruism and self-sacrifice. For that lack, for their egoism, they suffer; Apollo's laurel bough is immolated, and fireworks prefigure hellfire—not the refining flames of Dante's purgatory. In mothlike fascination, Marlowe keeps returning to the blaze that prefigures—even more than love or ambition— sin purged by sacrifice. No wonder Chapman eulogizes Marlowe's intellectual fire, while Drayton affirms that "his raptures were / All air and fire." Air, the sky, the combining element, is no less important for Marlowe, hypersensitive as he was to brightness and altitude. The sun, the first cause of both heat and light, beats continually upon his metaphors. It is the fiery chariot of Phaëton, swinging from the upsurge of triumph into the peripety of suffering. It is the vehicle that sweeps Goethe's Faust through the ether into new spheres of pure activity:

> *Ein Feuerwagen schwebt auf leichten Schwingen*
> *An mich heran! Ich fühle mich bereit,*

Auf neuer Bahn den Äther zu durchbringen,
Zu neuen Sphären reiner Tätigkeit.

(702-5)

[As if on wings, a chariot of fire
Draws near me. I am ready to be free.
Piercing the ether, new-born, I aspire
To rise to spheres of pure activity.
(trans. Philip Wayne)]

There could be no more luminous image for the audacity of a mind which, as Lamb declared of Marlowe, "delighted to dally with interdicted subjects." Marlowe was playing with fire, after all, in no innocuously figurative sense; men were burned at the stake in his day for lesser heresies than those he is recorded as professing. Moreover, if he practised the homosexuality he seems to have preached and preoccupied himself with, that was another crime punishable by burning. If it was not the unpardonable sin of Faustus, if it was not the Olympian theft of Mercury, it was the vice avenged by Edward's flaming spit. Mario Praz, a leading expert on problems of literary pathology, has diagnosed Marlowe's obsession as a "Ganymede complex." What other critics have designated as his thirst for the impossible, Professor Praz would interpret as a sublimation of Marlowe's attitude toward sex.

Such interpretations are relevant, but marginal, to the understanding of Marlowe's creative processes. His preoccupation with beautiful youths is an idyllic mood, which he is repeatedly forsaking for more ambitious and realistic themes. It would be more appropriate to borrow a phrase which Dr. Henry A. Murray has introduced into clinical psychology, and to classify Marlowe's case as an "Icarus complex." The disposition to isolate one's self on a higher plane, while attracting the admiration of others, is not an infrequent pattern of motivation, although competitiveness and exhibitionism—even when channelized into the theatre—rarely lead to such coruscating results. If individuals of this type are attracted less to the opposite sex than to their own, it is chiefly because they are animated by self-love; therein they are akin to another prototype; they are narcissists. In their autistic fantasies they fly, and their chief anxiety is the dread of falling. Since Icarus was the archetype of the overreacher, Marlowe was by temperament a tragedian. This is explicitly acknowledged when the prologue attributes Faustus' downfall to waxen wings which mount beyond his reach, or when Dido calls after Æneas:

Ile frame me wings of waxe like *Icarus,*
And ore his ships will soare vnto the Sunne,
That they may melt and I fall in his armes:
Or els Ile make a prayer vnto the waues,

> That I may swim to him like *Tritons* neece:
> O *Anna*, fetch *Orions* Harpe,
> That I may tice a Doplhin to the shoare,
> And ride vpon his backe vnto my loue.
>
>   (1651-8)

It was not fire but water, the quenching element, that killed Icarus; unscorched by the sun, he was drowned in the sea; Neptune prevailed over him, as over Leander—of whom we are reminded by Dido, sea-changed into a Nereid. The dolphin reminds us, not of Queen Elizabeth serenaded, nor of Antony's dolphin-like sensuality, but of Arion's musical enchantments and of the poet's powers over nature. The demonic familiars of Faustus are conceived in the shape of lions or horsemen or giants, and sometimes of women or unwed maids,

> Shadowing more beautie in their ayrie browes,
> Then has the white breasts of the queene of Loue.
>
>   (157-8)

This is a highly revealing preference. The brows of the spirits, who seem as sexless as angels, are preferred to the breasts of Venus. It might be inferred that Marlowe's sensibilities were less intrigued by sexual than by intellectual beauty—the beauty of Lucifer in his radiant pride. Venus' brows are invidiously compared with Tamburlaine's crest, and Zenocrate's brows shadow triumphs and trophies—in other words, her eyes, which reflect his actions. His own "frowning browes and fiery lookes," on the other hand, are a foretaste of death (252); and so is the frown of the Guise. So Edward sees his tragedy written in Lightborne's brows; and the wrath of God appears to Faustus in the ireful brows, the watchful eyes, the face of an estranged and angry father. That parallels the struggle, embodied in Helen and the Old Man, between beauty and truth. Dido offered Æneas as many soldiers as there were drops in the ocean. Faustus' last thoughts leap from combustion to liquefaction, with his yearning to lose his identity, to change his soul into "little water drops" (1472).

Icarus is a rebellious son, like Phaëthon, for whom the sun is a father-image; and Marlowe is capable of punning upon this association. Both sons are iconoclasts, unfilial rebels against the cosmic order. Hence Thomas Heywood mentions them, together with the Titans, as awful examples of "vaine Curiosity" in his *Hierarchy of the Blessed Angels:*

> Either like bold aspiring *Phaeton,*
> To aime at the bright Chariot of the Sun?
> Or with his waxen wings, as *Icarus* did,
> Attempt what God and Nature haue forbid?

What is this lesse, than when the Gyants stroue
To mutiny and menace war 'gainst *Ioue*.

The caveat against intellectualism was potent even in the seventeenth century. Pascal, that ascetic scientist, revived the warnings of Saint John and Saint Augustine against the lusts of the mind, the flesh, and the will—rivers of fire which bounded the wasteland of worldliness. It has been convenient for us to borrow Pascal's terminology, in characterizing the triad of basic urges that Marlowe so impenitently expressed. We have watched his genius devising poetic modes for each of them: the lyric plea for *libido sentiendi,* the epic vaunt for *libido dominandi,* and the tragic lament for *libido sciendi.* The most damnable appetite of all, which subsumed all the others because it wholly possessed the ego, was what Pascal's Jansenist masters termed *libido excellendi.* What could characterize Marlowe more succinctly, or better sum up his Icarian desire for flight? For the Jansenists, the urge to excel was the very temptation that had spoken through the serpent to Adam and Eve: "And yee shall bee as Gods, knowing good and euill" (Genesis, iii, 5). The subtle tempter, Mephostophilis, argues that man is more excellent than heaven. In their pursuit of excellence Marlowe's protagonists are goaded, like Captain Ahab, by the devilish tantalization of the gods. In effect, they partake of ambrosia; they violate divine authority; and the jealousy of the gods is visited upon their prideful heads. Theirs is the archetypal dilemma of *Prometheus Bound.* Tragedy, which ends by accepting the universe, cannot begin without challenging it; and Marlowe sounded this challenge for England as Æschylus did for Greece. If Marlowe seems the more iconoclastic, it is because the idols had accumulated; it was not a question of smashing rejection or chastened submission; a man could not come to his own terms with the cosmos except by risking charges of impiety.

"Tragedy is only possible to a mind which is for the moment agnostic or Manichæan," as I. A. Richards has acutely remarked. "The least touch of any theology which has a compensating heaven to offer the tragic hero is fatal." This applies with especial pertinence to *Doctor Faustus,* where the god-in-the-machine refuses to descend and the Evil Angel is a better theologian than the Good. Some would hold that tragedy, like so many other perspectives, is a substitute for religion; yet religion itself is a substitute for precise knowledge of the human condition; and the tragic view, as a branch of knowledge, faces existence without recourse to supernatural assumptions. "What certifies Olympus and reconciles the gods?" asks Goethe, in the prologue to *Faust,* and answers: "The might of man as revealed by the poet" (156-7). Tragedy is the ripened growth of a humanistic, as distinguished from a theological, culture. The tragic dramatist is not a high priest, but rather what Nietzsche would term a dragon-slayer, disposing of the illusions while enlarging the sympathies of his fellow men. Had Marlowe survived for a few years more and absorbed the new philosophy, Marjorie Nicolson surmises, it might have inspired an optimistic body of poetry and counterbalanced the pessimism of Donne. That engaging surmise may be warranted by Marlowe's imaginative response to the old-fashioned science he knew, though it does not take account of either the formal intention or the ethical purport of his tragedies. Since man is born to trouble as the sparks fly upward, one may well be more interested in the sparks than in the trouble. But *Doctor Faustus* is, to say the least, not an expression of scientific optimism. Less room is left for chance, nemesis closes in further, with every successive work. Leander, predestined to be a victim, ironically pleads for the inevitable:

> It lies not in our power to loue, or hate,
> For will in vs is ouer-rul'd by fate.

(I, 167-8)

The Play-King in *Hamlet* puts it less peremptorily:

> Our Willes and Fates do so contrary run,
> That our Deuices still are ouerthrowne.

(III, ii, 221-2)

Heretofore, virtue and fortune have been Marlowe's names for character and plot in the universal drama. If fortune was providence, virtue was acceptance; if fortune was luck, virtue was drive; in any event, the dramatic confrontation is between circumstance and the individual, the personality and the situation he confronts. Now, it would seem, an inexorable fatality looms behind a capricious fortune, limiting the range of man's potentialities, and humbling his virtue by weakening his free will. "Our erected wit maketh vs know what perfection is," wrote Sidney, "and yet our infected will keepeth vs from reaching vnto it." Will, over-reaching itself, encounters the limitation superimposed by fate. But wit, the intellect, climbing toward the infinite, is not so readily circumscribed. It is forever striving to refute the geographers, to prove cosmography, to resolve ambiguities. If it cannot probe unsearchable mysteries, it can push to the outside limits of the known; and there it can speculate, as Hamlet did, on "thoughts beyond the reaches of our Soules" (I, iv, 56). Every man is limited by conditions, as if—like Faustus—he had signed a contract; but his recognition of those realities which frame his life is, in its way, a victory over them; and the incongruity between them and his ideals of perfection is the wisdom of Mephostophilis, irony. Mephostophilis, in the last analysis, transcends Marlowe's heroes because he transcends the ego; he likewise retains his detachment from the inscrutable forces he is condemned to serve. As agent he bears his burden of complicity, as ironic commentator he frees himself. We cannot act without incurring guilt, we cannot think without transcending ourselves. The vista that Mephostophilis opens to us is a grasp of all that is not within the self, the encroachments and complications and contingencies that men over-simplify when they imprecate the bitch-goddess, Fortuna. Often she seems more intelligent than they. "Seemeth she not to be a right artist?" inquired Montaigne. But, as he keenly realized, it is their intelligence that discerns a pattern in her fortuitous ironies. It is their art that limns those circumstantial artistries which, as Hardy insists, repeat themselves timelessly. Tragedy is a ritual which initiates men into reality, and irony is the perspective of tragedy.

While science, capitalism, imperialism were at the beginning of their modern development, Marlovian tragedy was able to project the inordinate courses they would pursue, through Marlowe's insight into the wayward individualist and into the life that is lived—as he would put it—"without control." Living in a day when controls were external and ubiquitous and high-handed, he boldly asserted the values of freedom. Subsequently, this became much easier; and, with facility, came devaluation. Faustianism has become the veritable ideology of liberal man, the principal myth of western civilization, as Oswald Spengler pointed out in predicting the decline of the historical epoch that arose with the Renaissance. Faust, in the twentieth century, is not the man he was in the nineteenth: he is the decadent aesthete of Thomas Mann or the intellectual snob of Paul Valéry. While the art of the drama has been mechanized and amplified, the scope and audience of the serious artist have diminished. If he has a hero, it is not the dynamic Faust but Flaubert's Saint Anthony, the resigned protagonist who secludes himself, yet is haunted by the desires he has resisted. If he takes a watchword from Goethe, uncharacteristically, it is renunciation. If he favours a figure of speech, it is understatement, *meiosis* rather than *hyperbole*. If he is a poet he takes his leave of hyperbole, with Mallarmé's *Prose pour des Esseintes*. It is only through mystical correspondences that he can link the symbolic world of poetry with the actual world of experience—the two worlds that Marlowe brought so much closer together. In the Middle Ages the distinction between them had been carefully upheld: literature coexisted with life on parallel planes that never quite touched. The movement toward naturalism, broadly speaking, was that gradual abandonment of the metaphysical plane for the literal which F. M. Cornford has called "infiguration," calling attention to Marlowe as one of its innovators. If this is so, Marlowe enjoyed his strategic position because his background was still sustained by the mythical and the universal, even while he was engaged in bringing the factual and the personal into the foreground.

We look back toward him from an austere vantage-point, from which the naturalistic impulse seems almost to have run its expansive course. Our writers, perhaps with good reason, do not glory in our world. Yet one of them, James Joyce, has suggested a happy ending to the tale of Icarus. The son, by trying his wings, learns to fly; growing up, he becomes the father, Daedalus; and mankind is richer by virtue of his craftsmanship. Knowledge may be power, and power may corrupt, yet beauty preserves—we are so much older than Marlowe, and so little wiser. T. S. Eliot authorizes us to believe that Marlowe had the most thoughtful and philosophical mind among the Elizabethan dramatists, albeit—Mr. Eliot adds—"immature." We know what Mr. Eliot means by maturity, since he has referred to Congreve in elsewhere defining it; and though it is not as common as it should be, it is not so rare as the gift of early ripeness we cherish in Marlowe. Young enough to retain the fresh perceptions of youth, old enough to have lived through its self-deceptions, he had in him—as Drayton perceived—"those braue translunary things / That the first poets had." With him we not only taste the alluring fruit; we walk in the sunlit innocence of the garden; and, plunging back farther into primordial darkness, we seem to witness the blinding flash of creation. It is Lucretius who gives us our best summation, when he eulogizes his master Epicurus:

> His vigorous and active Mind was hurl'd
> Beyond the flaming limits of *this* World
> Into the mighty Space, and there did see
> How things begin, what can, what cannot be;
> How all must die, all yield to fatal force,
> What steddy limits bound their natural course;
> He saw all this and brought it back to us.

This is quoted from the seventeenth-century translation of Thomas Creech, but some of the Latin phrases seem nearer to the letter and to the spirit of Marlowe's English—the *vivida vis animi* of his heroes, the *flammantia moenia mundi* against which they hurl themselves, and the *finita potestas* that overwhelms them. Conversely, in Marlowe's phraseology, Lucretius was indeed a forward wit, divinely discontent, fruitful in aspiring, running to regions far. If Marlowe learned the lyric mode from Ovid and the epic mode from Lucan, it may well have been Lucretius who schooled him in tragic discernment of the nature of things. For Lucretius, too, life was grand and grave and harsh, and death was premature. Neither poet took the middle way; poetry takes the way of fine excess. Excess tempts youth to stray from the *via media,* the *mediocritas,* the mean between extremes that Bacon recommends. But in his parables, *De Sapientia Veterum* (xxvii), the prosaic Bacon concedes that age goes astray through defect; and whereas defect crawls upon the earth like a serpent, excess makes itself at home in the skies like a bird. The course of Icarus, defying the laws of gravity and common sense, was obviously uncertain and unsafe; yet even Bacon was compelled to admire it, because its youthful swiftness kindled a certain magnanimity.

Marlowe's Map

by Ethel Seaton

"Giue me a Map." These words, put into the mouth of the dying Tamburlaine, bring Christopher Marlowe into line with all those "aspiring minds" to whom a map can be a satisfaction of curiosity and a source of delight. They are a great and varied company, from Charlemagne studying his "fair silver tables," to the schoolboy Hakluyt having his first lesson in map-reading in the Middle Temple, even to Mr. Conrad in our own day, if one may venture to identify him with his mouthpiece, yet another Marlow. Before him, no one has expressed in prose the stay-at-home's pleasure in such a study more fully than Burton; he "never travelled but in map or card," and could not but think "that it would please any man to look upon a geographical map, . . . to behold, as it were, all the remote provinces, towns, cities of the world, and never to go forth of the limits of his study. . . . What greater pleasure can there now be, than to view those elaborate maps of Ortelius, Mercator, Hondius, &c.?"

Burton is the inheritor of the Elizabethan interest in maps, fostered in all readers of early voyages, and satisfied in students by the fine productions of the cartographers of Venice and Antwerp. That Marlowe shared this educated taste is suggested by the demand of his hero for a map in which to tread again the "interminable roads" of a life's conquests, to lament over "the little done, the much to do." That his interest had some thoroughness seems to be attested by the frequency with which, in locating countries, he refers to the Tropic Circles, and by an actual reference to the science of map-making. When Tamburlaine is encamped before Damascus (Part I, IV. iv), he boasts that with his sword for pen, he will anew reduce the countries to a map, of which the meridian-line will pass through that city:

> Here at *Damascus* will I make the Point
> That shall begin the Perpendicular.

"Marlowe's Map," by Ethel Seaton. From *Essays and Studies by Members of the English Association*, X (1924), 13-35. Copyright 1924 by Ethel Seaton. Reprinted by permission of the author.

Marlowe knew that the cartographer of his time had a wide choice for his initial meridian of longitude, his perpendicular, though already the island of Ferro in the Canaries was becoming standardized. He knew also that it was a sign of territorial conquest; for a quarter of a century controversy on spheres of influence had raged between Spaniards and Portuguese round the meridian, the Line of Demarcation, or Repartition.

These seem unmistakable signs that Marlowe used a map with pleasure and intelligence. Yet his geographical knowledge is one of the points on which his editors have been most severe. "Marlowe's notions of geography are as vague as Æschylus's," said Bullen despairingly, when he caught his author letting the Danube flow into the Mediterranean; and when it came to Zanzibar being on the west coast of Africa, he accepted the emendation to east without even a note. In guessing at the whereabouts of some of Marlowe's towns commentators evidently felt that the one thing safely to be assumed was an indifference to exactitude. German scholars seem to stand almost alone in suggesting that it would be fairer to Marlowe to seek his sources, and find whether his knowledge and his ignorance are those of the man or the period.

All the names in the Jacobean Burton's list of "elaborate maps" might have been known to the Elizabethan Marlowe. Mercator's fame has best withstood the tooth of time, but in his own day it was no greater than that of his friend and fellow-worker, Abraham Ortelius. The vast monument of Ortelius's industry, the *Theatrum Orbis Terrarum,* published in 1570 at Antwerp, was constantly re-issued, revised, translated, in the attempt to keep pace with discovery and to supply the demand for geographical knowledge. Both the man and his atlas were well known in England, and by the ordinary inquirer of the time the work was accepted as authoritative, however some seamen might question its accuracy in the minutiæ of coast-lines. Sir Humfrey Gilbert and his friend Gascoigne the poet consulted it for the North-west passage; Daniel Rogers, diplomatist, antiquarian, and kinsman of the compiler, wrote dedicatory poems for it; Humfrey Lluyd sent from his deathbed his description of Anglesey and map of Wales for insertion in it; Mulcaster asked Ortelius for advice on the teaching of elementary drawing; Camden had the substantial honour of a presentation copy; Hakluyt reproduced its map of the world, as the best available, in his *Principal Navigations,* and later wrote to Ortelius begging him to make a panoramic map, such as might be contained in small compass, rolled on rollers in a wooden frame; this would be of great service to politicians, citizens, and students of Oxford and Cambridge!

Ortelius received many a compliment, including one from Dr. Dee, on the beauty of his maps, and they are indeed a triumph of clearness and elegance, and comparatively modern in general outline. The orientation sometimes differs from that familiar to us, since there was no necessity to identify the North with the top of the page. It is disconcerting to our

prejudices to find, for instance, the coastline of Palestine displayed horizontally instead of perpendicularly; or Asia Minor hanging like a great pendant instead of jutting out squarely above Cyprus. The coloured copies, painted in Ortelius's own workshop, vary in preciseness and beauty, but all, whether plain or coloured, show the legibility that was one of his chief aims. Another aim, accuracy of nomenclature, is less well attained, but the difficulties were well-nigh insuperable, especially in half-known lands, or in countries like those of the Levantine seaboard, where conquest upon conquest has blurred a clear map into an ill-rubbed palimpsest. This conscientiousness fortunately did not make Ortelius despise the pictorial flourishes that turn the medieval map into an ideal playground. In his seas, mermaids, dolphins, and flying-fish rise above the surface, the whale waits open-mouthed to swallow Jonah, caravels and galliasses scud before the wind, slaves ply the oar in "pilling brigandines," and galleons grapple, with bursts of smoke and flame. In his eastern countries, strange animals roam about and "fill the gaps," as Swift complains, and in China beyond the Great Wall, as Milton remembered,

> across the barren plains
> Of Sericana, the Chineses drive
> With sails and wind, their cany waggons light.

All this, though geographically reprehensible, must have been of untold value in stimulating the fancy and imagination of the student.

It is difficult to compute how many copies of the *Theatrum* found their way into England; that Englishmen did buy it, we know from the letters of Ortelius himself.[1] Some college libraries would acquire it, and the collections of diplomatists and antiquarians could hardly afford to be without it. The close relations existing between noblemen, adventurers, scholars, and poets of the period make it probable that the latter had little difficulty in consulting such a book. Lord Lumley's library, to which Hakluyt had access, and of which Humfrey Lluyd was librarian, would almost certainly have a copy. Sir Walter Raleigh, who, according to Aubrey, always took a box full of books on his voyages, was not the man to be deterred from possessing one by its high cost.

There is then every possibility that Marlowe could see and even consult the *Theatrum,* although the library of Corpus Christi College has now no copy;[2] the query, can it be proved that he did so, is more searching. The proof seems to lie in one of his very "mistakes." In the map of Africa, Zanzibar the island is duly marked on the east coast as Zenzibar,

---

[1] One copy was bought by a certain Mr. Garth, surely that Mr. Richard Garthe, "one of the Clearkes of the Pettie Bags," in whose cabinets Hakluyt delightedly beheld "strange curiosities."

[2] For this information I am indebted to the courtesy of the Librarian of the College.

but a far more imposing Zanzibar, a province, appears in large t,
the "Westerne part of Affrike," precisely where Marlowe places
closer survey of the map shows that Techelles, in the account oi
triumphal march (II *Tamburlaine*, i. 6), is merely transcribing into v
some of the salient names of the map. His first march passes

> along the riuer *Nile,*
> To *Machda,* where the mighty Christian Priest,
> Cal'd *Iohn* the great, sits in a milk-white robe.

The eye is drawn to Machda, an Abyssinian town on a tributary of the
Nile, by the neighbouring note: *Hic longe lateq; imperitat magnus
princeps Presbiter Iões totius Africę potentiss: Rex.* Techelles continues:

> From thence vnto *Cazates* did I martch,
> Wher Amazonians met me in the field.

Where the Nile rises in a great unnamed lake, the district Cafates has
for its chief town Cazates, and is called *Amazonum regio.* Then comes the
crux:

> And with my power did march to *Zansibar*
> The Westerne part of *Affrike,* where I view'd
> The Ethiopian sea, riuers and lakes:
> But neither man nor child in al the land.

Beside Cape Negro appears in large print the province-name ZANZIBAR,
with the note: *hęc pars Africę meridionalis quę veteribus incognita fuit,
a Persis Arabibusq; scriptoribus vocatur.* Between this western part and
South America the sea is named *Oceanus Æthiopicus* in flourished letters;
in the province small rivers abound, and to north and south of the name
Zanzibar is that word so useful to the cartographer in difficulties, *Deserta.*
Marlowe, it must be observed, is therefore vindicated when he speaks of
Zanzibar as not *on* the western coast, but as itself the western part. He
is equally explicit later, when Tamburlaine examines his map and accepts his general's conquests as his own; reversing the actual order of
march, he passes

> along the Ethiopian sea,
> Cutting the Tropicke line of *Capricorne,*
> I conquered all as far as *Zansibar.*
>
> (Part II, v. iii.)

Actually the name Zanzibar is to the north of the Tropic, but the coloured maps make it clear that the province includes the whole southern

...ent, from Cape Negro to the Cape of Good Hope
...ozambique. In this location of the province Zanzibar,
...y Zanguebar, on the western coast, Ortelius is at vari-
...y contemporary authorities, and the map of Africa by
...4), which otherwise he followed very closely, does not in-
...l. Later cosmographers, such as Livio Sanuto, make its east-
...n quite clear. The transference is possibly due to a confused
...ding of Marmol, who, with Barros, is referred to in the intro-
...y notes to the map. In any case, the responsibility for that oft-
...ded *western* rests with Ortelius, not with our Marlowe.

...echelles has reached his southernmost point; turning northwards, he
...sses successively through Manico, by the coast of Byather, and so "to
...ubar, where the Negros dwell." On the map, Manico, curtailed by Marlowe for his metre, appears in full style as the province Manicongo,
Byather the province in its more correct and modern form of Biafar,
while above the province and town of Guber is printed in bold type
Nigritarum Regio. Then comes the last stage of the journey:

> [I] made haste to *Nubia,*
> There hauing sackt *Borno* the Kingly seat,
> I took the king, and lead him bound in chaines
> Vnto *Damasco.*

In the map, Borno, the chief town of Nubia, lies near the shore of *Borno
lacus,* that *"Borno* Lake" which Tamburlaine himself mentions later. So
ends a passage in which one can almost follow Marlowe's finger travelling
down the page as he plans the campaign; it is difficult to know whether
his memory or the printer is responsible for the slight differences of
spelling.

Almost beyond doubt, then, Marlowe knew Ortelius's map of Africa,
for he could not have obtained all this detail from the representation
of Africa in the much-reproduced map of the world, from which many of
his chosen names are omitted, notably Zanzibar itself. It does not, however, follow that he knew the whole atlas, for separate maps were commonly reproduced in cosmographies. *Tamburlaine* is sown almost as
thick with place-names as the sky with stars; can it be shown that any of
these, outside Africa, are derived from Ortelius?

A close examination of the geographical names in *Tamburlaine* leads
to an interesting conclusion. In Part I, Marlowe works on a large scale,
without much detail; his armies move through continents and countries,
and the provinces mentioned are such as were familiar to men of any
education: Media, Armenia, Syria, Tartary. Not more than ten towns
are named, and most of these were commonplaces to an Elizabethan:
Constantinople, Argier, Damascus, Venice, Morocco. Many of the names
and epithets, such as Græcia, Parthia, the Euxine, the ever-raging Caspian

Lake, would be familiar to any student of the classics, and Persepolis plays the part later taken by Samarkand, Tamburlaine's own town, which is not so much as named here. The setting is almost completely bounded by medieval geography; only twice does the Elizabethan, with his knowledge of a new hemisphere, break away beyond "Alcides' posts," as when, with a side-glance at Drake's exploit, and a lordly disregard of chronology, he makes Tamburlaine's ambition reach

> to th' Anta[r]tique Pole,

and again

> Euen from *Persepolis* to *Mexico*,
> And thence vnto the straightes of *Iubalter*.

In Part II, however, provinces of more recent interest are called by their contemporary names, such as Natolia, Amasia, Caramania. The Euxine becomes also the *Mare Magiore,* the Red Sea is also named *Mare Roso*. Some thirty towns are mentioned, many of which are written off a modern map, and some are so little known that commentators have either passed them over in silence, or else have arbitrarily identified them by mere resemblance of sound, with slight regard for the importance of their site in the action. Did Ortelius furnish Marlowe with any of these? A glance at the titles of his maps shows that many could well be useful: *Tartaria, Persiæ Regnum, Terra Sancta, Egyptia, Natolia, Turcicum Imperium*.[3] Within these bounds the characters of Part II have their being, as a brief survey of the action will recall.

Two lines of movement can be followed, that of the Turkish army and that of Tamburlaine's forces. The play opens with the Turks at their outposts on the Danube. Under fear of Tamburlaine's pressure on their eastern frontiers, they make a truce with the Christians, withdraw their troops into Asia Minor, are checked by news of treacherous pursuit, and, halting, give battle at a place not precisely named, but apparently in the neighbourhood of Mount Orminius. Meanwhile Tamburlaine, who at the close of Part I was in Egypt, at "truce with al the world," is after many years again on the march, and we hear of him at Alexandria, Larissa, and Aleppo. The gradual approach of the two armies draws to a meeting, and a battle is fought, again unnamed, but seemingly near the confines of Natolia, not far from Aleppo. Then Tamburlaine, with his train of captive kings, turns to subdue Babylon, to conquer the rallying Turks, his last victory, and to oppose "the wrath and tyranny of death," his only defeat.

[3] The early date, and the frequency of editions and translations of the *Theatrum* with its *Parergon,* make it difficult to draw conclusions for the date of either Part of *Tamburlaine*. I have cited here a coloured copy of 1584 (British Museum, Maps, C. 2. d. 1) as being near in time to the assumed date of the play.

Such is the main outline of the action; whether Marlowe shows reason-
able exactitude in his plan and in the details, is a question that Ortelius
may help to resolve. It would be well first to recall the rather different
nomenclature of the sixteenth century. Natolia is much more than the
modern Anatolia; it is the whole promontory of Asia Minor, with a
boundary running approximately from the modern Bay of Iskenderûn
eastward towards Aleppo, and then north to Batum on the Black Sea.
Of this region Marlowe only twice uses the names Asia Minor or Asia
the Less, while Asia and Asia Major denote either the whole continent,
or the part of Asia beyond this boundary. Orcanes, king of Natolia,
exactly describes its importance when he says:

> My realme, the Center of our Empery,
> Once lost, All Turkie would be ouerthrowne.
>
> (Part II, i. i.)

In Part I, however, there are signs that Marlowe follows medieval authority in using Africa to denote the Turkish empire, and making Memphis
its centre. Soria, the name regularly used by Italian writers and by
Ortelius, represents Syria, or more narrowly Syria north of Palestine; it
replaces in Part II the form Siria of Part I. Egyptia in Part I includes
Siria, for Damascus is Egyptian; in Part II, Egypt is distinct from Soria,
and its capital is. Cairo, named for the first time.

Commentators, crediting Marlowe with neglectful vagueness, have
themselves neglected the indications that he has been careful to give.
There seem to be two chief causes of confusion. The belief that the
Turco-Hungarian battle was fought in Europe has led to the search for
Natolian towns in Bulgaria, and for Mount Orminius in Transylvania.
Similarly, the apparent failure to identify Larissa, and more pardonably
Balsera, has led to utter misunderstanding of Tamburlaine's movements.

The first of the two muddles is the easier to deal with. As I have elsewhere shown,[4] Marlowe boldly "lifted" all the circumstances of this apparently imaginary campaign from the famous battle of Varna in 1444, a
date actually some forty years later than Tamburlaine's death. From the
chroniclers of Varna are drawn the truce and its terms, the Christians'
treachery and the excuses for it, the Turkish wrath, disillusionment, and
triumph. Marlowe does not, however, commit himself to the site of Varna
for this anachronistic battle, but seems purposely to transport it into Asia
Minor, and to prefer indication to precise location. The Turkish troops
were in fact withdrawn into Asia Minor, and it was a lightning-move by
the Sultan that hurled them back into Europe to meet the truce-breakers
at Varna; Marlowe seems content to leave them in Natolia. When the
treachery is hatched, Frederick reports that Orcanes has dismissed

---

[4] *Times Lit. Suppl.,* 16 June, 1921 (correspondence).

                              the greatest part
              Of all his armie, pitcht against our power
              Betwixt *Cutheia* and *Orminius* mount:
              And sent them marching vp to *Belgasar,*
              Acantha, Antioch, and *Cæsaria,*
              To aid the kings of *Soria* and *Ierusalem.*

                                                    (Part II, ɪɪ. i.)

That, as Ortelius reveals, precisely describes the movement of the Turkish
army through Asia Minor. Cutheia is the modern Kutayeh, the classical
Cotyaeum, and appears in the map of Natolia as Chiutaie, both district
and town. As the capital of Natolia, it was an important place; Leun-
clavius, in his notes to the *Annales Turcici* (1588), gives the many forms of
its name current. Mount Horminius is shown only in the map of *Græcia*
in the *Parergon,* situated in Bithynia east and slightly south of the modern
Scutari. For the single use of these two names, however, Marlowe had
probably yet another source. Belgasar and Acantha appear in the map of
Asia as Beglasar and Acanta, in a line leading roughly south-east through
Asia Minor, while the former is to be found again as Begbasar in *Natolia,*
and as Begasar in *Turcicum Imperium.* When, in the next scene, Orcanes
with the rear-guard ("the [little] power I haue left behind") hears of the
Hungarians' treacherous advance, he is on the point of marching "from
proud *Orminus* mount To faire *Natolia.*" Here Marlowe seems, in disac-
cord with Ortelius, to speak as if there were also a town Natolia, an invention that he repeats later, or else to consider the mountain as only on
the outskirts of Natolia proper. The battle seems to take place near here,
for after it Orcanes still has to haste and meet his army.
    Meanwhile Tamburlaine is also on the move. In the first scene, the
Turk Gazellus says of him that he

                            now in *Asia,*
              Neere *Guyrons* head doth set his conquering feet,
              And means to fire Turky as he goes.

But he must be referring to Tamburlaine's outposts, for almost immediately he gives other news of him:

                  Tamburlaine hath mustred all his men,
              Marching from *Cairon* northward with his camp,
              To *Alexandria,* and the frontier townes.

Guyron is not an invention of Marlowe's, but occurs twice in the
Theatrum, as Giuron in the map of Asia, and as Guiron in *Turcicum
Imperium;* it is a town near the upper Euphrates, north-east of Aleppo,
in the latter map not far from the confines of Natolia, and therefore a

possible outpost. The report of Tamburlaine proves correct; having travelled from Cairo *via* Alexandria, he is encamping at Larissa, as his first speech in Act I, scene 4, tells us:

> Now rest thee here on faire *Larissa* Plaines,
> Where Egypt and the Turkish Empire parts,
> Betweene thy sons that shall be Emperours.

Broughton was very "hot" when he quoted Milton to illustrate this: "The scene here seems to lie

> 'Twixt old Euphrates and the brook that parts
> Egypt from Syrian ground."

It is in fact by the brook itself, but Marlowe's exact description of the site has been obscured by the frequent omission of the comma after *parts,* that in the Octavo of 1590 completes the needed isolation of the line. It gives the exact position in which we find Larissa in the map of the Turkish Empire, a sea-coast town, south of Gaza; in the map of Africa already cited, it lies a little to the north of the dotted boundary line. It is on the biblical Brook of Egypt, and is the Rhinocolura of the classical period, the "most ancient city Larissa" of the Crusades, the El Arîsh of the modern map. By more perhaps than mere coincidence, Marlowe chooses for the scene of Zenocrate's death the town where the soldiers wept for the death of Baldwin of Jerusalem. It is fitting that the pillar placed in memory of her should be inscribed in "Arabian, Hebrew, Greek," for, Greek being the speech of Egypt to an Elizabethan classical student, these are the languages of the three lands which almost meet in "faire *Larissa* Plaines."

As a boundary town, Larissa is suitable also for the meeting place of Tamburlaine with his generals, and for the starting-point of their concerted operations against the Turks. Delayed there by his grief and vengeance, Tamburlaine sends on ahead a flying column; when the last scene at Larissa closes, he sets out

> Towards *Techelles* and *Theridamas,*
> That we haue sent before to fire the townes,
> The towers and cities of these hatefull Turks.
>
> (III. ii.)

These words prepare us definitely for the next scene, of which equally definitely the opening lines tell us the situation, the speaker being Theridamas:

> Thus have wee martcht Northwarde from *Tamburlaine,*
> Vnto the frontier point of *Soria:*

> And this is *Balsera* their chiefest hold,
> Wherein is all the treasure of the land.
>
> (III. iii.)

Here is a difficulty at first sight, for Balsera or Balsara (which Milton scans as Balsára) is undoubtedly the common Elizabethan form of the modern Basra; yet Basra is certainly not "Northwarde from *Tamburlaine*," nor can it by any stretch of geographical imagination be called a "frontier point of Soria." It is significant that the name of this besieged fortress is given only this once, and with no unfamiliar name is a printer so likely to err as with one that ignorance immediately assumes to be well-known; "security is mortals' chiefest enemy." It is an obvious absurdity that Tamburlaine, advancing from Egypt against Asia Minor, should send a skirmishing party right off his line of march, across the dreaded Arabian Desert, to the very country that he is reserving for his next campaign. We have seen once already that Marlowe can be trusted in his points of the compass; if, before emending to southward, we take him on trust here, we must assume that the unknown town is on the northern or Natolian frontier of Soria, for the column has started from Larissa on the southern frontier. Ortelius can help us out with a suggestion. In the map of Natolia, especially noticeable in the coloured copies as a frontier point, is the town Passera, with the first "s" long. This may well be Marlowe's Balsera. The objection occurs that the arbitrary choice of an insignificant town is not probable, but, as will be shown, Marlowe often makes just such a choice. Moreover, this particular episode is a patchwork of borrowed scraps, and it seems to be his practice to situate his invented episodes in places unimpeachable by their very obscurity.

When the hold has been seized, Theridamas prepares to meet Tamburlaine,

> Who by this time is at *Natolia*,
> Ready to charge the army of the Turke.

Again the scenes are strictly linked; the next (III, v) brings us to the Turkish camp, where a messenger breaks in and is the first speaker:

> Here at *Alepo* with an hoste of men
> Lies *Tamburlaine*, this king of *Persea*: . . .
> Who meanes to gyrt *Natolias* walles with siege,
> Fire the towne and ouerrun the land.

That "Here" is a splendid southward gesture, telling whence the messenger has come hotfoot, for the enemy is at his heels, and enters upon this very scene. The Turks themselves are "in Natolia," and on its eastern confines, for the snake-like trail of their army covers the land

from the bounds of *Phrigia* to the sea
Which washeth *Cyprus* with his brinish waues.

Now comes a difficulty. Again Marlowe uses caution and refrains from committing himself to a definite site for his invented battle. The only indication of place comes later, when Tamburlaine reminds his pampered jades of *"Asphaltis,* where I conquer'd you," and rewards with queens apiece his common soldiers that fought "So Lion-like vpon *Asphaltis* plaines." The name that springs unbidden to the mind is *Lacus Asphaltites,* but a moment's reflection shows its unsuitability. Tamburlaine is last heard of at Aleppo, the Turks are in Natolia, and the battle must take place in that direction. The only reference in the Marlovian canon to the Dead Sea is in *Edward II,* where the English name is used with a play upon its Latin equivalent. When Marlowe speaks later in *Tamburlaine* of *Limnasphaltis,* and of *Asphaltis lake,* he is referring to the bituminous waters of the Euphrates near Babylon. For the first time Ortelius affords no help; Marlowe seems, like a mischievous "hare," to have succeeded in putting us off the scent. He has done two things to confuse: he speaks of Natolia as if it were a town; then he introduces for the site of his battle Asphaltis, a place apparently not known to classical or modern geography.

Yet there is a clue left. Twice, and with some emphasis, does the Sultan Callapine refer boastfully to the coming conflict as "the Perseans sepulchre." To any classical student poring over this cockpit of the world, remembrance would inevitably come of other campaigns, other conquerors, and of these the greatest is that "Chiefe spectacle of the world's preheminence," Alexander the Great, the most familiar of all ancient worthies to the Elizabethan. Issus and Arbela, Alexander's two great defeats inflicted on the Persians, lie roughly to west and to east of that area north of Aleppo whither Marlowe has led his Tamburlaine. Each of these battlefields could suggest the phrase, "the Perseans sepulchre." Again, Abraham Hartwell, the Elizabethan translator of the chronicler Minadoi, uses the very word when he describes the defeat, in Marlowe's lifetime, of the Persians by the Turks, as "the perpetuall sepulcher of a couragious and warlike people." But, even granted that Alexander's victories may be in Marlowe's mind, why Asphaltis? The bituminous nature of the Euphrates basin is a commonplace of cosmography and of the history of Alexander's campaign. Plutarch's life of the conqueror describes his naïve surprise and still more naïve experiment, when, after leaving Arbela, he first saw what Tennyson has called "the Memmian naphtha-pits." Marlowe, like Hakluyt, might have heard the contemporary testimony of the merchant, John Eldred, who journeyed from Babylon to Aleppo in 1583, and heard the many "springs of tarre" blowing and puffing like a smith's forge.

After this break, which leaves us with the area between Aleppo and the Tigris on which to exercise conjecture, the thread can be picked up again with the help of Ortelius. Tamburlaine, on his expedition to Babylon, halts with his harnessed captives at Byron (IV, iii). It is the last stage of his journey, for in the maps of Asia and *Turcicum Imperium*, Biron is only a few miles up-stream from Babylon or Bagdet itself; it is the town of which Gazellus, who so strangely drops out of the play after Act II, is viceroy. Finally Tamburlaine reaches the eternized city of Babylon:

> Where *Belus, Ninus* and great *Alexander*
> Haue rode in triumph, triumphs *Tamburlaine.*

Hither to "*Asia Maior,* where the streames, Of *Euphrates* and *Tigris* swiftly runs," Callapine pursues with a fresh army, and halts so near that he can "behold great Babylon, Circled about with *Limnasphaltis* Lake"; Ortelius portrays the lake, but does not name it. Callapine falls upon the Persians, trusting to their being "faint and weary with the siege," but his army flees "Like Summers vapours, vanisht by the Sun," and Callapine owes his escape only to his great and unseen ally who "Giues battile gainst the heart of *Tamburlaine.*"

The conqueror's legacy to his sons is the extent of the world yet left for conquest. On the map he traces the five thousand leagues of his journeys, arrogating to himself the campaigns of his under-kings through Africa and beyond *Græcia.* Regretfully he sees worlds yet to conquer:

> see what a world of ground
> Lies westward from the midst of *Cancers* line, . . .
> And from th' Antartique Pole, Eastward behold
> As much more land, which neuer was descried.

The gold mines, spices, and jewels of the New World, the glittering ice-wall of the Antarctic, lure him still: "And shal I die, and this vnconquered?" It is the cry of Alexander, reversed in accordance with those new world conditions that nothing brings home to the mind so forcibly as a map. The play ends on the note of the aspiring motto adopted by Charles V, *Plus ultra,* There *is* more beyond.

With the aid of Ortelius, we can thus make our own plan of the campaigns of Tamburlaine in Part II; only twice are we left in comparative uncertainty and each time it is for an invented battle. Marlowe's caution in battle sites had begun even in Part I, for where the defeat of Bajazeth was located by one at least of his authorities as Mount Stella near Ancyra, he is never more explicit than "in Bithynia."

Encouraged, we turn to Ortelius for help in identifying names that have no place on the lines of march, but are scattered lavishly through the play, and we find that, without a single exception, every non-classical name appears in the *Theatrum.* Marlowe must have turned the atlas to and fro, and picked out a name here and there, attracted partly, but not entirely, by its sonority.

When Callapine plans his escape from Egypt (I, iii), a Turkish galley lies waiting for him in *"Darotes* streames" that run "By *Cario . . .* to *Alexandria* Bay." In *Africa* and *Turcicum Imperium,* Darote or Derote is a town at the bend of the westernmost arm of the Nile delta, that is, on the river-way from Cairo to Alexandria.[5] Callapine has to buy over his jailer with the bribe of kingship, and later (III, v) he keeps his promise by investing him

> king of *Ariadan,*
> Bordering on *Mare Roso* neere to *Meca.*

This exactly describes the position in the map of Africa of this unimportant town that Marlowe arbitrarily selected; it appears again in *Turcicum Imperium,* but much less conspicuous, and the sea there is not called *Mar Rosso.* Again another example: Tamburlaine's son Amyras, reproaching his brother for cowardice, vows that he would not so incur his father's fury for

> all the lofty mounts of *Zona Mundi,*
> That fill the midst of farthest *Tartary.*

>   (IV, i.)

In *Europe* and *Russia,* the range of *Zona mundi montes,* or *Orbis Zona montes,* runs southwards through northernmost Tartary from the coast near Waygatz and Petsora, in the coloured maps most obviously "farthest *Tartary."*

The journeys of Tamburlaine's three generals (I, vi) were evidently planned by Marlowe with the *Theatrum* before him. The southward march through Africa of Techelles has already been traced. In the same map Marlowe would find the towns conquered by Techelles and Usumcasane in the north of Africa: Azamor, Fes, Tesella (south of Oran), the province Gualata, and *Canariȩ Insulȩ.* Just as he shortened Manicongo into Manico for his metre, so here he shortens Biledulgerid into Biledull, with the excuse that the name of this province is so divided here in two layers. *Estrecho de Gibraltar* here, and in *Europe* and *Spain,* gives him "the narrow straight of *Gibralter,"* so that it is not necessary even for the metre to replace this new form by that of *Tamburlaine,* Part I, *Jubaltér.*

For the last series of exploits Marlowe seeks variety and forsakes *Africa* for *Europe;* Theridamas tells how by the river *Tyros* he subdued

> *Stoka, Padalia,* and *Codemia.*
> Then crost the sea and came to *Oblia,*

[5] In the half-page map, *Ægypti Recentior Descriptio,* Deruti is on an arm of the river branching eastwards to Rosetta.

> And *Nigra Silua,* where the Deuils dance, . . .
> From thence I crost the Gulfe, call'd by the name
> *Mare magiore,* of th' inhabitantes.

With some variations of spelling that make one wonder whether Marlowe's o's and a's were almost indistinguishable, all these names cluster round the north-west shore of the Black Sea, the *Mare Magiore*. The River Tyros (the Dniester) acts as the southern border of the province Podolia; Stoko is on it, and Codemia lies to the north-east on another stream. Partly separating Codemia from Olbia, and thus perhaps suggesting an otherwise unnecessary sea journey, is the thick, green, hollow square of Nigra Silva, but even in this picture atlas there is never a devil dancing there. It is disconcerting to find the Black Forest cropping up thus near Odessa, but a quotation given by Mercator in his later atlas explains both the position and the ill repute: "La Forest Hercynie va iusques . . . a ce qu'elle aye atteint les derniers Tartares, ou elle se nomme la Forest noire ou obscure, sans bornes, sans chemins, ny sentiers fraiez: et tant pour la cruauté des bestes farouches, que pour *les monstrueuses terreurs des Faunes espouventables,* du tout inaccessible aux humains." [6]

With the map of Europe still open, Marlowe plays the same game on a smaller scale with the petty kings of the Turkish army, gathering their levies from their subject-towns (III, i). The king of Jerusalem naturally raises his from "*Iudæa, Gaza,* and *Scalonians* bounds"; that the town of Ascalon appears in the map as Scalona effectively disposes of the 1605 Quarto's absurd change to *Sclauonians,* apparently a confused reminiscence of the earlier enumeration of Sigismond's composite army of "Sclauonians, Almans, Rutters, Muffes, and Danes."

For the king of Trebizond, Marlowe's finger traces from west to east the northern seaboard of Asia Minor: Chia, Famastro, Amasia (here the province only), Trebisonda, Riso, Santina. For the king of Soria, he passes from Aleppo south-westward to the sea-coast near Cyprus, and chooses Soldino and Tripoli, and so inland again to Damasco; and in passing it may be said that this form Damasco, which is that of four out of five of the modern maps in the *Theatrum,* replaces in Part II, except for a single genitive use, the form Damascus regular in Part I. When the king of Soria is enumerating later his further reinforcements (III, v), he adds Halla; this might well be thought to be one of the many variants of Aleppo (Alepo, Halep, Aleb), but it appears in the map of the world as a separate town to the south-east of Aleppo.

With the same geographical justice does Marlowe treat his Christian leaders; Frederick complains of the cruel Turkish massacres done

---

[6] French text of 1619, p. 227. Cf. A. H. Gilbert, *A Geographical Dictionary of Milton,* *s.v.* Hercynian Wilderness.

> Betwixt the citie *Zula* and *Danubius,*
> [And] through the midst of *Verna* and *Bulgaria*
> And almost to the very walles of *Rome.*
>
> (II, i.)

Zula, which has vanished from the average modern map, appears in the *Europe* of Ortelius to the north of the Danube, in the province of Rascia; the same map offers a possible explanation of that puzzling *Rome,* which cannot mean Rome though it may mean Constantinople: the word may have been suggested by ROMA in large type just north of Constantinople, violently and ludicrously separated from its NIA.

The last of all these scattered names carries us farther afield; the passage must be quoted in full, for a very pretty problem of punctuation is involved:

> He brings a world of people to the field,
> From *Scythia* to the Oriental Plage
> Of *India,* wher raging *Lantchidol*
> Beates on the regions with his boysterous blowes,
> That neuer sea-man yet discouered:
> All *Asia* is in armes with *Tamburlaine,*
> Euen from the midst of fiery *Cancers* Tropick,
> To *Amazonia* vnder *Capricorne.*
> And thence as far as *Archipellago*:
> All *Affrike* is in Armes with *Tamburlaine.*
>
> (I, i.)

Broughton's note, "Lantchidol was the name of the part of the Indian Ocean lying between Java and New Holland," was possibly due to the reproduction of the *Typus Orbis Terrarum* in Hakluyt, or to the mention of the sea in Willes's translation of Pigafetta's voyage in his *History of Travayle* (1577, f. 446 *verso*). Marlowe could read of it there or could, before Hakluyt, find it in the original map, where *Lantchidol Mare* borders a promontory of yet unexplored land, in outline suggesting the north-west of Australia, but here merely designated *Beach.* The name, apparently a native one, may have recalled to Marlowe's mind, through its English synonym, the phrase that he knew from other sources, "Oriental Plage." But with that map of the world before him, and with the map of Africa in his head, Marlowe did not make the mistake that almost every editor has made for him by altering the punctuation of the Octavo of 1592. He did not think that Asia, or even its farthest isles, extended "under *Capricorne";* yet that is how almost every editor punctuates the lines. No, the sense-division is at *"Tamburlaine";* from Scythia to the farthest

East Indies, all Asia is in arms with Tamburlaine; from the Canaries (the juncture of Cancer and the Meridian) southward to *Amazonum Regic* and the land under Capricorne, and thence northward again to the islands of the Mediterranean, all Africa is in arms with Tamburlaine. The second part is a summary of the generals' campaigns in Africa, to be expanded and detailed later. The colons at *discouered* and at *Archipellago* are attractive examples of their use to denote the "actor's pause," the rhetorical upward intonation and emphasis at the end of the line, before the drop to the end of the sense-paragraph, such as is still heard at the *Comédie Française*. Here they do not imply a division of sense; that comes on the name that tolls four strokes throughout the speech like a knell of doom.

Emboldened by this evidence of knowledge and reasonableness on Marlowe's part, we can attack at last that apparently insuperable difficulty of the Danube flowing into the Mediterranean. Knowing as we do that Marlowe had studied the shores of the Black Sea, north, south, east, and west, we cannot believe that he made such a blunder. Yet there it is. Orcanes, when actually "on *Danubius* banks," utters himself thus:

> Our Turky blades shal glide through al their throats,
> And make this champion mead a bloody Fen.
> *Danubius* stream that runs to *Trebizon*,
> Shal carie wrapt within his scarlet waues,
> As martiall presents to our friends at home
> The slaughtered bodies of these Christians.
> The Terrene main wherin *Danubius* fals,
> Shall by this battell be the bloody Sea.
> The wandring Sailers of proud *Italy*,
> Shall meet those Christians fleeting with the tyde,
> Beating in heaps against their Argoses.
>
> (I, i.)

As an act of faith, inspired by the trustworthiness of Marlowe on other points, we may assume that he intends some meaning. Here are two statements, mutually contradictory, and equally absurd: first the Danube flows to Trebizond, then it falls into the Mediterranean. Yet Shakespeare says almost the same thing and no modern editor cries out on his ignorance:

> Like to the Pontick Sea,
> Whose icy current and compulsive course
> Ne'er feels retiring ebb, but keeps due on
> To the Propontick and the Hellespont,

> Even so my bloody thoughts, with violent pace,
> Shall ne'er look back, ne'er ebb to humble love.
>
> (*Othello*, III, iii.)

Annotators quote from Philemon Holland's version of Pliny, but an even clearer description of the violent flow of the Bosporus from north to south is given by the sixteenth-century traveller, Petrus Gyllius, who sums up quaintly thus: "The Mæotis is the mother of the Pontus, and the Pontus the father of the Bosporus, the Propontis, and the Hellespont. . . . So great is the rapidity of the Bosporus that the current is visible as it is forced out into the Propontis." This last is precisely Marlowe's idea. He sees the waters of the Danube sweeping from the river-mouths in two strong currents, the one racing across the Black Sea to Trebizond, the other swirling southwards to the Bosporus, and so onward to the Hellespont and the Ægean. Both currents bear the slaughtered bodies of Christian soldiers, the one to bring proof of victory to the great Turkish town, the other to strike terror to the Italian merchants cruising round the Isles of Greece. Nicholas Nicholay, one of Marlowe's recognized authorities, definitely connects the "compulsive course" with the flow of rivers: "But for so much as many great rivers . . . from Europe doe fall into the Blacke and Euxine Sea, it commeth to pass that beyng full, she gusheth out through the mouth of her wyth great vyolence intoo the Sea Pontique (i. e. Propontic) and from thence through the streit of Hellesponthus . . . into the Sea of Egee." Perondinus, another source, in speaking of Bajazeth's defeat by Tamburlaine, uses an expression that may have given the idea to Marlowe: *Eufrates . . . maiore sanguinis et aquarum vi ad mare Rubrum volveretur;* here, like Marlowe, he considers the main sea into which the inland sea opens to be the outlet of the river, for *Mare Rubrum* can include the modern Arabian Sea, as it does in the *Turcicum Imperium* of Ortelius.

The whole question of the Mediterranean was much debated in the sixteenth century, cosmographers being divided in opinion on the westerly or the north-easterly source of its waters. Gyllius, sent to Constantinople to collect information for the French king, thinks the subject worth some chapters. The matter was so much a commonplace of educated knowledge that Marlowe takes its familiarity for granted, and goes a step beyond. Shakespeare describes the process, and characteristically uses it as a metaphor for the feelings of an individual. Marlowe assumes the process, sees with poetic clairvoyance what might actually be the grim result, and paints the picture, partly for its own sake and partly for its effect. It is an example of what Mr. Lewis Einstein has said: "Marlowe regarded eloquence as the instrument by which the imagination should be freed."

As we follow these tracks through the *Theatrum,* the conviction grows that Marlowe used this source at least with the accuracy of a scholar and the common sense of a merchant-venturer, as well as with the imagination of a poet. The assurance is all the more welcome as it supports the growing belief, expressed by such a critic as Swinburne, and by such an authority on Marlowe as Professor Tucker Brooke, that he was something more than a dramatist of swashbuckling violence and chaotic inconsequence—a *Miles Gloriosus* of English drama. Here we find order for chaos, something of the delicate precision of the draughtsman for the crude formlessness of the impressionist. Panoramic though his treatment still may be, there is method in his seven-league-booted strides. We wrong Marlowe if, in our eagerness to praise his high moments of poetic inspiration, we mistakenly depreciate his qualities of intellect, of mental curiosity, and logical construction. We do him wrong, being so majestical, to see in him only this show of violence. Here are a careful setting of the stage, and a linking of scene with scene by place-indications as capable, though not as beautiful, as those of Shakespeare.

This precise handling of a source need not be thought a sign of pedantry in Marlowe; scholarly he was, but not pedantic, not the type to

love a cell
And—like a badger—with attentive looks
In the dark hole sit rooting up of books.

The proof of this seems to lie in the fact that, after the Second Part of *Tamburlaine,* he did not thus use the *Theatrum* again, although the map of the Mediterranean was clear in his mind when he wrote *The Jew of Malta.* The book had served his purpose, and with the royal "forward view" of genius, he passed on. De Quincey's words are illustrated: "All action in any direction is best expounded, measured, and made apprehensible by reaction": the completeness of Marlowe's reaction is the measure of his growth. The impulse came rather, as has been suggested to me, from an interest in strategy. He was playing a great game of chess, with kings and conquerors for pieces, and for chess board the *Theatrum Orbis Terrarum:* a *Kriegspiel,* such as many recently have played with the aid of flags on pins; but his game, being imaginary, without our bitter urgency, was excellent sport. It has been said that the Second Part is a mercenary afterthought, that the parade of geographical terms covers a weakening of poetic impulse. Yet at the least it was a final effervescence of boyishness, of satisfaction in youthful cleverness, in "pulling the thing off," pardonable in a young graduate of twenty-four. At most, it was something more. Even in this his poetic power found outlet. Even here, from the bare outlines of maps, and perhaps from the dry statements of cosmographers, he "bodied forth the forms of things unknown." He saw the Polar cliffs as "rocks of shining pearl"; he heard the boisterous waves of raging Lantchidol beat on an uncharted coast. He pored over this great atlas until the countries "came alive," and the creatures of his brain went through such adventures as fell to the lot of many an Englishman of his time. His Techelles, halting on the western coast of Africa *"view'd* The Ethiopian sea"; the word is significant. It is the same experience of poetic apprehension as Keats more strongly felt, and more felicitously expressed, when he saw the rapt wonder of his Cortes, "Silent upon a peak in Darien."

Tamburlaine's Passions

by Roy W. Battenhouse

When we read attentively what the Elizabethans had to say in criticism of the human passions, it becomes very clear why Fortescue could think Tamburlaine an "incarnate devil." The tragic flaw in Tamburlaine's nature goes deep. As judged by sixteenth-century standards, his passions have fallen victim to three ills: immoderation, misdirection, and delusion. Or, to put the matter another way, his tragedy is explainable in terms of the degenerate source of his inspiration, the mistaken goal of his aspiration, and the intemperate course of his desire. Let us examine in turn each of these considerations.

I

In studying Elizabethan theory of the passions we need to observe, first of all, that literary opinion was on the side of Aristotle and the Platonists, as opposed to the Stoics. That is to say, it was held by most authors that man's passions are beneficial, provided they are kept temperate. Philemon Holland refers to

the absurdities of the said Stoicke Philosophers, who instead of well governing and ruling the soule of man, have as much as lieth in them, extinguished and abolished the same! [1]

As champion against the Stoics, Holland recommends Plutarch; for Plutarch proclaims that virtue arises not from the abolition of the unreasonable part of the soul, but from its ordering and moderation.[2] On this same question Nashe tells us that he holds to the Peripatetic view of the passions as against the Stoic.[3] And Chapman, also, is not the Stoic

[1] Holland's "Summarie" of chap. iv. of his translation of Plutarch's *Morals* (1603), p. 64.
[2] *Morals*, p. 68.
[3] *Anatomie of Absurditie*, ed. McKerrow, I, 27.

many critics have thought him to be: instead of *apatheia* we get from his
Tears of Peace the declaration that "Homer hath told me that there
are / Passions in which corruption hath no share. . . . To stand at
gaze / In one position, is a stupid maze, / Fit for a statue." [4]

A typical Elizabethan historian such as Higgins rests his judgments of
tragedy on the view of the passions taught by Plotinus. In introducing
The First Parte of the Mirrour for Magistrates (1574) Higgins declares
that the desire of glory is admirable, provided it is kept within bounds:

> *Plotinus* that wonderfull and excellent Philosopher hath these wordes: The
> property of Temperaunce is to couet nothing which may be repented: not to
> excede the bands of measure, & to kepe Desire vnder the yoke of Reason. . . .
> For to couet without consideration: to passe the measure of his degree, and to
> lette will run at random, is the only destruction of all estates. . . . Will you
> that I rehearse *Alexander* the Great, *Caesar, Pompey, Cyrus, Hannibal,* &c. All
> which (by desier of glorye) felte the rewarde of theire immoderate and in-
> satiable lustes. . . . I surely deme those Princes above specified (considering
> their factes, estates, fortunes, fame and exploytes) had neuer come to suche
> ende, but for wante of temperance.[5]

The view may be compared with that of John Davies of Hereford, who in
the midst of a long discussion of the passions declares that Choler, if kept
at a mean, "yeeldes most sweet effects," making the Wit and Courage
great.

> And if with *fury* it be not disgrac'd,
> It should by al *meanes,* by *all* be embrac'd.[6]

Temperance, moderation, "mediocritie," the mean—these constitute
the recurring theme of Renaissance writers. Greville speaks of "medioc-
rity, that reciprocall paradise of mutuall humane duties." [7] He complains
that "in man's muddy soule the meane doth not content. . . . This makes
some soare and burne." [8] Amiot, the great translator of Plutarch's *Lives,*
declares that "the commendation of all doinges" consists in "the meane
poynt, betweene the two faultie extremities of too much and too little." [9]
La Primaudaye says he takes his stand with Socrates: Temperance is "the
ground-worke and foundation of all vertues," for "no man can find out
any thing that is so excellent and woonderfull as temperance, the guide
and gouernor of the soule." [10] Most succinctly, perhaps, the reasons for

---

[4] Chapman's *Poems* (London, 1875), p. 113, col. 2.
[5] "To the Nobilitie and all other in office," ed. Haslewood, I, 3-4.
[6] *Microcosmos,* ed. Grosart, I. c. 74.
[7] *Life of Sidney,* ed. Grosart, IV, 179.
[8] The Chorus of Good Spirits in *Alaham,* Act 1, ed. Grosart, III, 194.
[9] "Amiot to the Readers," Plutarch's *Lives* (1579), trans. North.
[10] *The French Academie,* pp. 180, 181.

giving moderation the primary place in ethical theory are stated by Sir William Cornwallis:

> without moderation, the wit of man will serue a wrong master; without modera-
> tion, the body will rebel against the soule, without moderation, the soule yeelds
> to the body; in a word, vnmoderated, both soule and body perisheth. This is
> shee that makes the distinction betwixt vertue and vice; this is she that makes
> courage valor, that without moderation would be anger, and then fury; this is
> she that separateth iustice and cruelty, prouidence from feare, power from
> tyranny, maiesty from pride.[11]

When we put Marlowe's Tamburlaine against the background of this commentary, it is plain that the conqueror's dramatic career is a notable example of lack of temperance. He belongs in the class of world conquerors lamented by Higgins—with Alexander, Caesar, and Hannibal— men who "lette will runne at random" to the destruction of the world and to their own self-misery. Lacking the moderation which Cornwallis says is necessary to prevent a man from serving a wrong master, Tamburlaine serves earthly glory. Lacking the moderation which distinguishes virtue from vice, his courage becomes, as Cornwallis predicts, not valor but anger and fury. Failure in moderation causes him, Greville would say, to "soare and burne."

II

But secondly, and more basically, we must be concerned with a further question: What was the reason for Tamburlaine's failure in moderation? Here, too, the Elizabethans have well-established theory. Immoderation, and all its attendant perturbations of the soul, are due, says La Primau-daye, to *misdirected* desire. Desire is natural to every soul; but those souls who through ignorance set their desire on worldly goods can never find contentment:

> The Philosophers teach vs by their writings, and experience doth better
> shew it vnto vs, that to couet and desire is proper to the soule, and that from
> thence all the affections and desires of men proceede, which draw them hither
> and thither diuersly, that they may attaine to that thing, which they thinke is
> able to lead them to the enioying of some good, whereby they may liue a
> contented and happie life. Which felicitie, the most part of men, through false
> opinion, or ignorance rather of that which is good, and by following the in-
> clination of their corrupted nature, do seeke and labor to finde in humane
> and earthlie things, as in riches, glorie, honor, and pleasure. But forasmuch as
> the enioying of these things doth not bring with it sufficient cause of contenta-
> tion, they percieue themselues alwaies depriued of the end of their desires, and

[11] *Discourses upon Seneca the Tragedian* (1961), Sig. L1, 4ᵛ.

are constrained to wander all their life time beyond all bounds and measure, according to the rashnes and inconstancie of their lusts. . . . Briefly, all men whose harts are set vpon worldly goods, when they are come to this estate of life, they would attaine to that: and being come thereunto, some other newe desire carrieth them farther, so that this mischiefe of continuall, vncertaine, and vnsatiable lustes and desires doth more and more kindle in them vntill in the ende death cut off the thred of their inconstant, and neuer contented life. . . . But they, who through the studie of wisdome are furnished with skill and vnderstanding, and know that all humane and earthlie things are vncertaine, deceitfull, slipperie, and so many allurements vnto men to drawe them into a downe-fall and destruction, they I say, doe laie a farre better and more certaine foundation of their chiefe GOOD, contentation, and felicitie. . . . And deliuering their soules by the grace of God, from all those perturbations, which besiege them in the prison of their bodies, they lift vp their wishes and desires, yea they refer al the ends of their intents and actions to this only marke, to be vnited and ioined to the last end of their soueraigne GOOD, which is the full and whole fruition of the essence of God. . . .[12]

Instead of "the full and whole fruition of the essence of God" which La Primaudaye recommends, Tamburlaine knows only "The sweet fruition of an earthly crowne." This blindness-of-mind we may regard as the cause of Tamburlaine's never contented life. His argument for thinking an earthly crown the sole felicity is that Nature teaches us to have aspiring minds. But La Primaudaye holds that "No man *by nature* [italics mine] can finde out the right way that leadeth to happines. . . . The word of God sheweth vs the right way to happines." [13] Tamburlaine's aspiration, obviously, is not rooted in the word of God. Fundamentally pagan, he knows what Nature's "foure Elements" teach him—no more. Therefore his desire looks toward a wholly earthly good and runs, naturally, head-long into Ambition.

But AMBITION, as Renaissance moralists never tired of pointing out, was the ruin of Phaëton and of Adam.

> Beware ambition, 'tis a sugred pill,
> That fortune layes, presuming minds to kill.[14]

Much of the detail with which Ambition's features were conventionally drawn has pattern-significance for the portrait of Tamburlaine. We should observe, for example, in La Primaudaye that

Ambition neuer suffreth those that haue once receiued hir as a guest, to enioy their present estate quietly. . . . And the more they growe and increase in

[12] The opening words of "The Author to the Reader" of *The French Academie* (1586).
[13] *Ibid.*, p. 31 marginally.
[14] Bodenham's *Belvedere* (1600), p. 109.

power and authoritie, the rather are they induced and caried headlong by their
affections to commit all kind of iniustice, and flatter themselues in furious and
frantike actions, that they may come to the end of their infinite platformes, and
of that proud and tyrannicall glory, which, contrarie to all dutie they seeke
after.[15]

Or if we look into Du Bartas, at the point where he is describing the dis-
eases of the soul in his poem *The Furies,* we find a picture of "secret-
burning" Ambition

> Pent in no limits, pleas'd with no Condition;
> Whom *Epicurus* many Worlds suffice not,
> Whose furious thirst of proud aspiring dyes not
> Whose hands (transported with fantastick passion)
> Bear painted Scepters in imagination.[16]

Pierre Charron[17] furnishes us a particularly detailed portrait of Ambition. Ambition, he says, is the strongest and most powerful passion that
is, surmounting all other passions. Alexander, who courageously refused
to touch the most beautiful damsel that was in his power, burned nevertheless with ambition, and indeed made his victory over love serve his
ambition. Ambition, furthermore, takes away a man's concern for his life;
it causes him to contemn religion; and it offers violence even to the laws
of nature, for it causes the murder of parents, children, and brothers.
Finally,

Ambition hath no limits, it is a gulfe that hath neither brinke nor bottome;
it is that vacuity which the Philosophers could neuer find in Nature; a fire
which increaseth by that nourishment that is giuen vnto it. Wherein it truly
payeth his master: for ambition is onely iust in this, that it sufficeth for his own
punishment, and is executioner to it selfe. The Wheele of Ixion is the motion
of his desires, which turne and returne vp and downe, neuer giuing rest vnto his
minde.
They that will flatter ambition, say it is a seruant or helpe vnto vertue, and
a spurre to beautiful actions; for it quitteth a man of all other sinnes, and in
the end, of himselfe too; and all for vertue: but it is so farre from this, that it
hideth sometimes our vices; but it takes them not away, but it couereth or
rather hatcheth them for a time vnder the deceitfull cinders of a malitious
hypocrisie, with hope to set them on fire altogether, when they haue gotten
authority sufficient to raigne publiquely and with impiety. . . . An ambitious
man putteth himselfe forth to great and honourable actions, the profit whereof

[15] *The French Academie,* p. 224.
[16] Lines 702-07, ed. Grosart, *Works of Sylvester,* I, 120.
[17] *Of Wisdome,* tr. Samson Lennard (1630), Bk. I, chap. xx. Charron's *Traité de la
Sagesse* was first published in 1595.

returneth to the publique good, but yet he is neuer the better man that per-
formes them, because they are not the actions of vertue but of passion. . . .[18]

These characteristic features of Ambition appear in Marlowe's portrait
of Tamburlaine. Tamburlaine can enjoy no rest. He is insatiably greedy
for glory. He loves to flatter himself in furious and frantic actions. His
hands may be said to "Bear painted Scepters in imagination" at the moment when, fingering the banquet cates of crowns, he indulges in dreams
of empire and bestows upon his lieutenants the as yet unconquered kingdoms of Egypt, Arabia, and Damascus.[19] Charron's point that Alexander
for ambition's sake kept himself chaste toward the beautiful damsel finds
parallel in Tamburlaine's boast that he has not violated Zenocrate:

> Her state and person wants no pomp you see,
> And for all blot of foule inchastity,
> I record heauen, her heauenly selfe is cleare.
>
> (*Tamb.* 2267-69.)

Charron's observation that those who flatter Ambition can say it is a spur
to beautiful actions also finds point, for Tamburlaine's ambition makes
him valorous, magnanimous, and eloquent. To his last moment he behaves
magnificently. However, his death scene also reveals plainly, fulfilling
Charron's portrait, the impiety and torment of unsatisfied desire. Ambition has burned to a fever of madness in Tamburlaine so that it
punishes itself.

Still there is, some of us feel, another aspect to Tamburlaine's soul. Besides his lust for power, there is his worship of beauty. We would like to
think that this latter quality is a point at which we may safely approve
his behavior. However, if we would be strictly fair to our Elizabethan
commentary, we must regard Tamburlaine's attitude toward beauty, too,
as instance of misdirected or corrupt desire. The beauties he worships are
earthly rather than heavenly. Pools of blood and tongues of fire, crowns,
"humaine" poetry, and Zenocrate—these his imagination exalts. He takes
them, mistakenly, for heavenly beauties: he supposes that wars illustrate
the life of gods, that the pursuit of crowns makes him and his men god-
like, that poetry is the human mind's distillation of some "heauenly
Quintessence," and that Zenocrate's beauty ranks her with the angels and
the "holy Seraphins." Each of these judgments is sturdily pagan—hence
(from a Christian point of view) false.

No Protestant humanist would say that Tamburlaine's pursuit of
earthly crowns or his love of earthly Zenocrate makes him genuinely god-

---

[18] *Ibid.*, p. 82.
[19] *Tamb.* 1747 ff.

like. On the contrary, these loves make him impious. It is a mad worship which causes him to threaten heaven and to burn Larissa. His Zenocrate is a beauty like Homer's Helen, not like Dante's Beatrice or Spenser's Una. Like Helen or Cressida, Zenocrate is beautiful, sentimental, inconstant, and vain, for her character is raised wholly on a naturalistic morality. But she has, superbly, the grace of pagan loveliness. And Tamburlaine's attachment is characteristically pagan: "this faire face and heauenly hew / Must grace his bed that conquers *Asia.* . . ."

Also in his devotion to poetry, proclaimed in an elegant and justly famous speech, Tamburlaine cannot get above a pagan understanding. Poetry is for him "The highest reaches of a humaine wit." [20] The view contrasts strikingly with that of John Davies of Hereford, for whom "Poetry [is] no skil humaine," but a divine skill; "For holy Raptures must the Head entrance." [21] According to the doctrine generally held by Elizabethan apologists, true Poetry is a matter not primarily of art, but of inspiration; not a labor, but a gift; not, as Tamburlaine says, a beauty digested by "restlesse heads," but, as Spenser says, a beauty infused into mortal breasts out of the Almighty's bosom.[22] And further, since this view of Tamburlaine's on poetry comes in the drama immediately after he has commanded the slaughter of the virgins, we may note that it does not fit with Spenser's view that true skill in poetry must arise out of "Love devoyd of villanie or ill."

Tamburlaine's worship of beauty, however, is dramatically very appropriate. Sidney had pointed out in his *Defence of Poesie* that poetry is "the companion of Camps," highly honored even by Turks and Tartars.[23] Tamburlaine himself explains that he is turning to beauty's just applause for the reason that

> euery warriour that is rapt with loue,
> Of fame, of valour, and of victory
> Must needs haue beauty beat on his conceites.
>
> (*Tamb.* 1961-63.)

His behavior accords with the Platonic theory that "Mars still doth after Venus move . . . because of Love / Boldness is handmaid"; that

[20] *Tamb.* 1949.

[21] *Microcosmos*, ed. Grosart, I. c. 81.

[22] *Teares of the Muses.* See the discussion of Spenser's theory of poetry by M. Bhattacherje, *Studies in Spenser* (Calcutta, 1929), pp. 48-9. The Elizabethan doctrine goes back to Plato's *Ion:* "All good poets compose their beautiful poems not as works of art, but because they are inspired and possessed." The root of all poetry is love, not wit.

[23] Feuillerat's edition, pp. 5 and 32. Greville makes the same point in *A Treatise of Monarchy*, stanzas 475-6, ed. Grosart, I, 171. Remember also that Milton attributes to the devils in Hell an interest in poetry.

> since men love, they therefore are more bold,
> And made to dare even death for their beloved;
> . . . All things submit to Love. . . .
> Celestials, animals, all corporeal things,
> Wise men and strong, slave-rich, and free-born kings
> Are love's contributories. . . .24

We can understand why Zenocrate is introduced into Marlowe's drama at the beginning of Tamburlaine's career: she provides the warrior a motive for his brave exploits. We find him saying that her beauty adds "more courage to my conquering mind." He boasts of the extensive conquests he will make "To gratify the sweet Zenocrate." 25 Later, her beauty furnishes inspiration for his battle against Bajazet. To fortify his mind for this critical test, he mediates on her beauty, exalts it above the heavens, and concludes:

> Stir not *Zenocrate* vntill thou see
> Me martch victoriously with all my men,
> Triumphing ouer him and these his kings,
> Which I will bring as Vassals to thy feete.
>
> (*Tamb.* 1224-27.)

That she may continue to inspire him and his men with boldness, he preserves a picture after her death:

> Thou shalt be set vpon my royall tent.
> And when I meet an armie in the field,
> Those looks will shed such influence in my campe.
> As if *Bellona*, Goddesse of the war
> Threw naked swords and sulphur bals of fire,
> Vpon the heads of all our enemies.
>
> (*Tamb.* 3227-32.)

A second aspect of Renaissance theory regarding Beauty's effect is neatly stated in a couplet of Chapman's:

---

24 *Andromeda Liberata* (1614), Chapman's *Poems*, pp. 188-9. Mr. F. L. Schoell, *Études sur L'Humanisme Continental en Angleterre* (Paris, 1926), p. 15, shows that the lines here are an almost literal translation from Ficinus' *In Convivium Platonis de Amore Commentarium*, V. viii.

25 *Tamb.* 2297 ff. Compare the anonymous play, *Caesar's Revenge*, I. vi. Caesar, struck by Cleopatra's "louely Tyranizing eyes," likens her to Helen of Troy, admits that his thoughts are "captiud to thy beauties conquering power," and declares that he will conquer Egypt and Africa for her.

> Beauty in heaven and earth this grace doth win,
> It supples rigour, and it lessens sin.[26]

In accord with this theory we note that Zenocrate's beauty, earthly though it is, can modify the sternness of Tamburlaine's spirit. Under the spell of her beauty he spares her father's life. When in Part II of the drama Zenocrate's death has deprived him of Beauty's softening influence, he becomes increasingly savage.

III

Finally, Elizabethan theory enables us to comment on the nature of Tamburlaine's fury. We have already remarked that Renaissance writers were not Stoic in their theory of the passions. Instead of flatly repudiating inspiration, they adopted the Platonic distinction of two types of inspiration. This doctrine, well stated by Du Bartas, is that fury can arise from two widely different sources:

> For euen as humane fury maks the man
> Les then the man: So heauenly fury can
> Make man pas man, and wander in holy mist,
> Vpon the fyrie heauen to walk at list.[27]

Elizabethans regarded this as an important distinction. Barnabe Barnes elaborates upon it in his *A Divine Centurie of Spirituall Sonnets*.[28] And Chapman applies the dichotomy to poetic inspiration:

[26] *Hero and Leander*, Third Sestyad, Chapman's *Poems*, p. 76. For other statements of this same theory, see Spenser, *Faerie Queene*, V. 8. 1; Bodenham, *Belvedere*, p. 44; and Nesca A. Robb, *Neoplatonism of the Italian Renaissance* (London, 1935), p. 218. The doctrine is Platonic.

[27] *The Urania*, stanza 30. The translation here is that of King James, published in *The Essayes of a Prentise, in the Divine Art of Poesie* (Edinburgh, 1585). For Sylvester's later translation, see *Works of Sylvester*, ed. Grosart, II, 4.

[28] He writes "To the Favourable and Christian Reader" (I quote from the reprint of London, 1815): "And if any man feele in himselfe, by the secret fire of immortal enthusiasme, the learned motions of strange and divine passions of spirite; let him refine and illuminate his numerous Muses with the most sacred splendour of the Holie Ghost: and then he shall, with divine Salust (the true learned Frenche poet,) finde, that as humane furie maketh a man lesse than a man, and the very same with wilde, unreasonable beastes; so divine rage and sacred instinct of a man maketh more than man, and leadeth him from his base terrestrial estate, to walke above the starres with angelles immortally."

There being in Poesy a twofold rapture (or alienation of soul, as the above-said teacher terms it) one *insania*, a disease of the mind, and a mere madness, by which the infected is thrust beneath all degrees of humanity: *et ex homine, brutum quodammodo redditur:* (for which poor Poesy, in this diseased and impostorous age, is so barbarously vilified); the other is *divinus furor*, by which the sound and divinely healthful, *supra hominis naturam erigitur, et in Deum transit*. One a perfection directly infused from God; the other an infection obliquely and degenerately proceeding from man. Of the divine fury, my Lord, your Homer hath ever been both first and last instance.[29]

The Elizabethans did not, like some twentieth-century liberals, adopt the notion that all things "spiritual" are divine. Instead, they recognized that the human spirit sometimes burns with what Fulke Greville called "false flames spirituall but infernal." [30] An age which was devoted to Plato was well aware that the tyrant can amazingly resemble his direct opposite, the philosopher king; that indeed the tyrant is simply the tragic caricature of the philosopher.[31]

Tamburlaine, it is true, asserts that his fury is inspired by heaven. It is Jove's spirit, he says, that living in him makes him "valiant, proud, ambitious." [32] But his enemies are not so sure Tamburlaine's inspiration is heaven-sent. The Governor of Babylon calls him "Vile monster . . . sent from hell to tyrannise on earth." [33] And the Souldan of Egypt thinks him a devil, since he is no man.[34] Ortygius, who raises the question "Whether from earth, or hell, or heauen he grow," is not sure whether Tamburlaine is a "God or Feend, or spirit of the earth, / Or Monster turned to a manly shape." [35]

If Elizabethans applied to the judgment of Tamburlaine's fury the current theory of the two types of inspiration which we have just cited, they must certainly have considered the conqueror's passion as arising from a human, not a divine, source. For as the drama proceeds, Tamburlaine becomes increasingly inhuman. His fury "none can quence but

---

[29] Epistle Dedicatory to his translation of the Odyssey, *Poems*, p. 238. The theory of the two types of ecstasy rests on a passage in Plato's *Phaedrus;* but Chapman has taken it from Ficinus' commentary on Plato's *Ion*. See Schoell, *Études*, pp. 1, 4-6. It is interesting to note that Burton, *Anat*. III. iv. 1. 1., applies the dichotomy to religion, saying that religion is of two kinds: false or true. He then points out that when false gods are worshipped or when God is falsely worshipped there results a furious disease of the soul, mere madness, *religiosa insania*.

[30] *Caelica*, CX, ed. Grosart, III, 143.

[31] See Plato's *Repub*., Bk. IX.

[32] *Tamb*. 3785 ff.

[33] *Tamb*. 4223.

[34] *Tamb*. 1414.

[35] *Tamb*. 826-34. Cf. 820-3.

blood and Emperie." [36] Finally, when the madness causes him "to dare
God out of heaven," as Greene put it, his inspiration is surely what Chapman called "an infection obliquely and degenerately proceeding from
man."

In making this candid analysis of Tamburlaine's pretensions, we will
find further support if we recall one of the central doctrines of the Elizabethans. It is stated, for example, in a sermon of Henry Smith, the popular
Elizabethan divine. Magistrates, says Smith,

> which use their power against God, which bear the Lawes against Gods Law,
> and be enemies to his servants . . . cannot so well be called *gods,* as Devils:
> such *gods* go to Hell.[37]

Or the pages of that popular Renaissance moralist, William Baldwin, will
also furnish us commentary for judging Tamburlaine. Kings, Baldwin
says, are given the name of gods because they have in charge the ministra-
tion of justice, but if they pervert this office, then they are not gods, but
devils:

> What a fowle shame wer it for any now to take vpon them the name and
> office of God, and in their doinges to shew them selves divyls? God can not of
> Iustice, but plage such shameles presumption and hipocrisy, and that with
> shamefull death, diseases, or infamy.[38]

Regarded from the Elizabethan vantage point, Tamburlaine's idealism
appears in quite another light than that in which modern criticism has
interpreted it. The great Scythian's tragedy, when measured by the canons
of Marlowe's day, is seen to be the result of uncontrolled, misdirected, and
diseased passions. The spectator feels *pity* when he beholds Tamburlaine's aspiration turned wholly toward things of earth, carrying a noble
man headlong into ambition and its attendant misery. And the spectator
experiences *fear* and takes warning when he sees Tamburlaine's inspiration, grounded in human passions rather than in divine wisdom, bringing
a fevered madness.

Certainly, however, there is no very good reason for identifying Mar-

---

[36] *Tamb.* 843-4.
[37] *Sermons,* p. 337 (editon of 1657). Smith's sermons were printed in many collected
editions, beginning as early as 1591. Nashe eulogizes "Siluer-tongu'd *Smith*" in *Pierce
Penilesse,* ed. McKerrow, I, 192-93.
[38] *Mirror for Magistrates* (1559), "To the nobilitye and all other in office," ed. L. B.
Campbell (Cambridge, 1938), p. 65.

lowe with his stage-character Tamburlaine. Drayton tells us[39] that Marlowe had "that fine madnes. . . . Which rightly should possesse a Poets braine." Why then may we not suppose that the dramatist had in him the "divinely healthful" madness which Chapman says Homer possessed?

[39] "To Henry Reynolds, of Poets and Poesie," *The Battaile of Agincourt, Elegies, etc.* (1627), p. 206.

Tamburlaine

by Eugene M. Waith

Hercules, as he appears in Sophocles, Euripides, and above all Seneca, is revitalized in Tamburlaine. No one of the older plays was used as a model, but Hercules was often in Marlowe's mind as he wrote. Several allusions in the play make this fact indisputable and, as Mario Praz pointed out many years ago, there are striking resemblances between Tamburlaine and Hercules Oetaeus.[1] However, it is finally less important to decide whether Marlowe was deliberately fashioning a Herculean hero than to remember that the traditional depictions of Hercules, especially those from Rome and Renaissance Italy, were thoroughly familiar to him. It is not surprising that Tamburlaine, who had already been used by Louis Le Roy and others as a symbol of the physical and intellectual vigour of the Renaissance,[2] should suggest the Greek hero to him. I believe that his attitude towards Tamburlaine, as expressed in the play, is very similar to the attitudes found in some of the portrayals of Hercules discussed in the previous two chapters. The images created by Seneca and Pollaiuolo can be of great assistance to the spectator of the twentieth century, partially cut off from the traditions in which Marlowe wrote; for they prepare the eye to discern the outlines of Marlowe's heroic figure.

The figure is vast. The very structure of the play conveys this impression, for the succession of scenes—some of them might almost be called tableaux—stretching over great expanses of time and space, presents the man in terms of the places he makes his and the time which at the last he fails to conquer. It is no accident that we always remember the effect of

[1] Mario Praz, "Machiavelli and the Elizabethans," *Proceedings of the British Academy,* XIV (1928), 71 ff. See also Battenhouse [*Marlowe's Tamburlaine*], pp. 196 ff., where the parallel to Seneca's Hercules is used to show that Marlowe depicts Tamburlaine as the type of insatiable conqueror who falls victim to his own covetousness. Since my interpretation of Seneca is totally different from Battenhouse's, the parallel does not seem to me to show anything of the sort.

[2] See Hallet Smith, "Tamburlaine and the Renaissance," *Elizabethan Studies, University of Colorado Studies,* Series B, II, 4 (Boulder, Colorado, 1945); Erich Voegelin, "Das Timurbild der Humanisten," *Zeitschrift für öffentliches Recht,* XVII (1937), 545-82.

Marlowe's resounding geography, for earthly kingdoms are the emblems of Tamburlaine's aspirations. At the end of his life he calls for a map, on which he traces with infinite nostalgia his entire career and points to all the remaining riches which death will keep him from:

> And shall I die, and this unconquered?
>
> (Part II, V. 3, 150.)[3]

To be a world conqueror in the various senses which the play gives to the term is the essence of Tamburlaine's character. That this insight is conveyed in part by the sprawling structure of the play is an important advantage to weigh against some of the obvious disadvantages of such a structure in the theatre. Although complication and even conflict in its fullest sense are almost missing, each successive episode contributes something to the dominant idea—the definition of a hero. There is a forward movement of the play in unfolding not only the narrative but the full picture of the hero. When the play is well acted and directed it has ample theatrical life, no matter how much the form is indebted to epic.

The first view we have of Tamburlaine is a kind of transformation scene. It is preceded by the brief, and basically snobbish descriptions given at the court of Mycetes, the ludicrously incompetent king of Persia, to whom Tamburlaine is a marauding fox,[4] a "sturdy Scythian thief," and the leader of a "Tartarian rout" (I, 1, 31, 36, 71). The Tamburlaine who walks on the stage dressed as a shepherd and leading Zenocrate captive has some of the outward appearance suggested by these descriptions, and the earlier impression of social inferiority is conveyed in the words of Zenocrate, who at first takes him for the shepherd he seems to be (I, 2, 8). However, his words and actions reveal a strikingly different man: he boasts like a genuine hero if not a gentleman, and exchanges his shepherd's weeds for complete armour and curtle-axe. Before our eyes he assumes the outward appearance which matches his warrior's spirit.

Tamburlaine is a proud and noble king at heart, yet his Scythian-shepherd origins give a clue to the absolute difference between him and the world's other kings. His is the intrinsic kingliness of the hero, associated with the ideal of freedom, whereas other kings are presented as oppressors, the products of a corrupt system. The garb of the Scythian

---

[3] All references to *Tamburlaine* are to the revised edition by Una Ellis-Fermor (London: Methuen, 1951). In the performance of *Tamburlaine* directed by Tyrone Guthrie in New York in 1956 a very large map was spread on the floor of the stage, making possible an extraordinarily effective theatrical image. Tamburlaine walked on the map as he pointed to his conquests, and at the end fell down on it, almost covering the world with his prone body.

[4] Battenhouse has pointed to the Machiavellian combination of the fox image in this scene with that of the lion in the following scene (p. 209). See also Harry Levin, *The Overreacher* (Cambridge, Mass.: Harvard University Press, 1952 [pp. 37-8], and London: Faber & Faber [p. 56]).

shepherd, even though he discards it, relates Tamburlaine to the simpler world of an earlier, mythical time. The king he becomes carries with him into a decadent world something of this primitive simplicity. Like his successors, Chapman's Bussy and Dryden's Almanzor, he is an early edition of the "noble savage."

Thus far Tamburlaine appears as a hero in the classic mode, but when he tells Zenocrate that her person "is more worth to Tamburlaine / Than the possession of the Persian crown" (ll. 90-1), the influence of the romance tradition is apparent. In fact, for the moment it seems that the "concupiscible power" of his soul dominates the "irascible power," though the subsequent action shows that this is not true. Tamburlaine's love, expressed in the poetry of the famous speech beginning "Disdains Zenocrate to live with me?" (ll. 82-105), further distinguishes him from his rival warriors. Their pride and their ambition are not accompanied by the imagination which informs his promises to Zenocrate:

> With milk-white harts upon an ivory sled
> Thou shalt be drawn amidst the frozen pools,
> And scale the icy mountains' lofty tops,
> Which with thy beauty will be soon resolv'd.
>
> (ll. 98-101)

The cold fire of this speech is the first testimony of Tamburlaine's imaginative scope and of the paradoxes of his nature; the icy mountain tops are the first memorable image of his aspiration.

The arrival of Theridamas with the Persian forces provides for another surprising revelation of the hero. We have just seen him in the guise of a lover; we now see him as an orator, overcoming Theridamas with words. Marlowe insists on the unexpectedness of these aspects of the hero. "What now? in love?" says Techelles (l. 106), and, when Tamburlaine asks whether he should "play the orator," replies disdainfully that "cowards and faint-hearted runaways / Look for orations" (ll. 130-1). In defiance of this advice, Tamburlaine delivers his brilliantly successful oration, winning from Theridamas the tribute that even Hermes could not use "persuasions more pathetical" (l. 210). Yet, surprising as this eloquence is to Tamburlaine's followers, it is not alien to the Renaissance concept of the Herculean hero. Cartari specifically reminds his readers that Hercules, like Mercury, whom he has just discussed, has been called a patron of eloquence. It is, so to speak, perfectly proper to present a Herculean hero as orator.

Tamburlaine begins his oration with a complimentary picture of Theridamas, but soon turns to himself with the famous boast "I hold the Fates bound fast in iron chains," and the comparisons of himself to Jove. The effect of the speech is double, for though it displays the hero as orator, it also presents, by means of eloquence, his self-portrait as conqueror of

the world and even as demigod. Such self-praise might be taken as Marlowe's way of portraying a man who will say anything to get ahead or of
pointing to the ironical contrast between a man's pride and his accomplishment, but one of the puzzling features of *Tamburlaine* is that the
hero's actions also show him in the guise of a demigod, and only his death
proves that he does not control the fates. Even death is not presented un-
equivocally as defeat. Tamburlaine's extravagant boasts, like those of
Hercules, are largely made good, so that he and his followers become the
amazement of the world. In Usumcasane's words, "These are the men that
all the world admires."

Before Tamburlaine unleashes his persuasive forces Theridamas comments on his appearance in words which emphasize the importance of
visual impressions in this play:

> Tamburlaine! A Scythian shepherd so embellished
> With nature's pride and richest furniture!
> His looks do menace heaven and dare the gods,
> His fiery eyes are fixed upon the earth,
> As if he now devis'd some stratagem,
> Or meant to pierce Avernas' darksome vaults
> To pull the triple headed dog from hell.
>
> (I, 2, 154-60)

Again we have the transformation of the Scythian shepherd into a noble
warrior, but here even the armour appears as part of nature's endowment
of the hero. The eyes fixed on the earth are the symbolic equivalent of
one of Tamburlaine's best-known speeches, in which he makes an earthly
crown the ultimate felicity, but this fixation on the earth is accompanied
by looks which menace heaven and also suggest a Herculean conquest of
hell. The description is perfect, though to use it when the character
described stands before the audience is to risk a ludicrous incongruity.[5]
Marlowe depends on unhesitating acceptance of the verbal picture.

Marlowe's heavy dependence on description is again illustrated in the
next scene, when Menaphon gives Cosroe an even fuller account of
Tamburlaine's looks than we have had from Theridamas. In this speech
the hero's body is made symbolic of his character. He is tall like his desire;
his shoulders might bear up the sky like Atlas; his complexion reveals his
thirst for sovereignty; he has curls like Achilles; and his arms and hands
betoken "valour and excess of strength" (II, 1, 7-30).

One of Tamburlaine's most important traits, his infinite aspiration, re-

[5] Passages describing action supposedly taking place onstage in Seneca's plays have
been used to support the contention that the plays were never intended for the stage.
It is interesting to see a technique so nearly approaching Seneca's here and later in
Dryden. This obviously proves nothing about Seneca, but it shows that such an effect
was accepted by certain audiences and conceivably might have been by Seneca's audience.

ceives its first major treatment in a much discussed speech in the second act about the "thirst of reign and sweetness of a crown" (II, 7, 12-29). Menaphon's encomium of Tamburlaine's physical beauty provides a clue to the understanding of this passage. Just as his body seems beautiful not simply in itself but in that it expresses his character, so Tamburlaine extols the "sweet fruition of an earthly crown" not because anything the earth has to offer has final value for him, but because domination of the earth represents the fulfilment of his mission—the fulfilment of himself. The speech is about the infinite aspiration taught us by nature and the never-ending activity to which the soul goads us. "The sweet fruition of an earthly crown" is indeed bathos, as it has often been called, unless the earthly crown means something rather special in this play.

There is a good deal of evidence that it does. In an earlier scene Usumcasane says, "To be a king, is half to be a god," and Theridamas replies, "A god is not so glorious as a king" (II, 5, 56-7). Tamburlaine never puts it quite thus, for it is clear that like Hercules he already considers himself partly divine, yet kingship is obviously glorious to him. The "course of crowns" which he and his followers eat in Act IV, Scene 4, is the visual equivalent of the constant references to sovereignty. The earth itself is despicable—inert—the negation of heroic energy, as appears in the speech of Theridamas immediately following the lines about the earthly crown:

> For he is gross and like the massy earth
> That moves not upwards, nor by princely deeds
> Doth mean to soar above the highest sort.
>
> (II, 7, 31-3)

but ruling the earth is not an end in itself. It is a manifestation of the will to "soar above the highest sort." When Tamburlaine seizes his first crown, the crown of Persia, he makes the act symbolic of his will:

> Though Mars himself, the angry god of arms,
> And all the earthly potentates conspire
> To dispossess me of this diadem,
> Yet will I wear it in despite of them . . .
>
> (II, 7, 58-61)

His contempt for earthly potentates and the assertion of his will combine in his conception of himself as the scourge of God, a conception which he shares with Hercules (III, 3, 41-54).[6] He is the avenger, nemesis to the mighty of the world, contemptuous demonstrator of the absurdity of their claims, liberator of captives. He is not so much the instrument as

---

[6] On the importance of this idea in *Tamburlaine,* see Battenhouse, pp. 99-113.

the embodiment of a divine purpose. His serene confidence that his will is seconded by destiny gives him the magnificence of the hero who transcends the merely human. The activities of such a hero are always confined to the earth, though always pointing, in some sense, to a goal beyond. Thus Seneca's Hercules Oetaeus, while rejoicing in his earthly deeds, never forgets that he is destined to become a star. Toward the end of Part II Tamburlaine begins to speak of an otherworldly goal,[7] but even before this time the thrones and crowns of the world stand for something which though *in* the earth is yet not *of* it. Their importance to Tamburlaine lies in taking them away from tyrants like Bajazeth, for whom they have intrinsic value. Tamburlaine's last instructions to his son are to sway the throne in such a way as to curb the haughty spirits of the captive kings (Part II, V, 3, 234-41). An earthly crown represents the sweet fruition of his purpose in being.

Tamburlaine's moving description of the aspiration for sovereignty has the utmost value in the play in presenting his double attitude towards the earth. And as he both seeks and despises earthly glory, he both claims and defies the power of the gods. "Jove himself" will protect him (I, 2, 179); not even Mars will force him to give up the crown of Persia (II, 7, 58-61). He does not belong entirely to either earth or heaven. Though he has distinctly human characteristics, both good and bad, he has something of the magnificence and the incomprehensibility of a deity.

Tamburlaine speaks of Mars as "the angry god of war," and the words might serve as self-description, for when he is angry the awe that his looks inspire is almost that of a mortal for a god. Agydas, when Tamburlaine has passed, *"looking wrathfully"* at him, expresses a typical reaction:

> Betrayed by fortune and suspicious love,
> Threatened with frowning wrath and jealousy,
> Surpris'd with fear of hideous revenge,
> I stand aghast; but most astonied
> To see his choler shut in secret thoughts,
> And wrapt in silence of his angry soul.
> Upon his brows was pourtrayed ugly death,
> And in his eyes the fury of his heart,
> That shine as comets, menacing revenge,
> And casts a pale complexion on his cheeks.
>
> (III, 2, 66-75)

Later a messenger speaks of "The frowning looks of fiery Tamburlaine, / That with his terror and imperious eyes / Commands the hearts of his associates" (IV, 1, 13-15), and the Governor of Damascus calls him "this

---

[7] Early in Part I he promises Theridamas friendship "Until our bodies turn to elements, / And both our souls aspire celestial thrones" (I, 2, 235-6), but here the reference seems more conventional.

man, or rather god of war" (V, 1, 1). Anger is the passion most frequently displayed in his looks, his words, and the red or black colours of his tents.

Not only is he a man of wrath, as the Herculean hero characteristically is; he is also fiercely cruel. This trait of character receives a continually increasing emphasis; it is strikingly demonstrated in Tamburlaine's treatment of Bajazeth. In Scene 2 of Act IV the defeated emperor is brought on in his cage, from which he is removed to serve as Tamburlaine's footstool. But Scene 4 is even more spectacular. Tamburlaine, dressed in scarlet to signify his wrath towards the besieged city of Damascus, banquets with his followers while the starving Bajazeth in his cage is insulted and given scraps of food on the point of his conqueror's sword. In the midst of these proceedings Tamburlaine refuses Zenocrate's plea that he raise the siege and make a truce with her father, the Soldan of Egypt. In the last act of Part I we see Tamburlaine order the death of the virgins of Damascus, who have been sent to beg for mercy after the black colours have already indicated Tamburlaine's decision to destroy the obstinate city. With inhuman logic he points out that it is now too late and that they "know my customs are as peremptory / As wrathful planets, death, or destiny" (V, 2, 64-5). At the end he says that his honour—that personal honour which is the basis of the hero's *areté*—"consists in shedding blood / When men presume to manage arms with him" (V, 2, 415-16). Tamburlaine's is a cosmic extension of the cruelty Achilles shows to Hector or Hercules to the innocent Lichas. Though it is a repellent trait, it is entirely consistent with the rest of the character. Instead of passing over it, Marlowe insists on it. One need not assume, however, that Marlowe himself loved cruelty nor, on the other hand, that he is depicting here a tragic flaw. It is an important part of the picture, a manifestation of Tamburlaine's "ireful Virtue," to use Tasso's phrase, and one of the chief occasions for wonder. One may disapprove and yet, in that special sense, admire.

Marlowe's method of constructing his dramatic portrait is essentially dialectical. Not only is love balanced against hate, cruelty against honour, but these and other traits are constantly brought out against a background of parallels or contrasts. Tamburlaine is contrasted with other monarchs and with Zenocrate. In the last act an entire city is his antagonist. Throughout the play his followers are like variations on the Tamburlaine theme, imitating his ferocity and zest for conquest, but incapable of his grandeur. The first three monarchs with whom the hero is contrasted are the foolish Mycetes, his brother, Cosroe, and the emperor Bajazeth. Mycetes is a grossly comic foil in his inability to act or speak well, to control others or himself. In the opening speech of the play he deplores his own insufficiency to express his rage, "For it requires a great and thundering speech" (I, 1, 1-3), a thing Tamburlaine can always provide.

In a low-comedy scene in the first act he comes alone on to the battlefield, the picture of cowardice, looking for a place to hide his crown.

This action in itself takes on great significance when we come, three scenes later, to Tamburlaine's praise of crowns. Mycetes curses the inventor of war and congratulates himself on the wisdom that permits him to escape its ill effects by hiding the crown which makes him a target. To put the censure of war and the praise of scheming wisdom in the mouth of such a character inclines the audience to see virtue in the hero's pursuit of war and in a kind of wisdom more closely allied to action.

The contrast with Cosroe is another matter. Patently superior to his brother Mycetes, Cosroe appears to be an ordinarily competent warrior and ruler. In fact, his one crippling deficiency is his inability to recognize the extraordinary when he sees it in the person of Tamburlaine. His attempt to pat Tamburlaine on the head and reward him for a job well done by giving him an important post in the kingdom, as any normal king might do, is as inept, given the nature of Tamburlaine, as the feckless gesturing of Mycetes. Cosroe is perfectly familiar with the rules of the game as it is generally played in the world, where the betrayal of a Mycetes is venial and competence has at least its modest reward. His cry of pain when Tamburlaine turns against him, "Barbarous and bloody Tamburlaine" (II, 7, 1), expresses the outrage of one who finds that the rules he has learned do not apply. Tamburlaine's strategy is so much more daring and his treachery so much more preposterous that they are beyond the imagination of Cosroe.

Bajazeth, Tamburlaine's third antagonist, is no mere moderately successful king. A proud and cruel tyrant, he rejoices in the sway of a vast empire. With his first words a new perspective opens up: "Great kings of Barbary, and my portly bassoes" (III, 1, 1). Here is a ruler served by kings. "We hear the Tartars and the eastern thieves, / Under the conduct of one Tamburlaine, / Presume a bickering with your emperor." The tone is superb. One notes the condescension of "one Tamburlaine" and the hauteur of "Presume a bickering." He is assured ("You know our army is invincible"); he is used to command ("Hie thee, my basso . . . Tell him thy lord . . . Wills and commands (for say not I entreat)"); and he is obeyed by thousands ("As many circumcised Turks we have, / And warlike bands of Christians renied, / As hath the ocean or the Terrene sea / Small drops of water").

If Cosroe is a little more like Tamburlaine than is his foolish brother, Bajazeth is decidedly more so. He speaks of "the fury of my wrath" (III, 1, 30), and shows his cruelty by threatening to castrate Tamburlaine and confine him to the seraglio while his captains are made to draw the chariot of the empress. The famous (and to a modern reader ludicrous) exchange of insults between Zabina and Zenocrate reinforces the parallel. Yet Marlowe emphasizes the ease with which this mighty potentate is toppled from his throne. The stage directions tell the story: "BAJAZETH *flies and he pursues him. The battle short and they enter.* BAJAZETH *is overcome*" (III, 3, 211 ff.). This contrast brings out what was suggested by the contrast with Cosroe, the truly extraordinary nature of Tamburlaine. For Bajazeth is what Mycetes would like to be but cannot be for lack of natural aptitude. He is what Cosroe might become in time with a little luck. As a sort of final term in a mathematical progression, he presents the ultimate in monarchs, and in himself sums up the others. That even he should fall so easily defines the limitations of the species and sets Tamburlaine in a world apart. He is not merely more angry, more cruel, more proud, more powerful. Though sharing certain characteristics with his victims, he embodies a force of a different order.

Zenocrate, by representing a scale of values far removed from those of the warrior or the monarch, provides further insights into Tamburlaine's character. Something has already been said of his courtship of her in the first act, when, to the surprise of Techelles, he shows that he is moved by love. The inclusion in his nature of the capacity to love is a characteristic Renaissance addition to the classical model of the Herculean hero. One recalls that Tasso's Rinaldo, though chiefly representing the "ireful virtue," is susceptible to the charms of Armida. Yet Zenocrate is not an enchantress like Armida nor is Tamburlaine's love for her presented as a weakness.[8] Love, as opposed to pure concupiscence, is a more important part of Tamburlaine than of Rinaldo. As G. I. Duthie has pointed out, it modifies considerably his warrior ideal,[9] leading him to spare the life of the Soldan and "take truce with all the world" (V, 2, 467).

Marlowe leaves no doubt that the commitment to Zenocrate is basic and lasting, but it is not allowed to dominate. Tamburlaine refuses Zenocrate's plea for Damascus, and when he also refuses the Virgins of Damascus he says:

> I will not spare these proud Egyptians,
> Nor change my martial observations
> For all the wealth of Gihon's golden waves,
> Or for the love of Venus, would she leave
> The angry god of arms and lie with me.
>
> (V, 2, 58-62)

This clear evaluation of the claims of Venus as opposed to those of Mars precedes by only a few lines the long soliloquy in which he extols the

---

[8] I cannot agree with Battenhouse (pp. 165 ff.), who believes that the comparison of her to Helen of Troy in Tamburlaine's lament for her death shows her to be a "pattern of pagan, earthly beauty" and "devoid of religion or conscience." Her attitude towards her father and towards the deaths of Bajazeth and Zabina leads to an opposite conclusion.

[9] "The Dramatic Structure of Marlowe's 'Tamburlaine the Great,' Parts I and II," *English Studies (Essays and Studies,* New Series), I (1948), 101-26. I do not wholly agree as to the extent of the modification Duthie sees. I am not so sure as he is that the marriage of Tamburlaine and Zenocrate symbolizes the establishment of an ideal relationship between beauty and the warrior.

beauty of Zenocrate. Here he admits that he is tempted to give in to Zenocrate, who has more power to move him than any of his enemies. By implication it is clear that this power is due to her beauty, which is so great that if the greatest poets attempted to capture it,

> Yet should there hover in their restless heads
> One thought, one grace, one wonder, at the least,
> Which into words no virtue can digest.
>
>   (V, 2, 108-10)

But on the verge, as it might seem, of capitulating to this softer side of his nature, he first reproves himself for these "thoughts effeminate and faint," and then presents beauty as the handmaid of valour. This passage is a textual crux,[10] and its syntax is so treacherous that a close analysis of the meaning is nearly impossible, but I think it is fair to say that Tamburlaine's convictions about the role of beauty are given in the lines:

> And every warrior that is rapt with love
> Of fame, of valour, and of victory,
> Must needs have beauty beat on his conceits . . .
>
>   (V, 2, 117-19)

The conclusion of the speech looks forward to what beauty may inspire Tamburlaine to do, and it is as important a part of his mission as the scourging of tyrants. This is to show the world "for all my birth, / That virtue solely is the sum of glory, / And fashions men with true nobility" (V, 2, 125-7); that is, that the hero's goal is to be attained by an innate power which has nothing to do with the accidents of birth. To Theridamas, Techelles and Usumcasane he has said much the same thing, assuring them that they deserve their titles

> By valour and by magnanimity.
> Your births shall be no blemish to your fame;
> For virtue is the fount whence honour springs.
>
>   (IV, 4, 129-31)

In several ways the power of love and beauty is subordinated to Tamburlaine's primary concerns. The encomium of Zenocrate leads to the statement of beauty's function in the warrior's life and then to Tamburlaine's intention of demonstrating true nobility. Furthermore the entire soliloquy is carefully framed. Before it begins, Tamburlaine orders a slaughter, and after his lines about true nobility he calls in a servant to ask whether Bajazeth has been fed. Tamburlaine's love for Zenocrate,

---

[10] See Ellis-Fermor's note, V, 2, 115-27.

extravagant as it is, is part of a rather delicately adjusted balance of forces.

Zenocrate is a pale character beside the best heroines of Shakespeare and Webster, but her attitude towards Tamburlaine is an important part of the meaning of the play. After her initial mistake—not wholly a mistake—of thinking he is just the Scythian shepherd he seems to be, her feelings towards him change rapidly. When she next appears she defends him to her companion, Agydas, who still sees Tamburlaine as a rough soldier. He asks:

> How can you fancy one that looks so fierce,
> Only disposed to martial stratagems?
>
> (III, 2, 40-1)

Zenocrate replies by comparing his looks to the sun and his conversation to the Muses' song. When Tamburlaine enters he rewards each of them with behaviour suited to their conception of him: *"Tamburlaine goes to her, and takes her away lovingly by the hand, looking wrathfully on Agydas, and says nothing"* (III, 2, 65 ff.).

Zenocrate enters enthusiastically into the exchange of insults with Bajazeth and Zabina, but it is her speeches after the sack of Damascus and the suicides of Bajazeth and Zabina which truly reveal her attitude towards Tamburlaine. Sorrowing for the cruel deaths of the Virgins of Damascus, she asks:

> Ah, Tamburlaine, wert thou the cause of this,
> That term'st Zenocrate thy dearest love?
> Whose lives were dearer to Zenocrate
> Than her own life, or aught save thine own love.
>
> (V, 2, 273-6)

His cruelty is recognized for what it is without its impairing her love. Similarly, when she laments over the bodies of the emperor and empress, she acknowledges Tamburlaine's pride, but prays Jove and Mahomet to pardon him. This lament is a highly effective set-piece, whose formality gives it a special emphasis. Its theme, the vanity of earthly power, is resoundingly stated in the refrain, "Behold the Turk and his great emperess!" which occurs four times, varied the last time to "In this great Turk and hapless emperess!" (V, 2, 292, 295, 300, 306). But within the statement of theme there is a movement of thought as Zenocrate turns from the most general aspect of the fall of the mighty to what concerns her more nearly, its bearing on Tamburlaine. The orthodoxy of the moral she draws from this spectacle of death is conspicuous, and nowhere more so than in the central section:

> Ah, Tamburlaine, my love, sweet Tamburlaine,
> That fightst for sceptres and for slippery crowns,
> Behold the Turk and his great emperess!
> Thou that, in conduct of thy happy stars,
> Sleep'st every night with conquest on thy brows,
> And yet wouldst shun the wavering turns of war,
> In fear and feeling of the like distress,
> Behold the Turk and his great emperess!

The culmination of the speech is its prayer that Tamburlaine may be spared the consequences of "his contempt / Of earthly fortune and respect of pity" (V, 2, 302-3).

When Tamburlaine's enemies inveigh against his pride and presumption, their protests have a hollow ring, and Marlowe may seem to be laughing at the point of view they express. He is certainly not doing so when he puts criticism of the same faults in the mouth of Zenocrate. Through her an awareness of the standard judgment of Tamburlaine's "overreaching" is made without irony and made forcefully. Through her it is also made clear that such an awareness may be included in an unwavering devotion, just as Deianira's devotion can digest even the grave personal slight she suffers from Hercules. Zenocrate both presents the conventional view of hubris more convincingly than any other character, and shows the inadequacy of this view in judging Tamburlaine.

A contrast on a larger scale forms the final episode of Part I: Tamburlaine is pitted against the great city of Damascus. Since Zenocrate pleads for the city, this is an extension of the contrast between the hero and heroine. Since the city is ruled by Tamburlaine's enemies, it is the climax in the series of contrasts between him and the representatives of corrupt worldly power. His first three enemies are individuals of increasing stature, but the Governor of Damascus and his allies, the Soldan and Arabia, are none of them imposing figures. Instead, the city of Damascus becomes the collective antagonist, to which Tamburlaine opposes his personal will. Much more than the individual monarchs of the first acts, the city seems to represent the point of view of society, which Zenocrate also adopts when she becomes the spokesman for conventional morality. When the delegation of virgins asks the conqueror for mercy, the appeal is in the name of the whole community:

> Pity our plights! O, pity poor Damascus!
> Pity old age . . .
> Pity the marriage bed . . .
> O, then, for these and such as we ourselves,
> For us, for infants, and for all our bloods,
> That never nourished thought against thy rule,

Pity, O pity, sacred emperor,
The prostrate service of this wretched town . . .

(V, 2, 17-37)

Tamburlaine's refusal is based on the absolute primacy of his will—
of the execution of whatever he has vowed. He is as self-absorbed as
Hercules, whose devotion to his areté obliterates any consideration for
Deianira or Hyllus, in *The Women of Trachis*. Homer portrays the hero's
uncompromising adherence to his own standard of conduct in the refusal
of Achilles to fight. In Book IX of the *Iliad*, when he is waited on by
the delegation of warriors, including his old tutor, Phoenix, heroic integrity directly opposes obligation to others—to friends and allies in war.
The "conflict between personal integrity and social obligation" was inherent in the story of the Wrath of Achilles, according to Cedric Whitman,
but Homer gave it special importance, seeing it "as an insolubly tragic
situation, the tragic situation *par excellence*." [11] In the Renaissance it
is not surprising to find "social obligation" represented by the city, but
in this case it is an enemy city. Instead of being urged to fight for friends
Tamburlaine is urged to spare citizens whose only fault is the acceptance
of the rule of their foolish, and finally weak, Governor. Hence the social
obligation denied by Tamburlaine is not that of supporting his friends'
cause but of conforming to an ideal of behaviour which places mercy
above justice. The code of Tamburlaine is a more primitive affair. His
word once given is as inflexible as destiny, and the imposition of his
will upon Damascus is also the carrying out of a cosmic plan. To the
demands of a segment of society he opposes a larger obligation to free
the world from tyrants. Marlowe's setting him against Damascus reaffirms
both his colossal individuality and his god-like superiority. The siege of
this city is used to present the core of the problem of *virtus heroica*.

Marlowe puts far less emphasis upon the benefactions of his hero's
career than was put upon the benefactions of Hercules; the punishment
of the wicked is what Tamburlaine himself constantly reiterates. Nevertheless, the punishment of Damascus is balanced by the hero's generosity
in sparing the Soldan. This is not a matter of just deserts. It is Tamburlaine's god-like caprice to spare Zenocrate's father. Because he does so
the end of Part I suggests a positive achievement. Zenocrate's greeting
of her "conquering love" is a mixture of wonder and gratitude, and even
the vanquished Soldan joins in the general thanksgiving.

Whether Part II was planned from the first, as some have thought, or
written in response to the "general welcomes Tamburlaine receiv'd," as
the Prologue says, its general conception is strikingly similar to that of

<hr/>

[11] *Homer and the Heroic Tradition* (Cambridge, Mass.: Harvard University Press,
1958 [p. 182], and London: Oxford University Press [p. 182]). See also C. M. Bowra,
The Greek Experience (London: Weidenfeld & Nicolson, 1957 [Chap. II], and New
York: Harcourt, Brace & World, Inc. [Chap. II]).

Part I. Its structure is again episodic, though the episodes are somewhat more tightly knit. The pattern is again a series of encounters between Tamburlaine and his enemies, leading at last to the one unsuccessful encounter—with death. To Mycetes, Cosroe and Bajazeth correspond the vaster alliance of Bajazeth's son Callapine and his allies. To the conflict between the factions in Persia corresponds the fight between Orcanes and Sigismund after a truce has been concluded. Here again, but even more circumstantially, we have the jealous struggles, the hypocrisies and the betrayals of conventional kings. Sigismund is a despicable figure, Orcanes a rather sympathetic one—even more so than his structural counterpart, Cosroe. He is portrayed as a religious man, is given some fine lines on the deity, ". . . he that sits on high and never sleeps, / Nor in one place is circumscriptible" (II, 2, 49-50), and, though born a pagan, acknowledges the power of Christ. That religion spares him none of the humiliations accorded to the enemies of Tamburlaine suggests that his religion, like his statecraft, is conventional. He is far from being the worst of men or the worst of rulers, yet, like the kings in Part I, he is given to boasting of his power and position and making snobbish remarks about Tamburlaine's lowly origin. It may be significant that he offers his partial allegiance to Christ as a means of obtaining the victory over Sigismund, who is a perjured Christian. This bargaining religion is the foil to Tamburlaine's impious self-confidence.

Other elements of the pattern of Part I are also imitated here. The siege of Damascus is matched by the siege of Babylon; Bajazeth in his cage is matched by the conquered kings in harness, to whom Tamburlaine shouts the famous "Holla, ye pampered jades of Asia!" (IV, 3, 1), so often parodied. Tamburlaine in his chariot, actually whipping the half naked kings who draw him, is a powerful theatrical image. Preposterous as the scene may be, it is satisfyingly right as a visual symbol of one of the principal themes of the play. Part II develops the theme more fully than Part I, giving it a prominent place in the dying hero's instructions to his eldest son:

> So reign, my son; scourge and control those slaves,
> Guiding thy chariot with thy father's hand.
>
> .   .   .   .   .
>
> For, if thy body thrive not full of thoughts
> As pure and fiery as Phyteus' beams,
> The nature of these proud rebelling jades
> Will take occasion by the slenderest hair,
> And draw thee piecemeal, like Hippolytus . . .
>
> (V, 3, 228-9, 236-40)

Another theme developed in Part II is the cruelty of Tamburlaine. It is so prominent here that it may seem to mark a loss of sympathy for the hero. Certainly the brutality to the conquered kings and to the Governor of Babylon, and above all Tamburlaine's murder of his son, constitute more vivid and more shocking examples than even the treatment of Bajazeth. Yet one need not conclude that Marlowe has changed his mind about his hero. All of these scenes may be understood as part of a rhetorical amplification of a theme which is, after all, unmistakable in Part I. Furthermore these scenes serve to emphasize other aspects of Tamburlaine's character indicated in Part I. The portrait is not changed: its lines are more deeply incised.

The scenes presenting Calyphas, the cowardly son, are perhaps the most shocking of all, and may be used as examples of the amplified theme of cruelty in Part II. In the first of them (I, 4) Celebinus and Amyras, the two brave sons, win paternal approval by vying with each other in promises to scourge the world, while Calyphas is furiously rebuked for asking permission to stay with his mother while the rest are out conquering. As in all the scenes with the three sons, the patterning is obvious to the point of being crude, and the humour in the depiction of the girlish little boy not much to our taste. Nevertheless, the scene does more than show how hard-hearted Tamburlaine can be. For members of the audience who have not seen Part I it presents Tamburlaine's relationship to Zenocrate, and for the rest it restates that relationship in different terms. The scene opens with a loving speech to Zenocrate, who replies by asking Tamburlaine when he will give up war and live safe. It is this question which the scene answers by asserting the primacy of the irascible powers in Tamburlaine's nature. In spite of his love he identifies himself with "wrathful war," and as he looks at her, surrounded by their sons, suddenly thinks that his boys appear more "amorous" than "martial," and hence unworthy of him. Zenocrate defends them as having "their mother's looks" but "their conquering father's heart" (I, 4, 35-6), and it is then that they proclaim their intentions. Tamburlaine's rebuke to Calyphas is a statement of his creed, glorifying the "mind courageous and invincible" (I, 4, 73), and drawing a portrait of himself comparable to several in Part I:

> For he shall wear the crown of Persia
> Whose head hath deepest scars, whose breast most wounds,
> Which, being wroth, sends lightning from his eyes,
> And in the furrows of his frowning brows
> Harbours revenge, war, death and cruelty . . .
>
> (I, 4, 74-8)

The furrowed brows belong to the angry demigod of Part I, and if the picture is somewhat grimmer, it is partly because of the hint that the demigod must suffer in the accomplishment of his mission.

The next scene with Calyphas (III, 2) takes place after the death of

Zenocrate, and like the former one, makes its contribution to the development of Tamburlaine's character. As the earlier scene began with the praise of Zenocrate, so this one begins with her funeral against the background of a conflagration betokening Tamburlaine's wrath. Again Calyphas is responsible for an unexpected note of levity when he makes an inane comment on the dangerousness of war just after his father has concluded stern instructions to his sons how to be "soldiers, / And worthy sons of Tamburlaine the Great" (III, 2, 91-2). The consequence is not only a rebuke but a demonstration. Never having been wounded in all his wars, Tamburlaine cuts his own arm to show his sons how "to bear courageous minds" (III, 2, 143). Here his cruelty and anger are turned against himself, as perhaps they always are in some sense in the scenes with Calyphas.

The last of these scenes (IV, 1) is the most terrible and by far the most important, for Calyphas here prompts Tamburlaine to reveal himself more completely than ever before. In the first part of the scene the boy has played cards with an attendant while his brothers fought with their father to overcome the Turkish kings. He has scoffed at honour and, like Mycetes, praised the wisdom which keeps him safe (IV, 1, 49-50). When the victors return, Tamburlaine drags Calyphas out of the tent and, ignoring the pleas of his followers and of Amyras, stabs him to death. It is almost a ritual killing—the extirpation of an unworthy part of himself, as the accompanying speech makes clear:

> Here, Jove, receive his fainting soul again;
> A form not meet to give that subject essence
> Whose matter is the flesh of Tamburlaine,
> Wherein an incorporeal spirit moves,
> Made of the mould whereof thyself consists,
> Which makes me valiant, proud, ambitious,
> Ready to levy power against thy throne,
> That I might move the turning spheres of heaven;
> For earth and all this airy region
> Cannot contain the state of Tamburlaine.
>
> (IV, 1, 111-20)

To interpret this murder as merely one further example of barbarous cruelty is to accept the judgment of Tamburlaine's enemies. The cruelty is balanced against one of the most powerful statements of the spirituality of Tamburlaine. It is the "incorporeal spirit" which makes him what he is, a hero akin to the gods, and which, because it cannot bear to be other than itself, pushes him to the execution of his cowardly son. As the great aspiring speech of Part I obliges us to see an earthly crown as the goal to which Tamburlaine's nature forces him, so this speech and its accompanying action oblige us to accept cruelty along with valour, pride and ambition as part of the spirit which makes this man great. The soul of Calyphas, by contrast, is associated with the "massy dregs of earth" (IV, 1, 123), lacking both courage and wit, just as Theridamas described the unaspiring mind as "gross and like the massy earth" (Part I, II, 7, 31).

So far does Tamburlaine go in asserting his affinity to heaven and contempt for earth, that for the first time he hints that sovereignty of the earth may not be enough for him. It is an idea which has an increasing appeal for him in the remainder of the play. He makes another extreme statement in this scene when his enemies protest the barbarity of his deed. "These terrors and these tyrannies," he says, are part of his divine mission,

> Nor am I made arch-monarch of the world,
> Crown'd and invested by the hand of Jove,
> For deeds of bounty or nobility . . .
>
> (IV, 1, 150-2)

To be the terror of the world is his exclusive concern.

The emphasis on terror is consistent with the entire depiction of his character. The denial of nobility is not. It is an extreme statement which the emotions of the moment and dialectical necessity push him to. Allowing for an element of exaggeration in this speech, however, the scene as a whole, like the other scenes with Calyphas, presents a Tamburlaine essentially like the Tamburlaine of Part I, and not seen from any very different point of view. As he grows older, as he encounters a little more resistance, his character sets a little more firmly in its mould. It remains what it has always been.

The death of Zenocrate is, as every critic has recognized, the first real setback to Tamburlaine. In view of her association with the city in Part I it is appropriate that Tamburlaine makes a city suffer for her death by setting fire to it. His devotion to her and to the beauty she represents appears in the speech he makes at her deathbed (II, 4, 1-37), in his raging at her death, in the placing of her picture on his tent to inspire valour (III, 2, 36-42), and in his dying address to her coffin (V, 3, 224-7). As G. I. Duthie says, death is the great enemy in Part II, and his conquest of Zenocrate is in effect his first victory over Tamburlaine.[12] As he had to make some concessions to Zenocrate in Part I, so in Part II he has to come to terms with the necessity of death. The process begins with the death of Zenocrate, to which his first reaction is the desire for revenge. Not only does he burn the town where she died; he also orders Techelles to draw his sword and wound the earth (II, 4, 97). This prepares us somewhat for his later order, when death has laid siege to him, to "set black

---

[12] "The Dramatic Structure of Marlowe's 'Tamburlaine the Great,' " pp. 118, 124.

streamers in the firmament, / To signify the slaughter of the gods" (V, 3, 49-50). By keeping always with him the hearse containing her dead body he refuses wholly to accept her death as he now defies his own.

Only in the last scene of Act V does cosmic defiance give way to acceptance, and when this happens Tamburlaine's defeat by death is partially transformed into a desired fulfilment. I have already mentioned his hint that the earth cannot contain him. It is followed by a suggestion that Jove, esteeming him "too good for earth" (IV, 3, 60), might make a star of him. Now he says:

> In vain I strive and rail against those powers
> That mean t'invest me in a higher throne,
> As much too high for this disdainful earth.

> (V, 3, 120-2)

and finally:

> But sons, this subject, not of force enough
> To hold the fiery spirit it contains,
> Must part . . .

> (V, 3, 168-70)

Like Hercules Oetaeus, he feels that his immortal part, that "incorporeal spirit" of which he spoke earlier, is now going to a realm more worthy of him, though imparting something of its power to the spirits of his two remaining sons, in whom he will continue to live. In these final moments we have what may be hinted at earlier in his self-wounding—a collaboration with death and fate in the destruction of his physical being. For the psychologist the drive towards self-destruction is latent in all heroic risks; it is the other side of the coin of self-assertion. Though Marlowe could never have put it this way, his insight may be essentially similar.

From the quotations already given it will be apparent that Tamburlaine's attitude toward the gods changes continually. He boasts of their favour or defies them to take away his conquests; likens himself to them, executes their will, waits for them to receive him into their domain, or threatens to conquer it. Tamburlaine's religious pronouncements, especially his blasphemies, have attracted a great deal of critical comment from his day to ours. Since Marlowe himself was accused of atheism, the key question has been whether or not Tamburlaine is a mouthpiece for his author. Some critics emphasize Tamburlaine's defiance of Mahomet and the burning of the Koran, but these episodes are surely no more significant than his "wounding" of the earth. As Kocher has pointed out (p. 89), his line, "The God that sits in heaven, if any god" (V, 1, 200) contains in its parenthetical comment more blasphemy for a Christian than does the whole incident of the Koran. Yet even this questioning of God's existence is only one of the changes of attitude just cited. To try to deduce Marlowe's religious position from these speeches is a hopeless undertaking, and to try to decide on the basis of the biographical evidence which of them Marlowe might endorse is risky and finally inconclusive. Somehow the relationship of these opinions to the rest of the play must be worked out. Either their inconsistency is due to carelessness (in this case carelessness of heroic proportions) or it has some bearing on the heroic character. Seneca's Hercules displays a similar variety of attitudes. In the earlier play he thanks the gods for their aid in his victory over the tyrant, Lycus, and offers to kill any further tyrants or monsters the earth may bring forth. Moments later, as his madness comes upon him, he says:

> To the lofty regions of the universe on high let me make my way, let me seek the skies; the stars are my father's promise. And what if he should not keep his word? Earth has not room for Hercules, and at length restores him unto heaven. See, the whole company of the gods of their own will summons me, and opens wide the door of heaven, with one alone forbidding. And wilt thou unbar the sky and take me in? Or shall I carry off the doors of stubborn heaven? Dost even doubt my power?
>
> (*Hercules Furens*, ll. 958-65)

In the first lines of *Hercules Oetaeus* he again boasts of his activities as a scourge of tyrants and complains that Jove still denies him access to the heavens, hinting that the god may be afraid of him. Later (ll. 1302-3) he almost condescends to Jove, remarking that he might have stormed the heavens, but refrained because Jove, after all, was his father. Greene could quite properly have inveighed against "daring God out of heaven with that atheist Hercules." At the end of *Hercules Oetaeus* the hero accepts his fate with calm fortitude and even helps to destroy himself amidst the flames. These changes in attitude are perhaps more easy to understand in Hercules, since his relationship to the gods was in effect a family affair. Tamburlaine is not the son of a god, but his facile references to the gods, sometimes friendly, sometimes hostile, may be interpreted as part of the heroic character of which Hercules is the prototype. He has the assurance of a demigod rather than the piety of a good man.

Such assurance, rather than repentance, breathes in the lines in which Tamburlaine advises his son Amyras:

> Let not thy love exceed thine honour, son,
> Nor bar thy mind that magnanimity

That nobly must admit necessity.
Sit up, my boy, and with those silken reins
Bridle the steeled stomachs of those jades.

                                                        (V, 3, 199-203)

The advice to admit necessity[13] may reflect Tamburlaine's own acceptance of his death, but in context it refers primarily to the necessity for
Amyras to take over Tamburlaine's throne. The whole speech shows
Tamburlaine's conviction of the rightness of what he has done. The
place of love is again made subordinate to honour, the hero's chief concern. Magnanimity is stressed as it is in Tamburlaine's advice to his
followers to deserve their crowns "By valour and magnanimity" (Part I,
IV, 4, 129). Even the bowing to fate is to be done nobly, as Tamburlaine himself is now doing. Finally, the heroic enterprise of controlling
tyrants is to be continued. There is no retraction here, no change in
the basic character. He has come to terms with death, but this is more a
recovery than a reversal. He has spoken earlier in the play of his old
age and death, but, very humanly, has rebelled when death struck at
Zenocrate and then at himself. Now he has regained calm with self-
mastery.

Though the suffering of Tamburlaine is so prominent from the death
of Zenocrate to the end, retribution is not what is stressed. The last scene
of the play presents a glorification of the hero approaching apotheosis.
It opens with a formally patterned lament, spoken by Theridamas,
Techelles and Usumcasane, the last section of which expresses the theme
of the scene, Tamburlaine as benefactor:

Blush, heaven, to lose the honour of thy name,
To see thy footstool set upon thy head;
And let no baseness in thy haughty breast
Sustain a shame of such inexcellence,
To see the devils mount in angels' thrones,
And angels dive into the pools of hell.
And, though they think their painful date is out,
And that their power is puissant as Jove's,
Which makes them manage arms against thy state,
Yet make them feel the strength of Tamburlaine,
Thy instrument and note of majesty,

[13] Helen L. Gardner has written about the importance of the theme of necessity
in Part II in an excellent essay, "The Second Part of 'Tamburlaine the Great,'"
Modern Language Review, 37 (1942), 18-24. I cannot agree with her that Marlowe's
sympathies are much changed, however, nor that the moral of Part II is "the simple
medieval one of the inevitability of death."

> Is greater far than they can thus subdue;
> For if he die, thy glory is disgrac'd,
> Earth droops and says that hell in heaven is plac'd.
>
> (V, 3, 28-41)

His sons live only in his life, and it is with the greatest reluctance that Amyras mounts the throne at Tamburlaine's command. When he speaks in doing so of his father's "anguish and his burning agony" (V, 3, 209), he seems to imply that Tamburlaine's sufferings are the inevitable concomitants of his greatness and his service to humanity. It is he who pronounces the final words:

> Meet heaven and earth, and here let all things end,
> For earth hath spent the pride of all her fruit,
> And heaven consum'd his choicest living fire!
> Let earth and heaven his timeless death deplore,
> For both their worths will equal him no more.
>
> (V, 3, 249-53)

Full of Herculean echoes, the lines form a perfect epitaph for the hero, the product of earth and heaven.

Three times in this scene Tamburlaine adjures his son to control the captive kings and thus maintain order. He compares the task with Phaëton's:

> So reign, my son; scourge and control those slaves,
> Guiding thy chariot with thy father's hand.
> As precious is the charge thou undertak'st
> As that which Clymene's brain-sick son did guide
> When wandering Phoebe's ivory cheeks were scorched,
> And all the earth, like Ætna, breathing fire.
> Be warned by him, then; learn with awful eye
> To sway a throne as dangerous as his;
>
> (V, 3, 228-35)

Despite his ambition and pride, Tamburlaine is no Macbeth to seek power "though the treasure / Of nature's germens tumble all together, / Even till destruction sicken. . . ." [14] Rather, he identifies himself with universal order, as does Seneca's Hercules. The very chariot which is a symbol of his cruel scourging is also the symbol of control and hence of

---

[14] *The Complete Works of Shakespeare,* ed. G. L. Kittredge (Boston: Ginn & Co., 1936 [IV, 1, 58-60]).

order. Compared to the chariot of the sun, it is also the bringer of light. In the depiction of the Herculean hero there is no relaxation of the tensions between his egotism and altruism, his cruelties and benefactions, his human limitations and his divine potentialities. Marlowe never lets his audience forget these antitheses. In the first scene of Act V this great benefactor orders the Governor of Babylon to be hung in chains on the wall of the town. He rises from his deathbed to go out and conquer one more army. It is Marlowe's triumph that, after revealing with such clarity his hero's pride and cruelty, he can give infinite pathos to the line, "For Tamburlaine, the scourge of God, must die" (V, 3, 248).

In obtaining a favourable reception for his hero among the more thoughtful members of his audience Marlowe could no doubt count on not only some familiarity with the heroic tradition in which he was working, but also on the often-voiced regard for the active life. Gabriel Harvey, it will be recalled, asks who would not rather be one of the nine worthies than one of the seven wise masters. He also expresses another attitude on which Marlowe could count, the Stoic regard for integrity—truth to oneself. Harvey prefers Caesar to Pompey because Pompey deserts himself, while Caesar remains true to himself. He notes that it was Aretine's glory to be himself.[15]

The last moments of the play appeal to the spectator's pity by insisting on the tragic limitation of Tamburlaine as a human being. "For Tamburlaine, the scourge of God, must die" is comparable to Achilles' lines: "For not even the strength of Herakles fled away from destruction, / although he was dearest of all to lord Zeus . . ." But the play's dominant appeal is to the wonder aroused by vast heroic potential. The very paradoxes of Tamburlaine's nature excite wonder, and this was supposed in Marlowe's time to be the effect of paradox. Puttenham, in his familiar *Arte of English Poesie,* calls paradox "the wondrer." Tamburlaine's "high astounding terms," for which the Prologue prepares us, clearly aim at the same effect. Many years later, Sir William Alexander, the author of several Senecan tragedies, wrote that the three stylistic devices which pleased him most were: "A grave sentence, by which the Judgment may be bettered; a witty Conceit, which doth harmoniously delight the Spirits; and a generous Rapture expressing Magnanimity, whereby the Mind may be inflamed for great Things." The last of these three he found in Lucan, in whose "Heroical Conceptions" he saw an "innate Generosity"; he remarked the power of "the unmatchable Height of his Ravishing Conceits to provoke Magnanimity."[16] Marlowe was undoubtedly influenced by the style of the *Pharsalia,* the first book of which he had translated, and in any case Alexander's words might justly

[15] *Gabriel Harvey's Marginalia,* pp. 134, 156.
[16] *Anacrisis* (1634?), in *Critical Essays of the Seventeenth Century,* ed. J. E. Spingarn (Bloomington: Indiana University Press, 1957 [I, 182, 183], and London: Oxford University Press [I, 182, 183]).

be applied to *Tamburlaine*. The epic grandeur of the style,[17] with its resounding catalogues of exotic names, its hyperboles, and its heroic boasts and tirades, "expresses magnanimity," that largeness of spirit so consistently ascribed to the great hero. Alexander testifies that such a style may inflame the mind "for great things," and general as this description is, it serves well for the feeling aroused by the play. Another name for it was admiration.

[17] Harry Levin has written brilliantly of this style in *The Overreacher* (Cambridge, Mass.: Harvard University Press [especially pp. 10 ff.], and London: Faber & Faber [pp. 30 ff.]), where he comments on the superb appropriateness of the term of Puttenham's for hyperbole. As he says, "It could not have been more happily inspired to throw its illumination upon Marlowe—upon his style, which is so emphatically himself, and on his protagonists, overreachers all" (p. 23). See also M. P. McDiarmid, "The Influence of Robert Garnier on some Elizabethan Tragedies," *Études Anglaises*, XI (1958), 289-302; and Donald Peet, "The Rhetoric of Tamburlaine," *ELH*, 26 (1959), 137-55. Commenting on Marlowe's use of amplification, Peet remarks that "there can be little doubt that Marlowe wants us to *marvel* at Tamburlaine," whether or not he seeks approval (p. 151).

The Damnation of Faustus

by W. W. Greg

When working lately on the text of *Doctor Faustus*, I was struck by certain aspects of the story as told in Marlowe's play that I do not remember to have seen discussed in the editions with which I am familiar. I do not pretend to have read more than a little of what has been written about Marlowe as a dramatist, and it may be that there is nothing new in what I have to say; but it seemed worth while to draw attention to a few points in the picture of the hero's downfall, on the chance that they might have escaped the attention of others, as they had hitherto escaped my own.

As soon as Faustus has decided that necromancy is the only study that can give his ambition scope, he seeks the aid of his friends Valdes and Cornelius, who already are proficients in the art—

> Their conference will be a greater help to me
> Than all my labours, plod I ne'er so fast.[1]

Who they are we have no notion: they do not appear in the source on which Marlowe drew—"The historie of the damnable life, and deserued death of Doctor Iohn Faustus . . . according to the true Copie printed at Franckfort, and translated into English by P. F. Gent."—and Cornelius is certainly not the famous Cornelius Agrippa, who is mentioned in their conversation. But they must have been familiar figures at Wittenberg, since on learning that Faustus is at dinner with them, his students at once conclude that he is "fallen into that damned art for which they two are infamous through the world." The pair are ready enough to obey

"The Damnation of Faustus" by W. W. Greg. From *The Modern Language Review*, XLI (1946), 97-107. Copyright 1946 by the Modern Humanities Research Association. Reprinted by permission of the Editors of *The Modern Language Review*.

[1] There is as yet no satisfactory critical text of *Faustus*, and I have had to do the best I could, in the light of my own study, to harmonize the rival versions as printed in the quartos of 1604 and 1616 respectively, taking from each what best illustrated the points I wished to make. In the case of such a necessarily eclectic text there seemed no object in attempting to follow the spelling of the originals, except where it possessed some significance. I have also felt free so to punctuate as best to bring out what I believe to be the sense of the original.

Faustus' invitation, for they have long sought to lead him into forbidden ways. "Know," says Faustus—

> Know that your words have won me at the last
> To practise magic and concealèd arts.

At the same time, though they are his "dearest friends," he is anxious not to appear too pliant, adding, a little clumsily (if the 1604 text is to be trusted)

> Yet not your words only, but mine own fantasy,

and he makes it plain that he is no humble seeker after instruction, but one whose personal fame and honour are to be their main concern—

> Then, gentle friends, aid me in this attempt,
> And I, that have with concise syllogisms
> Gravelled the pastors of the German church,
> And made the flowering pride of Wittenberg
> Swarm to my problems, as the infernal spirits
> On sweet Musaeus when he came to hell,
> Will be as cunning as Agrippa was,
> Whose shadows made all Europe honour him.

His friends are content enough to accept him on these terms. Valdes, while hinting that common contributions deserve common rewards—

> Faustus, these books, thy wit, and our experience
> Shall make all nations to canonize us—

paints a glowing picture of the possibilities before them, adding however—in view of what follows a little ominously—

> If learned Faustus will be resolute.

Reassured on this score, Cornelius is ready to allow Faustus pride of place—

> Then doubt not, Faustus, but to be renowmed,
> And more frequented for this mystery
> Than heretofore the Delphian oracle—

but only on condition that the profits of the enterprise are shared—

> Then tell me, Faustus, what shall we three want?

However, it soon appears that for all their sinister reputation the two are but dabblers in witchcraft. They have, indeed, called spirits from the deep, and they have come—

> The spirits tell me they can dry the sea
> And fetch the treasure of all foreign wracks,
> Yea, all the wealth that our forefathers hid
> Within the massy entrails of the earth—

but they have made no use of this knowledge, they have never become the masters—or the slaves—of the spirits. Even to raise them they must, of course, have run a mortal risk—

> Nor will we come unless he use such means
> Whereby he is in danger to be damned—

but they have been careful not to forfeit their salvation for supernatural gifts; they have never succumbed to the temptation of the spirits or made proof of their boasted powers. Nor do they mean to put their own art to the ultimate test. When Faustus eagerly demands,

> Come, show me some demonstrations magical,

Valdes proves himself a ready teacher—

> Then haste thee to some solitary grove,
> And bear wise Bacon's and Albanus' works,
> The Hebrew Psalter, and New Testament;
> And whatsoever else is requisite
> We will inform thee ere our conference cease—

and guarantees to make him proficient in the art—

> First I'll instruct thee in the rudiments,
> And then wilt thou be perfecter than I.

Knowing the depth of Faustus' learning, and satisfied of his courage and resolution, they are anxious to form a partnership with one whose potentialities as an adept so far exceed their own. But Cornelius leaves us in no doubt of their intention to use Faustus as a cat's-paw rather than run into danger themselves—

> Valdes, first let him know the words of art,
> And then, all other ceremonies learned,
> Faustus may try his cunning by himself.

The precious pair are no deeply versed magicians welcoming a promising beginner, but merely the devil's decoys luring Faustus along the road to destruction.[2] They serve their purpose in giving a dramatic turn to the scene of his temptation, and except for a passing mention by the students, we hear no more of them.[3]

Faustus goes to conjure alone, and alone he concludes his pact with the devil. What use will he make of his hazardously won powers? His dreams, if self-centred, are in the heroic vein:

> Oh, what a world of profit and delight,
> Of power, of honour, and omnipotence,
> Is promised to the studious artizan!
> All things that move between the quiet poles
> Shall be at my command: emperors and kings
> Are but obeyed in their several provinces,
> But his dominion that exceeds in this
> Stretcheth as far as doth the mind of man:
> A sound magician is a demi-god!

More than mortal power and knowledge shall be his, to use in the service of his country:

> Shall I make spirits fetch me what I please?
> Resolve me of all ambiguities?
> Perform what desperate enterprise I will? . . .
> I'll have them read me strange philosophy
> And tell the secrets of all foreign kings;
> I'll have them wall all Germany with brass, . . .
> And chase the Prince of Parma from our land . . .

---

[2] There is a hint that Faustus' downfall was planned by Mephostophilis from the start. Quite near the end, gloating over Faustus' despair, he says (in the 1616 text):
> when thou took'st the book
> To view the scriptures, then I turned the leaves
> And led thine eye.

The only incident *in the play* to which this could refer is the collocation of biblical texts that prompts Faustus to renounce divinity in the opening scene.

[3] Of course, the theatrical reason for this is that Marlowe has no further use for them, but like a good craftsman he was careful to supply a dramatic reason in his delineation of the characters.

Whatever baser elements there may be in his ambition, we should, by all human standards, expect the fearless seeker after knowledge and truth, the scholar weary of the futilities of orthodox learning, to make at least no ignoble use of the power suddenly placed at his command.

Critics have complained that instead of pursuing ends worthy of his professed ideals, Faustus, once power is his, abandons these without a qualm, and shows himself content to amuse the Emperor with conjuring tricks and play childish pranks on the Pope; and they have blamed this either on a collaborator, or on the fact of Marlowe's work having been later overlaid and debased by another hand. The charge, in its crudest form, involves some disregard of the 1616 version, which is not quite as fatuous as its predecessor, but in broad outline there is no denying its justice. As to responsibility: it is of course obvious that not all the play as we have it is Marlowe's. For my own part, however, I do not believe that as originally written it differed to any material extent from what we are able to reconstruct from a comparison of the two versions in which it has come down to us. And while it is true that the middle portion, to which objection is mostly taken, shows little trace of Marlowe's hand, I see no reason to doubt that it was he who planned the whole, or that his collaborator or collaborators, whoever he or they may have been, carried out his plan substantially according to instructions. If that is so, for any fundamental fault in the design Marlowe must be held responsible.

The critics' disappointment is quite natural. Although it is difficult to see how any dramatist could have presented in language and dramatic form the revelation of a knowledge beyond the reach of human wisdom, there is no question that much more might have been done to show the wonder and uphold the dignity of the quest, and so satisfy the natural expectation of the audience. Marlowe did not do it; he deliberately turned from the attempt. Instead he showed us the betrayal of ideals, the lapse into luxury and buffoonery.

And what, in the devil's name, would the critics have? I say "in the devil's name," because all that happens to Faustus once the pact is signed is the devil's work: "human standards" are no longer relevant. Who but a fool, such a clever fool as Faustus, would dream that any power but evil could be won by a bargain with evil, or that truth could be wrung from the father of lies? "All power tends to corrupt, and absolute power corrupts absolutely," is indeed an aphorism to which few Elizabethans would have subscribed; but Marlowe knew the nature of the power he put into the hands of his hero and the inevitable curse it carried with it.

Of course, Faustus' corruption is not a mechanical outcome of his pact with evil. In spite of his earnest desire to know truth, and half-hidden in the Marlowan glamour cast about him, the seeds of decay are in his character from the first—how else should he come to make his fatal bargain? Beside his passion for knowledge is a lust for riches and pleasure and power. If less single-minded, he shares Barabbas' thirst for wealth—

> I'll have them fly to India for gold,
> Ransack the ocean for orient pearl,
> And search all corners of the new-found world
> For pleasant fruits and princely delicates . . .

Patriotism is a veil for ambition: he will

> chase the Prince of Parma from our land
> And reign sole king of all our provinces . . .

> I'll join the hills that bind the Afric shore
> And make that country continent to Spain,
> And both contributary to my crown:
> The Emperor shall not live but by my leave,
> Nor any potentate in Germany.

His aspiration to be "great emperor of the world" recalls Tamburlaine's vulgar desire for

> The sweet fruition of an earthly crown.

But Faustus' ambition is not thus limited; the promptings of his soul reveal themselves in the words of the Bad Angel:

> Be thou on earth, as Jove is in the sky,
> Lord and commander of these elements.

If there is a sensual vein in him, it is hardly seen at this stage; still his demand to "live in all voluptuousness" anticipates later desires—

> Whilst I am here on earth let me be cloyed
> With all things that delight the heart of man;
> My four and twenty years of liberty
> I'll spend in pleasure and in dalliance—

and it may be with shrewd insight that Valdes promises "serviceable" spirits,

> Sometimes like women or unwedded maids
> Shadowing more beauty in their airy brows
> Than in the white breasts of the Queen of Love.

But when all is said, this means no more than that Faustus is a man dazzled by the unlimited possibilities of magic, and alive enough to his own weakness to exclaim:

> The god thou serv'st is thine own appetite . . .

After Faustus has signed the bond with his blood, we can trace the stages of a gradual deterioration. His previous interview with Mephostophilis struck the note of earnest if slightly sceptical inquiry with which he entered on his quest:

> This word Damnation terrifies not me,
> For I confound hell in Elizium:
> My ghost be with the old philosophers!

He questions eagerly about hell, and the spirit replies:

> Why, this is hell, nor am I out of it:
> Think'st thou that I who saw the face of God
> And tasted the eternal joys of heaven,
> Am not tormented with ten thousand hells
> In being deprived of everlasting bliss? . . .
>   *Fau.* What, is great Mephostophilis so passionate
> For being deprivèd of the joys of heaven?
> Learn thou of Faustus manly fortitude,
> And scorn those joys thou never shalt possess.

After the bond is signed the discussion is renewed, but while the devil loses nothing in dignity of serious discourse, we can already detect a change in Faustus; his sceptical levity takes on a more truculent and jeering tone. Asked "Where is the place that men call hell?" Mephostophilis replies:

> Within the bowels of these elements,
> Where we are tortured and remain for ever.
> Hell hath no limits, nor is circumscribed
> In one self place, but where we are is hell,
> And where hell is, there must we ever be:
> And to conclude, when all the world dissolves
> And every creature shall be purified,
> All places shall be hell that is not heaven.
>   *Fau.* Come, I think hell's a fable.
>   *Meph.* Ay, think so still, till experience change thy mind. . . .
>   *Fau.* . . . . Think'st thou that Faustus is so fond to imagine

That after this life there is any pain?
Tush! these are trifles and mere old wives' tales.
   Meph. But I am an instance to prove the contrary;
For I tell thee I am damned and now in hell.
   Fau. Nay, and this be hell, I'll willingly be damned:
What? sleeping, eating, walking, and disputing!

In the next scene there follows the curiously barren discussion on astronomy. It has probably been interpolated and is not altogether easy to follow, but the infernal exposition of the movements of the spheres calls forth an impatient,

> These slender questions Wagner can decide

and at the end Mephostophilis' sententious

> Per inaequalem motum respectu totius

and Faustus' half-satisfied

> Well, I am answered!

leave in the mouth the taste of dead-sea fruit. The quarrel that follows on the spirit's refusal to say who made the world leads to the intervention of Lucifer and the "pastime" of the Seven Deadly Sins. There seems to me more savour in this than has sometimes been allowed; still it is a much shrunken Faustus who exclaims:

> Oh, this feeds my soul!

He had been no less delighted with the dance of the devils that offered him crowns and rich apparel on his signing the bond: we do not know its nature, but from his exclamation,

> Then there's enough for a thousand souls!

when told that he may conjure up such spirits at will, we may perhaps conclude that it involved a direct appeal to the senses. That would, at least, accord with his mood soon afterwards; for while it would be rash to lay much stress on his demanding "the fairest maid in Germany, for I am wanton and lascivious" (this being perhaps an interpolation) we should allow due weight to Mephostophilis' promise:

> I'll cull thee out the fairest courtesans
> And bring them every morning to thy bed;
> She whom thine eye shall like, thy heart shall have,
> Were she as chaste as was Penelope,
> As wise as Saba, or as beautiful
> As was bright Lucifer before his fall.

So far Faustus has not left Wittenberg, and emphasis has been rather on the hollowness of his bargain in respect of any intellectual enlightenment than on the actual degradation of his character. As yet only his childish pleasure in the devil-dance and the pageant of the Sins hints at the depth of vulgar triviality into which he is doomed to descend. In company with Mephostophilis he now launches forth into the world; but his dragon-flights

> To find the secrets of astronomy
> Graven in the book of Jove's high firmament,

and

> to prove cosmography,
> That measures coasts and kingdoms of the earth,

only land him at last in the Pope's privy-chamber to

> take some part of holy Peter's feast,

and live with dalliance in

> the view
> Of rarest things and royal courts of kings . . .

It is true that in the fuller text of 1616 the rescue of "holy Bruno," imperial candidate for the papal throne, lends a more serious touch to the sheer horse-play of the Roman scenes in the 1604 version, and even the "horning" episode at the Emperor's court is at least developed into some dramatic coherence; but this only brings out more pointedly the progressive fatuity of Faustus' career, which in the clownage and conjuring tricks at Anhalt sinks to the depth of buffoonery. If, as may be argued, the gradual deterioration of Faustus' character and the prostitution of his powers stand out less clearly than they should, this may be ascribed partly to Marlowe's negligent handling of a theme that failed to kindle his wayward inspiration, and partly to the ineptitude of his collaborator. But the logical outline is there, and I must differ from Marlowe's critics, and believe that when he sketched that outline Marlowe knew what he was about.

Another point to be borne in mind is that there is something strange and peculiar, not only in Faustus' situation, but in his nature. Once he has signed the bond, he is in the position of having of his own free will renounced salvation. So much is obvious. Less obvious is the inner change he has brought upon himself. Critics have strangely neglected the first article of the infernal compact: "that Faustus may be a spirit in form and substance." Presumably they have taken it to mean merely that he should be free of the bonds of flesh, so that he may be invisible at will, invulnerable, and able to change his shape, ride on dragons, and so forth. But in this play "spirit" is used in a special sense. There is, of course, nothing very significant in the fact that, when the "devils" dance before him, Faustus asks:

> But may I raise such spirits when I please?

that he promises to

> make my spirits pull His churches down

and bids Mephostophilis

> Ay, go, accursèd spirit to ugly hell!

or that the latter speaks of the devils as

Misled.

> Unhappy spirits that fell with Lucifer—

though it is noticeable how persistently devils are called spirits in the play,[4] and it is worth recalling that in the *Damnable Life* Mephostophilis is regularly "the Spirit." What is significant is that when Faustus asks "What is that Lucifer, thy lord?" Mephostophilis replies:

> Arch-regent and commander of all spirits

which Faustus at once interprets as "prince of devils"; and that the Bad Angel, in reply to Faustus' cry of repentance, asserts:

> Thou art a spirit; God cannot pity thee

[4] Even in stage directions: the first entry of the Good and Bad Angels is headed in 1616: 'Enter the Angell and Spirit.'

—a remark to which I shall return. And if there could be any doubt of the meaning of these expressions, we have the explicit statement in the *Damnable Life* that Faustus' "request was none other than to become a devil." Faustus then, through his bargain with hell, has himself taken on the infernal nature, although it is made clear throughout that he still retains his human soul.

This throws a new light upon the question, debated throughout the play, whether Faustus can be saved by repentance. Faustus, of course, is for ever repenting—and recanting through fear of bodily torture and death—and the Good and Bad Angels, who personate the two sides of his human nature, are forever disputing the point:

> *Fau.* Contrition, prayer, repentance: what of these?
> *Good A.* Oh, they are means to bring thee unto heaven.
> *Bad A.* Rather illusions, fruits of lunacy

and again:

> *Good A.* Never too late, if Faustus will repent.
> *Bad A.* If thou repent, devils will tear thee in pieces.
> *Good A.* Repent, and they shall never raze thy skin.

There are two passages that are particularly significant in this respect: and we must remember, as I have said, the double question at issue—Faustus' nature, and whether repentance can cancel a bargain. First then, the passage from which I have already quoted:

> *Good A.* Faustus, repent; yet God will pity thee.
> *Bad A.* Thou art a spirit; God cannot pity thee.
> *Fau.* Who buzzeth in mine ears, I am a spirit?
> Be I a devil, yet God may pity me;
> Yea, God will pity me if I repent.
> *Bad A.* Ay, but Faustus never shall repent.

The Bad Angel evades the issue, which is left undecided.[5] Later in the same scene, when Faustus calls on Christ to save his soul, Lucifer replies with admirable logic:

---

[5] Faustus' words are perhaps intentionally ambiguous. "Be I a devil" may mean "What though I am a devil," or it may mean "Even were I a devil." Ward insisted on the second sense, but it is not borne out by the evidence. Boas shows a correct understanding of the passage when he glosses "spirit" as "evil spirit, devil."

> Christ cannot save thy soul, for he is just:
> There's none but I have interest in the same.[6]

Thus the possibility of Faustus' salvation is left nicely poised in doubt—like that of the archdeacon of scholastic speculation.

It is only when, back among his students at Wittenberg, he faces the final reckoning that Faustus regains some measure of heroic dignity. Marlowe again takes charge. But even so the years have wrought a change. His faithful Wagner is puzzled:

> I wonder what he means; if death were nigh,
> He would not banquet and carouse and swill
> Among the students, as even now he doth . . .

This is a very different Faustus from the fearless teacher his students used to know, whose least absence from the class room caused concern—

> I wonder what's become of Faustus, that was wont to make our schools ring with *sic probo.*

One good, or at least amiable, quality—apart from a genuine tenderness towards his students—we may be tempted to claim for him throughout: a love of beauty in nature and in art:

> Have not I made blind Homer sing to me
> Of Alexander's love and Oenon's death?
> And hath not he that built the walls of Thebes
> With ravishing sound of his melodious harp
> Made music—?

and the climax of his career is his union with the immortal beauty of Helen, to measures admittedly the most lovely that flowed from Marlowe's lyre. Is this sensitive appreciation something that has survived uncorrupted from his days of innocence? I can find no hint of it in the austere student of the early scenes. Is it then some strange flowering of moral decay? It would seem so. What, after all, is that "ravishing sound" but the symphony of hell?—

> Made music—with my Mephostophilis!

And Helen, what of her?

[6] Compare Faustus' own lines near the end:
Hell claims his right, and with a roaring voice
Says, "Faustus, come; thine hour is almost come":
And Faustus now will come to do thee right.

Here we come, if I mistake not, to the central theme of the damnation of Faustus. The lines in which he addresses Helen are some of the most famous in the language:

> Was this the face that launched a thousand ships
> And burnt the topless towers of Ilium?
> Sweet Helen, make me immortal with a kiss! . . .
> Here will I dwell, for heaven is in these lips,
> And all is dross that is not Helena.
> I will be Paris, and for love of thee
> Instead of Troy shall Wittenberg be sacked;
> And I will combat with weak Menelaus,
> And wear thy colours on my plumed crest:
> Yea, I will wound Achilles in the heel,
> And then return to Helen for a kiss.
> Oh, thou art fairer than the evening's air
> Clad in the beauty of a thousand stars,
> Brighter art thou than flaming Jupiter
> When he appeared to hapless Semele,
> More lovely than the monarch of the sky
> In wanton Arethusa's azured arms;
> And none but thou shalt be my paramour!

In these lines Marlowe's uncertain genius soared to its height,[7] but their splendour has obscured, and was perhaps meant discreetly to veil, the real nature of the situation. "Her lips suck forth my soul," says Faustus in lines that I omitted from his speech above.[8] What is Helen? We are not told in so many words, but the answer is there, if we choose to look for it. When the Emperor asks him to present Alexander and his paramour before the court, Faustus (in the 1604 version) laboriously explains the nature of the figures that are to appear:

> My gracious lord, I am ready to accomplish your request so far forth as by art and power of my spirit I am able to perform. . . . But, if it like your

[7] Besides a number of incidental passages of great beauty, some of which I have quoted, the play contains three that stand out above the rest and I think surpass all else that Marlowe wrote. The address to Helen is of course pure lyric; the final soliloquy is intense spiritual drama: with these, and in its different mode little below them, I would place the farewell scene with the students, which seems to prove that, had he chosen, Marlowe could have been no less an artist in prose than he was, in verse.

[8] "Her lips suck forth my soul: see where it flies!" Faustus of course intends the words in a merely amorous sense, confusing the physical and the spiritual in an exaggerated image that is not perhaps in the best taste. But I wonder whether Marlowe may not have had, at the back of his mind, some recollection of the *Ars Moriendi*, with its pictures of a devil dragging the naked soul out of the mouth of a dying man.

grace, it is not in my ability to present before your eyes the true substantial bodies of those two deceased princes, which long since are consumed to dust. . . . But such spirits as can lively resemble Alexander and his paramour shall appear before your grace in that manner that they best lived in, in their most flourishing estate . . .

He adds (according to the 1616 version):

> My lord, I must forewarn your majesty
> That, when my spirits present the royal shapes
> Of Alexander and his paramour,
> Your grace demand no questions of the king,
> But in dumb silence let them come and go.

This is explicit enough; and as a reminder that the same holds for Helen, Faustus repeats the caution when he presents her to his students:

> Be silent then, for danger is in words.

Consider, too, a point critics seem to have overlooked, the circumstances in which Helen is introduced the second time. Urged by the Old Man, Faustus has attempted a last revolt; as usual he has been cowed into submission, and has renewed the blood-bond. He has sunk so low as to beg revenge upon his would-be saviour—

> Torment, sweet friend, that base and aged man,
> That durst dissuade me from thy Lucifer,
> With greatest torments that our hell affords.

And it is in the first place as a safeguard against relapse that he seeks possession of Helen—

> One thing, good servant, let me crave of thee
> To glut the longing of my heart's desire;
> That I may have unto my paramour
> That heavenly Helen which I saw of late,
> Whose sweet embraces may extinguish clear
> Those thoughts that may dissuade me from my vow,
> And keep mine oath I made to Lucifer.

Love and revenge are alike insurances against salvation. "Helen" then is a "spirit," and in this play a spirit means a devil.[9] In making her his

---

[9] This fact has perhaps been obscured for critics by recollections of Goethe's *Faust.* Thus Ward, in a note on Faustus' address to Helen, writes: "The outburst of Faust

paramour Faustus commits the sin of demoniality, that is, bodily inter-
course with demons.[10]

The implication of Faustus' action is made plain in the comments of
the Old Man and the Angels. Immediately before the Helen episode the
Old Man was still calling on Faustus to repent—

> Ah, Doctor Faustus, that I might prevail
> To guide thy steps into the way of life!

(So 1604: 1616 proceeds:)

> Though thou hast now offended like a man,
> Do not persever in it like a devil:
> Yet, yet, thou hast an amiable soul,
> If sin by custom grow not into nature . . .

But with Faustus' union with Helen the nice balance between possible
salvation and imminent damnation is upset. The Old Man, who has
witnessed the meeting (according to the 1604 version), recognizes the
inevitable:

---

on beholding the real Helena (whom he had previously seen as a magical appari-
tion) . . . should be compared." There is, of course, no such distinction between
the two appearances of Helen in Marlowe's play. It is curious, by the way, how persistently critics and editors commit the absurdity of calling the spirit in Marlowe's
play "Mephistophiles," as if this were the correct or original form and not a variant
invented by Goethe a couple of centuries later.

[10] The *Oxford English Dictionary* defines *demoniality* as "The nature of demons; the
realm of demons, demons collectively. (Cf. *spirituality*.)" But this is not supported by
the only two quotations it gives. The first, curiously enough, is the title: "Demoniality;
or Incubi and Succubi . . . by the Rev. Father Sinistrari, of Ameno . . . now first
translated into English" (1879). This, even by itself, is suggestive, and anyone who
has looked beyond the title of this curious and long unprinted work by the seventeenth century theologian Lodovico Maria Sinistrari, knows that the analogy of
demoniality is not with "spirituality" but with "bestiality." The worthy casuist is
quite explicit. "3. Coitus igitur cum Dæmone, sive Incubo, sive Succubo (qui proprie
est Dæmonialitas), specie differt a Bestialitate, nec cum ea facit unam speciem . . .
8. Ulterius in confesso est apud omnes Theologos Morales, quod longe gravior est
copula cum Dæmones, quam quolibet bruto . . ." . The writer also draws a distinction, repeated in his better known work *De Delictis et Poenis* (Venice, 1700), between
two varieties of demoniality, that practised by witches and warlocks with devils, and
that which others commit with incubi and succubae. According to Sinistrari the first
to use the term *daemonialitas*, and to distinguish it from *bestialitas*, was Johannes
Caramuelis in his *Theologia Fundamentalis* (Frankfort, 1651). The other quotation
given in the dictionary is from *The Saturday Review* (1891), "The old wives' fables . . .
are those of demoniality, black masses, etc.," in which the meaning is presumably the
same.

> Accursèd Faustus, miserable man,
> That from thy soul exclud'st the grace of heaven
> And fliest the throne of his tribunal-seat!

The Good Angel does no less:

> O Faustus, if thou hadst given ear to me
> Innumerable joys had followed thee . . .
> Oh, thou hast lost celestial happiness . . .

And Faustus himself, still haunted in his final agony by the idea of a salvation beyond his reach—

> See, see, where Christ's blood streams in the firmament!
> One drop would save my soul—

shows, in talk with his students, a terrible clarity of vision:

> A surfeit of deadly sin, that hath damned both body and soul. . . . Faustus' offence can ne'er be pardoned: the Serpent that tempted Eve may be saved, but not Faustus

and Mephostophilis echoes him:

> Ay, Faustus, now hast thou no hope of heaven!

It would be idle to speculate how far the "atheist" Marlowe, whom gossip accused of what we call "unnatural" vice, may have dwelt in imagination on the direst sin of which human flesh is capable. But in presenting the fall and slow moral disintegration of an ardent if erring spirit, he did not shrink from depicting, beside Faustus' spiritual sin of bartering his soul to the powers of evil, what is in effect its physical complement and counterpart, however he may have disguised it in immortal verse.

The Equilibrium of Tragedy

by Una Ellis-Fermor

Finally, there is the rare negative form which might be called Satanic tragedy, the drama which oversets tragic balance, not merely by denying immanent good, but by implying a Satanic universe, a world-order behind the manifestation of event as evil as the event itself. To this kind belong, among others, some of the plays of Euripides, Marlowe's *Faustus,* some of Strindberg; among the more recent writers Lenormand sometimes approaches it.[1] This group of plays contrasts sharply with the two we have just considered, in that, at its height, magnitude of theme and power of passion again appear as distinguishing characteristics. This was true also of its direct opposite, religious drama,[2] for there also some attempt at interpretation of life formed a background of thought and found its way directly or indirectly into the total effect even of the outer action. But in the drama of Satanism not only is there a more or less clearly implied interpretation of the universe surrounding the events, but, by reason of its conflict with the systems of positive religion, this interpretation will generally be original to the writer. Thus, in the major Satanic drama there is presupposed a mind both comprehensive and original, strong and wide enough in scope to synthesize disparate material into an organic system and with an individualism tenacious enough to withstand the imaginative force of prevailing assumptions. Nevertheless, even the plays of this group disturb, in greater or less degree, that supreme balance which characterizes tragedy "of the centre." Though in less degree than the other negative plays, those of materialistic pessimism, they fall short by presenting a universe—even though pat-

[1] The vision of an evil world-order in *Medea* and *The Troades* appears consistent enough to justify regarding them as Satanic drama. Strindberg at his most coherent and forcible makes a similar reading of life (in *Miss Julia* and *The Father*), while Lenormand, slender as is his contribution in general, approaches it in *A L'Ombre du Mal.*

[2] Provided always that we continue to restrict that term to the drama of religious experience and do not extend it to include all drama written in terms of given theological assumptions.

terned and not chaotic—which corresponds but imperfectly with the dual, if contradictory, experience of man.

The peculiar Satanic negation appears in different ways in the plays of Euripides and of Marlowe. Euripides uses the facilities of the Greek chorus to comment upon a universe controlled now by an evil world-order and now by mixture of casualty and cause, while Marlowe, in *Dr. Faustus,* uses the more consistently dramatic Jacobean form to present a steadfast picture of an evil world-order on which there is no comment except by implication.

Euripides, through the familiar imagery of the old gods, reveals the irresponsible, meaningless or even malevolent forces that overbear man's valour. His gods, it is true, are more powerful than man, but certain of them are less noble, and from them comes the frustration which annuls creation, confuses valour, and cripples wisdom.[3]

Even in those plays where this interpretation is less clearly defined, the perception of pain and the poet's sympathy with it outweigh all else. And Euripides' nearest approach to a vindication of life's processes would appear to be Hecuba's in *The Troades,* where she justifies the sufferings of Troy as the raw material of art.[4]

Marlowe, whose tragedy appears at its height and in characteristic form in *Faustus,* takes up a unique position as a tragic thinker, because of the implacable paradox on which his reading of the universe rests; man's innate fallibility on the one hand, and, on the other, the infallibility demanded by inflexible law.[5] To this paradox there is only one conclusion: "Why then belike we must sin and so consequently die." The precision and finality of this deduction indicate a vision terrifying alike in its assumptions and in its omissions. For implicit in Marlowe's premiss is the predestination of man to destruction by some determinate power capable of purpose and intention, and, as such purpose can only be sadistic, the world order it implies must derive from a Satanism more nearly absolute than that of Euripides.[6]

But neither in this play nor elsewhere does Marlowe state this assumption in explicit terms and the implication itself rests on a few passages

---

[3] Some at least of the repetitions of this passage must be presumed to be Euripides' intention. (*Medea* 1415-19, *Alcestis* 1159-63, *Helen* 1688-92, *Bacchae* 1388-92, *Andromache* 1284-88.)

[4] *Troades,* 1240-45. Just so Deirdre, in the Cuchulainn cycle and in Synge's play, thinks of her sorrow as a song 'that shall be sung for ever.'

Both these passages put briefly and explicitly an estimate of the function of art in which is implicit the conclusion drawn a few pages earlier in discussing the relation of form to tragic balance in the Sophoclean tragedy.

[5] Like Fulke Greville after him, Marlowe, in the opening argument of the play, sees the

> Wearisome condition of humanity,
> Born under one law, to another bound.

[6] More nearly, indeed, than that of any dramatist known to me.

in *Faustus*.[7] Even there it is rather by silence and omission that he reveals his belief that evil is not only inherent in man's destiny but both irremediable and predetermined. Only a consistent vision of a Satanic universe could beget the initial paradox; never does Marlowe raise the question: Why, if the laws of the universe be such, should man, himself a part of that universe, be so irreconcilably opposed to them? To a convinced Satanist it is, in fact, no paradox. Given a sadistic and malevolent power directing the world-order there is no inducement to postulate a further transcendent power or intelligence, relating or reconciling the contradictions of man's capacity and God's demands. And so Marlowe achieves, not a balance between two interpretations of the universe, but immobility and rigidity of protest. In his drama the spirit of man is set against the universe, but there is no equilibrium between two worlds of thought. For Marlowe, at the time of *Faustus,* did not question the nature of the world-order. He saw it steadily and saw it evil.

So complete does Marlowe's Satanism seem in its direct and outward expression that it is almost impossible to reconcile with its finality our persistent impression of tragic mystery in *Faustus*. How are we to reconcile the absence of tragic equilibrium in this, perhaps the most notable Satanic play in literature, with this recurrent and obstinate conviction that here, if anywhere, is tragedy? In part because the absence, even here, is more apparent than real. The framework of Marlowe's thought, the deductive process by which he arrives at his conclusion, is consistent and, within its limits, unassailable.[8] But there are indications that it did not take into account the whole of his experience. The Satanic reading of life may, it is true, permit Faustus (and Marlowe) to confound Hell in Elysium and see Helen's beauty fairer than the evening air; for if these are themselves destructible, by so much is the mockery of man's fate more hideous. But there is one thing that Marlowe cannot subjugate to that world-order that predestines universal damnation—his own inarticulate and hardly acknowledged conviction that it is evil. From what source springs this passionate judgement, he does not appear to consider; but "Christ's blood streams in the firmament" and there escapes—coherently, it may be, only in this single line—the implication of a deeper division in his mind, that his otherwise consistent, Satanic interpretation has left unresolved. In that division, imaginatively revealed, though excluded from the logical demonstration of his thought, lie the dualism and conflict essential to the tragic mood. It does not constitute a balancing of one interpretation against another, but the absolute Satanism is flawed and the reader left with the impression of a potential balancing force to challenge its absolutism. Thus, even in the extreme case of *Faustus,* the most nearly

---

[7] Principally I, i, I, iii, II, ii, V, i and ii. (The references are to Boas's edition.)

[8] It is remarkable, indeed, that so clear a piece of deduction should be conveyed (even though, of necessity, piecemeal) in strict dramatic form.

Satanic tragedy that can be found, it would appear that in so far as drama is Satanic it loses tragic balance and in so far as it is tragic it is not Satanic. Moreover, in Marlowe's play, though in less degree than in the tragedies of the centre, there is to be found the same balancing of content by form that we remarked in the work of Sophocles. A partial challenge to the suffering and evil in the outer action comes from that beauty of form and style which itself gives the lie to the implication that the fundamental order of things is evil. For this itself implies harmony; as in the work of Sophocles, though not so fully, the revelation of beauty in form is an unwitting testimony to that beneficence or immanent good of which beauty and form are manifestations.

Nevertheless, in the plays of this last group, absolute tragic balance is overset, although magnitude of passion and thought again become possible, since the action is related to a surrounding universe greater in scope and significance than the figures and events that make up that action. And even though the direct inference be to a universe of implacable evil, this does not detract from the grandeur, though it may from the wholeness and saneness of the final impression. Moreover, beyond this direct influence lies the indirect and seemingly unwitting testimony to the "world of profit and delight" that, residing in beauty, in form and in the unacknowledged sources of the poet's vision, maintains a partial balance in the play, despite his logical and intentional Satanism.

The Damnation of Faustus

by J. P. Brockbank

Pico, in his *Oration*, recalls "that it was a saying of Zoroaster that the soul is winged and that, when the wings drop off, she falls again into the body; and then, after her wings have grown again sufficiently, she flies back to heaven." After his headlong fall into the body, Faustus's wings seem to grow again in the last act.

The Vision of Helen

When "music sounds" and Helen passes across the stage her sanctity is mirrored in the awed calm of the scholars' judgments. Her "heavenly beauty passeth all compare"; she is "the pride of nature's work" and a "blessed sight." This vision lends intensity and compassion to the austere admonitions of the Old Man, who speaks to Faustus when the scholars have left. Marlowe anticipates Milton in finding a poetry of "kind rebuke," a moral music, to efface the magic that charms the soul to hell. And in the Scholar's "Too simple is my wit to tell her praise" and the Old Man's "No mortal can express the pains of hell," he seems to set himself new tasks for language to perform.

When Faustus resumes his communion with Helen the context in the scene and the play calls for an extreme and simultaneous celebration of the rival values of the heroic and moral orders; and this is accomplished with marvellous economy. From a moral point of view Faustus's will is viciously egocentric: "let me crave of thee To glut the longing of my heart's desire"; and his eagerness to "extinguish clear Those thoughts that do dissuade me from my vow" is a manifest sin against the Holy Spirit. And yet it is a dedicated will, and the self seems transcended by the sanctity of its aspiration and allegiance. Thoughts that would dissuade from a vow to a seemingly unfallen Lucifer are extinguished for the sake of clearness and purity, and the "sweet embracings" of "heavenly Helen" suggest a divine wedding in the mode of the *Song of Solomon* rather than (for example) the whoredoms of Samaria and Jerusalem in *Ezekiel* (xxiii). Mephostophilis performs his last trick "in twinkling of an eye." Is Marlowe recalling St. Paul? "In a moment, in the twinkling of an eye, at the last trump: for the trumpet shall sound, and the dead shall be raised incorruptible . . . this mortal must put on immortality" (I *Cor.* xv. 52).

When Helen comes again in pageant style "between two Cupids" Marlowe endows Faustus with Tamburlaine's and Dido's passions for heroic immortality. Tamburlaine had remembered from "Homer's Iliads," "*Hellen,* whose beauty sommond Greece to armes, And drew a thousand ships to *Tenedos*" (2 *Tamb.* 3054). Dido recalls the "thousand ships" that desolated Troy and cries that her lover will make her "immortall with a kisse," while Aeneas calls waves "toples hilles" and speaks of a thousand Grecians "In whose sterne faces shin'd the quenchles fire, That after burnt the pride of *Asia*" (*Dido*, 1612, 1329, 1162, 481). Marlowe tells Helen's praises by recalling from the heroic past the power that moved on her behalf and, endowing the scholar with a soldier's imagination, he allows Faustus's resolution to renew it for the future: "And I will combat with weak Menelaus. And wear thy colours on my plumed crest." We feel too that Marlowe is vindicating his time's innocent love of tournament and chivalry.

But rival feelings are awakened also. Without alluding to the Old Testament, Marlowe moves in the same territories of the imagination, and feels Ezekiel's fascination for conjunctions of beauty, passion and destruction (see *Ez.* xxiii). Unlike the Sabean harlots, Helen is divine; but the sacking of Troy and Wittenberg for her sake is related to the Biblical image of the refining fire purging precious metals: "All is dross that is not Helena." The speech looks back not only to Valdes on "the queen of love," Faustus's hope to "live in all voluptuousness" and the Prologue's exequy to "proud audacious deeds" but also to Mephostophilis's Last Judgment "when all the world dissolves And every creature shall be purified." The purity is characteristically evoked by "the evening's air," "a thousand stars," "flaming Jupiter" and "wanton Arethusa's azured arms," reconciling "sweet pleasure" with Faustus's delight in beholding the heavens.

When Faustus kisses Helen he reconciles present with future satisfactions—the large Romantic cry "I will." Shakespeare's Cleopatra will say "Eternity was in our lips and eyes," and Blake that "The Gates of the Senses open upon Eternity"; and Marlowe here persuades us that Gluttony and Lechery have carried Faustus through hell to a prospect of Heaven. "Her lips suck forth my soul" may make Faustus a witch and Helen a succuba, but "see where it flies!" is a Simonian cry of triumph. Marlowe will not easily over-reach his own verbal magic.

The Plight of the Man

Faustus is "but a man condemned to die" (IV v. 21), has "offended like a man" (V. i. 40) and has a "distressed soul" (V. i. 65). His plight is expressed in a scrap of soliloquy, in his dealings with the Old Man and in his last talk with the scholars.

The comedy requires that Faustus should fall asleep and lose his leg (IV. v), and the opportunity is taken to remind us that his "fatal" time draws to a final end. His distress is intense, but its nature uncertain—we cannot tell if the "distrust" that despair drives into his thoughts is of God or of the devil. The passions of conscience, however, are in any case salutary, and Faustus is to blame for (very humanly) trying to "Confound" them with a quiet sleep. Sleep, like sloth, can be a sin. Faustus settles down for a nap in the hope of dodging moral conflict; and his "Tush, Christ did call the thief upon the cross" is not as Greg supposes "a sentimental piety" but a complacent blasphemy; in the Spira story and play the same sentiment is gravely weighed.

The Old Man's compassionate censure of Faustus adds a new dimension to our sense of the human predicament: "Yet, yet, thou hast an amiable soul If sin by custom grow not into nature." Augustine says, "For the law of sin is the violence of custom, whereby the mind is drawn and holden, even against its will; but deservedly, for that it willingly fell into it." (*Confessions* VIII. 12) Faustus is in this state of being "deservedly" held against will. Yet it is a bitter irony that the will in its freedom can more readily fall than climb. In putting so strong a stress on the will, it is easy to court the Pelagian heresy, which held that the human will can win salvation without grace. Marlowe encounters some difficulty in distinguishing dramatically between repentance by an act of free will and repentance through grace. The Old Man dissuades Faustus from using the devil's dagger by telling him of a hovering angel "with a vial full of precious grace" and pleading with him to "call for mercy and avoid despair." Is it that Faustus cannot repent because he is without grace, and cannot have grace because he will not repent? Or is it that he cannot receive the grace of justification from the angelic vial because he has too often denied the promptings of prevenient grace? Either way, the human relationship has its own dignity and power, and leaves us to wonder why a graceless man should be so moved by another's compassion.

As "hell strives with grace" for conquest in Faustus's breast, the powers of light and darkness seem matched in the Manichean way. But to patient judgment it appears that Faustus's yielding to evil is voluntary, while the Old Man's resistance to it makes it assist in the perfection of virtue. Faustus is again trapped by the metaphor of Lucifer as "sovereign lord" with Mephostophilis an emissary empowered to punish a "traitor." He can only conceive "presumption" as an offence against the tyranny of Pride, and it is his own pride that commits him to "proud Lucifer." The same pride moves his address to Helen with its presumptions of immortality and magnificence; it would be admirable were it not a last vain bid to escape from the human condition as the Old Man represents it. In the futility of his pride Faustus commands that the "base and aged man" should suffer the "greatest torments that our hell affords."

But the Old Man triumphantly endures the torments that in this life pride inflicts on humility. "Satan begins to sift me with his pride" recalls *Luke* xxii. 31, "Satan hath desired to have you, that he may sift you as wheat." It is another image of purifying ordeal, and it is suffered on earth in "our hell"—"As in this furnace God shall try my faith" (see *Is.* xlviii. 10). The Old Man will "fly unto my God" while the scholar Faustus remains below. As Augustine has it, "The unlearned start up and take heaven by force, and we with our learning, and without heart, lo, where we wallow in flesh and blood." (*Confessions* VIII. 19.)

When Lucifer and his henchmen take up their positions to witness Faustus's end they are like the figures of revenge-play (e.g. *The Spanish Tragedy*) who gloat upon the ironic justice they exact from men. Here, however, as Mephostophilis looks forward to a spectacle of "desperate lunacy" as man's "labouring brain" begets "idle fantasies To overreach the devil," the gloating takes the form of a pitiless objectivity about the nature of evil.

But the talk with the scholars supplies no "idle fantasies" as Faustus movingly reassumes his humanity and his fellowship with other men. Yet both are flawed by his isolation and sense of his unique doom: "had I lived with thee, then had I lived still." We recognise humility stirring in his courtesy, but his resolute apartness is subtly touched with pride. He blames the devils for the paralysis of his moral being: "I would weep, but the devil draws in my tears. . . . I would lift up my hands, but see, they hold 'em, they hold 'em"; but when the scholars chorus "Who Faustus?" we are more persuaded of the reality of the incapacities for grief and penitence than of the power of the invisible spirits. Self-assertion and self-effacement meet in, "Talk not of me, but save yourselves and depart"; as in the will he leaves for Wagner, there is a touch of irony in his magnanimity. And there is keen pathos in his farewell as it salvages a last pretext of reassurance, "If I live till morning I'll visit you."

A Last Judgment

After the scholars have left, the mockery of Mephostophilis administers a last turn of the screw: " 'Twas I, that when thou wert i' the way to heaven, Dammed up thy passage; when thou tookst the book To view the scriptures, then I turned the leaves And led thine eye." Faustus weeps.

It is a terrifying speech, recoiling upon our whole experience of the play. But without it the exploration of the mystery of evil would not be complete; it is the dramatic equivalent of the gospel's equally disturbing, "Then entered Satan into Judas" (*Luke* xxii. 3). From one point of view the play's devils are only symbols of "aspiring pride and insolence," and it is simply Faustus's wilful pride that turned the leaves and led his eye. It is *as if* the devil were directing him. But when Christianity externalised and personalised pride in its dramatic mythology of Satan it exposed itself to the hazard it meets here: man is prey to an adversary whose power daunts even Faustus and, as we have seen, daunted even Peter in his contests with Simon. In the tragic tradition, Satan's power is like a malignant fate (man is punished for the pride he was born with); in the Morality tradition it has grown into an inexplicable challenge to the power and mercy of God.

Yet the Good Angel denies the devil's ultimate power over man: "Hadst thou affected sweet divinity Hell or the devil had had no power on thee"; and Faustus's failure to affect divinity is manifestly voluntary and culpable. But whether we take Mephostophilis's claim literally or metaphorically, we are left to repeat Augustine's unanswerable question: "what can cause the will's evil, the will being sole cause of all evil?"

The final angelic pronouncements are, as Greg says, a Last Judgment upon Faustus. After it Faustus's death is not the natural death of the body only, but also what Augustine calls "the eternal, penal second death" (referred to in *Rev.* xx. 14), and his soul tumbles directly into "confusion." The hell-fire and the tormented glutton of the Bad Angel's description retain their traditional power (see *Luke* xvi. 24) and there is no need to attribute them to a collaborator.

Damned Perpetually

Faustus's great final soliloquy consummates the play in both its aspects —Morality and Heroic Tragedy—and each in its own way triumphs over the other. In fear we acquiesce in the littleness and powerlessness of man, and in pity we share his sufferings and endorse his protest.

The horrible prospect of a man being burnt alive, which Marlowe (like the Christianity he honours) does not spare us, accounts for little of the pathos and power. In the first lines we are much more moved by the magnificent futility of the human protest against the inexorable movement of time as it enacts an inexorable moral law. We are reminded that "All things that move between the quiet poles" are at the command of the process Faustus would escape: the "ever-moving spheres" cannot by definition "stand still." Faustus had explained the seasonal "circles" to the Duchess, who marvelled at the winter grapes (IV. vii. 23), and he had numbered the cycles of the spheres, but now his knowledge is of a different order. The cosmic rhythms evoked by the sense of the poetry seem to hold dominion over its movement. The first equably stressed eleven words echo the striking clock—"Ah Faustus, Now hast thou but one bare hour to live"; the "perpetually" that falls with finality at the end of the first sentence returns in the mocking oxymoron "Perpetual day"; and "rise, rise again" invokes precisely the diurnal motion it seeks to arrest.

The irony of the quotation from Ovid has long been celebrated. In the *Amores* (I. xiii. 40) it is the plea of ecstatic love, *Clamares, "lente currite, noctis equi,"* which Marlowe had poorly translated, "Then wouldst thou cry, stay night and runne not thus." But here the Latin words in their English setting sound like a last attempt to cast a spell whose vanity is betrayed by the rhythm as the horses seem to quicken pace through the line, and confessed in "The stars move still, time runs, the clock will strike." Were the soliloquy to end here we should feel that confinement to time is the cruellest fact of man's condition.

In the next lines, however, his ordeal is confinement to earth: "Oh, I'll leap up to my God! Who pulls me down?" The image affirming the immensity of Christ's Testament also declares its unreachable remoteness: "See see where Christ's blood streams in the firmament." Marlowe may be remembering both the gulf between heaven and hell (*Luke* xvi. 26) and Tamburlaine, defiant in his mortal sickness:

> Come let vs march against the powers of heaven,
> And set blacke streamers in the firmament,
> To signifie the slaughter of the Gods.
> Ah friends, what shall I doe? I cannot stand.
>
> (2 *Tamb.* 4440)

Christ has accomplished the triumph over mortality that Tamburlaine's labouring brain could only imagine. The imperial pageant hyperbole of the earlier play has in the later been made to express the superhuman power of Christ; but he conquers by sacrifice not by slaughter—humility has become heroic. Even without appeal to Christian symbolism, the play has made the streaming blood emblematic of eternal life. Blood refuses to flow when Faustus cuts his arm, it "dries with grief" as his "conscience kills it," and it gushes forth from his eyes "instead of tears." As Faustus pleads that "one drop" then "half a drop" would save his soul, he confesses his barren littleness of life in the vastness of the moral universe.

As the vision of blood fades, Faustus meets the unappeased wrath of God and cries for the mountains and hills to fall on him (see, e.g., *Luke* xxiii. 30, *Rev.* vi. 16, *Hos.* x. 8). Burial in earth becomes a privilege refused to the last paroxysms of Faustus's will. He is again re-enacting the fall of Lucifer, the figure in Isaiah who is "brought down to hell, to the

sides of the pit" and "cast out of the grave like an abominable branch"
(*Is.* xiv). When Faustus hopes for a refining ordeal of dissolution and re-
birth in "the entrails of yon labouring clouds" which might "vomit forth"
his limbs and let his soul "ascend to heaven" his words seem haunted by
Lucifer's—"I will ascend above the heights of the clouds, I will be like the
Most High"; and the same chapter could supply the stretching arm of God
and the smoke of the Last Day (*Is.* xiv). Marlowe has assimilated and re-
created the Biblical imagery, however, and it is dramatically valid whether
or not we suppose it allusive. Faustus, the damned hero as the play has
fashioned him, has become the fittest witness of apocalyptic vision. No
chorus could speak with such moving authority, for Faustus alone has
enacted all the futilities of pride.

The first phase of the soliloquy discovers the futility of human pretensions to power in the face of overwhelming cataclysm, the second makes us
feel the futility of knowledge and speculation. Faustus's plea for "some
end to my incessant pain" (recalling the Faust-book and the Spira story
and play) sums up that side of the Christian tradition which, with
Augustine, is "Against those that exclude both men and devils from pain
eternal" (*City of God,* XXII. xxiii). Like Pythagoras' "metempsychosis" it
is wishful thinking. *The French Academy* (II. 85) could have occasioned
the allusion to Pythagoras and supplied the distinction between the souls
of brutes (made of "elements") and those of men ("created of nothing").
And it would challenge Faustus's readiness to accuse the stars that reigned
at his nativity by asking, "how should the heavens, stars and planets give
that to the soul which they themselves have not?" (II. 87).

Faustus moderates his struggle to escape the pain of responsibility as
he curses his parents (see *Luke* xxiii. 29) and then checks himself: "No
Faustus, curse thyself, curse Lucifer That hath deprived thee of the joys
of heaven." Again, if we read "Lucifer" as a metaphor for Pride, the problem of responsibility recedes; but it returns when we think of the devil as
a person and evil as a power outside the consciousness of man. In either
case, it is fitting that the pride of knowledge should be finally purged with
"I'll burn my books!" and the fellowship of sin perpetuated with "Ah,
Mephostophilis!"

In the last scene, as in Shakespeare's tragedies, normal life must resume
as best it can. Marlowe (there is no need to suppose a collaborator)
abstains from the grotesque nastiness of the Faust-book catastrophe, and
strikes an apt balance between horror, dismay, and due reverence. If the
noise that the scholars report seems a concession to popular taste, we may
reflect that it might be a clue to the acting of Faustus's closing words, from
"My God, my God! Look not so fierce on me," and remember *Psalm* xxii:

My God, my God, why hast thou forsaken me? why art thou so far from
helping me, and from the words of my roaring?

Epilogue

The Epilogue seals both the Heroic-play and the Morality. In "Cut is the branch that might have grown full straight" we feel that the pruning has been done to maiming purpose. Marlowe may have remembered the image from Churchyard's *Shore's Wife*, where it also suggests wanton destruction, "And bent the wand that mought have grown full streight." But the Bible haunts the lines too, and the branch may be dead because it has failed to take nourishment from the tree (see *John* xv. 4-7, *Psalm* lxxx). The next line, "And burned is Apollo's laurel bough" alludes perhaps to the frustration of Faustus's pre-eminence in the hidden mysteries, but again the destruction may be wanton. The last lines are a due and weighty warning against emulating "forward wits" who "practise more than heavenly power permits"; yet they leave the wise still to wonder at the enticing deepness of unlawful things.

Faustus's ordeal is specifically that of the aspiring mind (the "unsatiable speculator" as the Faust-book has it), of that part of our nature which is dissatisfied with being merely human and tries vainly to come to rest in fantasies of omnipotence and omniscience. It is a romantic agony which oscillates across an abyss between extremities of hope and despair. Marlowe, seeing it for what it was, related the hope to the imperial and speculative ambitions of his time, and the despair to that side of Christianity which brings home to us the inescapable mortality and doom of man. Goethe, in a self-confessedly romantic age, was independently to take up the story again and, after many oscillations, endorse its potential of hope. Marlowe stuck to the basic shape of the story and accepted the damnation of his hero. But not complacently. D. H. Lawrence, who also understood the value of extreme commitments, said that a work of art "must contain the essential criticism on the morality to which it adheres. And hence the antinomy, hence the conflict necessary to every tragic conception." *Dr. Faustus* adheres to the rich and searching morality of Augustinian thought; but it does not allow us to come comfortably to rest in it. In the Heroic-play the reaching mind that is punished by hell is also the mind that apprehends heaven, and Faustus—the playwright's figment —suffers the one and glimpses the other on the audience's behalf.

The Jew of Malta and Edward II

by M. C. Bradbrook

The Jew of Malta is one of the most difficult of Elizabethan plays. Mr Eliot's explanation[1] will not cover the obvious change of tone between Acts 1 and 2 and the rest of the play. The first part of the play is, like *Faustus,* concerned only with the mind of the hero: Barabas' actions are comparatively unimportant. In the last part of the play actions supply nearly all the interest: there is an attempt to make the narrative exciting in itself, to connect the various episodes causally and consecutively to produce something of a story. This is the technique of that very different play, *Edward II.* I shall indicate below the most striking parallels in constructive method.

The first part of *The Jew of Malta* has a theme similar to *Faustus* and *Tamburlaine.* Barabas' sponsor, like Faustus, says:

> I count religion but a childish toy,
> And hold there is no sin but ignorance.
>
> (Prologue)

The hypocrisy of his enemies is Machiavelli's justification: "Admired I am of those that hate me most." This is also Barabas' case as he puts it to the merchant and to Abigail (1. 1. 110-18 and 1. 2. 290-3), and as it is illustrated by Ferneze and the friars. In the opening scene the glory of his wealth is given with a precision far from the indefinite splendours of *Tamburlaine:*

> Bags of fiery opals, sapphires, amethysts,
> Jacinths, hard topaz, grass green emeralds,
> Beauteous rubies, sparkling diamonds. . . .
>
> (1. 1. 25 ff.)

"*The Jew of Malta* and *Edward II.*" From *Themes and Conventions of Elizabethan Tragedy* by M. C. Bradbrook. Copyright 1935 by the Syndics of the Cambridge University Press. Reprinted by permission of the Syndics of the Cambridge University Press. The pages reprinted here are part of the chapter entitled "Christopher Marlowe."

[1] "A Note on the Blank Verse of Christopher Marlowe," in *The Sacred Wood,* reprinted in *Selected Essays.*

This elastic movement improves even on *Faustus;* and the movement of the following lines shows the same flexibility:

> why, then, I hope my ships . . .
> Are gotten up by Nilus' winding banks:
> Mine argosy from Alexandria,
> Loaden with spice and silks, now under sail,
> Are smoothly gliding down by Candy-shore
> To Malta, through our Mediterranean Sea.
>
>   (1. 1. 41 ff.)

The jerky laboured movement of the first line is set in opposition to the slurred glide of the last. So far as the action is concerned there is also a distinct advance. Barabas' asides to the other Jews should be compared with those of Faustus to the Pope and the knight.

The scene between Barabas and Ferneze (1. 2) develops a satiric tone: the Christian hypocrisy is contrasted with Barabas' open wickedness, and their greed with his. It is a development of the quarrel between Christians and infidels in *Tamburlaine*, Part II. Ferneze does not keep faith with infidels, and though the famous invocation of Orcanes is too heroic for a wronged merchant, it is the same theme treated at a different level.

> Open, thou shining veil of Cynthia . . .
> That he that sits on high and never sleeps,
> Nor in one place is circumscriptible . . .
> May, in his endless power and purity,
> Behold and venge this traitor's perjury!
>
>   (II *Tamburlaine*, 2. 2. 47 ff.)

The Christians here accuse the Jews of being responsible for the plague of the Turks (1. 2. 63 ff.) and of being doomed to misfortune (1. 2. 108-10). They end with a virtuous repudiation of any desire to shed blood and assurances to Barabas that he has had "nought but right."

In Barabas' laments there is a new and poignant note which recalls Faustus. Some of his phrases are out of all proportion to a material loss: they express general disillusion, like that of Job[2] from which they derive.

> only I have toil'd to inherit here
> The months of vanity, and loss of time,
> And painful nights, have bin appointed me.
>
>   (1. 2. 197-9)

The soliloquy which opens Act 2 is full of such passages:

---

[2] Cf. *The Book of Job*, 7. 3.

> The incertain pleasures of *swift-footed* time
> Have ta'en their flight, and left me in *despair;*
> And of my former riches rests no more
> But bare remembrance; like a soldier's scar,
> That has no further comfort for his maim.

(2. 1. 7-11)

It is the vocabulary of Faustus, but after this scene it appears no more. Not only the character of Barabas but the quality of the verse is changed; pity and human values are dropped.

What happens may be defined (but not explained, of course) as the substitution of a technique of action for a technique of verse. The last half of the play shows an interest in stage situations and the manipulation of the narrative.[3] The use of asides depends largely on stage effectiveness, and on a close intrigue. Such effects as the sudden revival of Barabas after he is thrown over the wall are parallel to the reversals of meaning achieved by giving him a final word to speak aside.

> Use him as if he were a—*Philistine.*

(2. 3. 229)

> And be reveng'd upon the—*governor.*

(2. 3. 145)

(He is speaking to the governor's son.)

The last three acts depend upon different kinds of reversals, verbal or narrative. The gulling of Lodowick and Mathias ("slaves are but nails to drive out one another"), of the friars, and of Ithamore, and the final series of cross betrayals between Ferneze, Calymath, and Barabas, are more in the style of Kyd than of anyone else. The "play of Pedringano" (with variations) is the basis of it, and the asides derive from those of Lorenzo (e.g. when he overhears Horatio's love-making) and of Hieronimo. To the influence of Kyd I think Marlowe's development of a new technique must be ascribed. It can be traced at the basic level of the versification. Marlowe uses the patterned speech of *The Spanish Tragedy* freely and depends a great deal on cut-and-thrust repartee, whereas in the earlier dramas his play on words had been of quite a different kind, and his flytings had not approached stichomuthia. The characters had flung long speeches at each other, like Marlowe's favourite simile of the giants throwing rocks at Jove.

"The hopeless daughter of a hapless Jew" (1. 2. 316) is not in *Tamburlaine*'s style (as Mr Bennett suggests) but an adaptation of

---

[3] This may or may not indicate revision by another hand. *Vide* H. S. Bennett's edition of the play, and *Thomas Heywood*, by A. M. Clark. I have assumed single authorship, feeling personally unfitted to pronounce judgment.

The hopeless father of a hapless son.

(*The Spanish Tragedy*, 4. 4. 84)

Lines like

And naught is to be look'd for now but wars,
And naught to us more welcome is than wars.

(3. 5. 35-6)

Will Barabas recover Malta's loss?
Will Barabas be good to Christians?

(5. 2. 75-6)

are quite unlike anything Marlowe had written before, but they can be
found on every page of *The Spanish Tragedy*.

It is generally admitted that the stage Machiavel, as Marlowe used him,
was descended from Kyd's Lorenzo, and that the earlier Marlovian plays
are not Machiavellian. It is in this play that the keyword "policy" first appears.

The Christians are consistently satirised in the last part of the play for
their "close hypocrisy." Ferneze, breaking his word with Selim as
Sigismund had with Orcanes, uses the same kind of virtuous flourish to
cover his treachery. Compare

take the victory our God hath given

(*II Tamburlaine*, 2. 1, ad fin.)

and

Proud daring Calymath, instead of gold,
We'll send thee bullets wrapt in smoke and fire:
Claim tribute when thou wilt, we are resolv'd—
Honour is bought with blood, and not with gold.

(2. 2, ad fin.)

Since they were deciding to keep their gold and break their word, the implications of the last line are directly ironical, especially if Ferneze's
protestations to Barabas are still remembered. At the end he profits by
Barabas' betrayal of Calymath to the extent of getting him into his own
power and murdering his soldiers, even while declaiming against the
treachery of the Jew and assuring Calymath that he has saved his life.
Barabas' soliloquies upon his villainy enforce the point.

This is the life we Jews are us'd to lead;
And reason too, for Christians do the like.

(5. 3. 115-16)

The "two religious caterpillars" are a more broadly farcical illustration of the same theme, with their competitive attempts to secure Barabas' wealth. The ease with which he plays on them is a measure of their contemptibility.

> —O good Barabas, come to our house!
> —O no, good Barabas, come to *our* house!
>
> (4. 1. 80-1)

This satire is persistent and unmistakable, and makes limited identification with Barabas' point of view possible to the very end.

Edward II is generally acclaimed as Marlowe's greatest dramatic success; but this is only possible by ignoring Elizabethan standards, and judging purely on "construction." As poetic drama, the last speech of Edward is inferior to the last speech of Faustus or even to the early soliloquies of *The Jew of Malta,* and how it is possible to fail as poetry and succeed as drama is not easy to understand.[4]

It is clear that Marlowe is developing in the manner suggested by *The Jew of Malta,* that is, the co-ordination of intrigue and the use of patterned speech. There is a new pattern, the "retort repetitive" and a use of little connective speeches which are not always successful.

Marlowe's compression of his sources and his articulation of the plot has been much praised: it is evidence of this new preoccupation with construction; but it is not always realised that it is responsible for the decline of the soliloquy. In his early plays only the heroes soliloquise and then not for the purpose of making the narrative clear, but for the purpose of expressing the central feelings of the play. In *Edward II* there is no central feeling or theme; it is merely a history. These soliloquies are merely pointers (especially Isabella's and Kent's) indicating when they are on Edward's side and when they are not. Sometimes the change is very clumsily done: the transformation of Isabella is not at all convincing. Mortimer, before his capture, is the most reckless of the Barons; afterwards he is a Machiavel. Kent vacillates more frequently but has less of a character to lose. Edward is really a different person before and after his capture: he even becomes much older (there are frequent references to "old Edward" and "aged Edward") to heighten the pathos.

The different kinds of feeling expressed in *Edward II* seem curiously unconnected and incongruent. Mortimer's use of irony and his worship of "policy" recall Barabas, while the speech of Lightborn—

---

[4] This passage was written before the publication of Charlton and Waller's edition of the play; it is very reassuring, and the more gratifying, to find that they have expressed the same opinion (pp. 53 ff.).

> I learn'd in Naples how to poison flowers;
> To strangle with a lawn thrust through the throat . . .
>
> (5. 4. 31-2)

is the completest expression of the Machiavellian mood of Tourneur and Webster to be found in the early drama.

There is also a new satiric observation of manners and habits which is very different from Marlowe's early style. It depends on the emphasis of detail to the point of caricature, and foreshadows Webster's use of the epigrammatic metaphor.

> The slave looks like a hog's cheek newly singed.
>
> (*The Jew of Malta*, 2. 3. 42)

> leaning on the shoulder of the king,
> He nods, and scorns, and smiles at those that pass.
>
> (1. 2. 23-4)

> 'Tis not a black coat and a little band,
> A velvet-cap'd cloak, fac'd before with serge,
> And smelling to a nosegay all the day . . .
> Or looking downward with your eyelids close,
> And saying "Truly, an't may please your honour"
> Can get you any favour with great men.
>
> (2. 1. 33 ff.)

This irony belongs to the "Machiavellian" attitude; it re-entered tragedy with the figure of the Malcontent, who was influenced by the critical heroes of Jonson. The feeling centred in Edward himself is quite different from this ironic Machiavellianism. The scene in which he is tortured and murdered produces an effect similar to the last scene of *Faustus;* the King knows that he is doomed, and his desperate efforts to pretend it is not so are overshadowed by the certainty that it will be so. The passage of time is important because the conflict between the two moods becomes sharper every instant. His speech at his deposition is a definite reminiscence of the earlier play:

> Continue ever thou celestial Sun;
> Let never silent night possess this clime:
> Stand still you watches of the element;
> All times and seasons, rest you at a stay,
> That Edward may be still fair England's king.
>
> (5. 1. 64 ff.)

(Compare *Faustus*, 5. 2. 140-6.)

Edward, in his refusal to face the implications of his actions and his belief that what he wants must necessarily happen, is close to that aspect of Faustus which is usually overlooked, but which seems important as a contrast to the fixed wills of Tamburlaine and Barabas. He oscillates between the lords and his favourites until, delivered up to Mortimer, he becomes simply a passive object of pity.

Throughout the play, Edward's feelings give what life there is to the verse. He seems to be describing an impersonal sorrow; his statements, that is, are always generalised. Gaveston or his ill-fortunes are only the cause, not really the subject.

> My heart is as an anvil unto sorrow. . . .
>
> (1. 4. 311)

The image is of a sensation rather than an emotion. When the King receives his favourite again, this note is stronger than that of joy, through the use of a comparison which professes to deny it.

> now thy sight
> Is sweeter far than was thy parting hence
> Bitter and irksome to my sobbing heart.
>
> (2. 2. 56 ff.)

Later, when he is defeated, the King says to the abbot:

> Good father, on thy lap
> Lay I this head, laden with mickle care.
> O might I never open these eyes again,
> Never again lift up this drooping head,
> O never more lift up this dying heart!
>
> (4. 6. 39 ff.)

This languorous repetition, and the use of such emotively powerful words as "drooping," "dying," "care," hardly escapes sentimentality. It is a preparation for the conscious pathos of "old Edward," of "My daily diet is heart-breaking sobs." This warm, naturalistic pity is certainly the strongest feeling in the play. It may be compared with the feeling in *The Jew of Malta* (2. 1. 1 ff.). That Marlowe, who reduced the human feelings to a minimum in *Tamburlaine,* should have come to rely on them so much has caused little comment; yet it seems remarkable enough, particularly when at the same time he maintained the completely unfeeling "Machiavellian" attitude also, in the character of Mortimer.

The structure of *Edward II* shows the unevenness of a transitional work.

It is evident that Marlowe was developing very rapidly, both technically and in the more important senses. It might even be hazarded that he was developing towards a more "Shakespearean" (that is, a more inclusive) style, for in *Edward II* there can be found the most formalised qualities of feeling, and the most naturally human.

The Massacre at Paris and Edward II

by F. P. Wilson

Edward II is the one play of Marlowe's—except *Dido*—which is not dominated by one character, and that a character with an aspiring mind: for the centre of this play is not Mortimer but Edward. Some have held that the reason for this change lies in the fact that Marlowe wrote *Edward II* for another dramatic company, not for the Admiral's men with the famous Edward Alleyn who distinguished himself in the parts of Tamburlaine, Barabas, and Faustus, but for Pembroke's men who were without an Alleyn. But the history and personnel of Pembroke's company in the plague years of 1592-3, when we first hear of them, is obscure: in those bad times for actors, companies broke up and re-formed in bewildering fashion. In this Serbonian bog of Elizabethan theatrical history I do not venture to tread, yet I must say that I find unconvincing the view that Marlowe changed his theme to suit his actors; for there never has been a company of professional actors which did not contain at least two men who thought themselves capable of playing star parts of the greatest magnitude. As probably, Marlowe may have been influenced by the success of Shakespeare's *Henry VI*, where the dramatic interest is spread over a yet wider range of characters.

But there is another chronicle play of Marlowe's about which a word or two may be said first. If *The Massacre at Paris* had survived as Marlowe wrote it, much more than a word or two would be necessary. It is our misfortune that the text is a reported text [1] so maimed in the reporting that criticism can only guess at Marlowe's intention and achievement. Some

[1] What appears to be a tentative draft of a single episode in the play, possibly in Marlowe's handwriting, exists in a fragment of a single leaf now in the Folger Library. It gives a fuller version of sc. xvi, ll. 1-16, followed by nine lines of verse not represented in the printed text. Once suspected of being one of J. P. Collier's forgeries, it is now accepted as genuine, thanks to J. Q. Adams (*The Library*, 1934, xiv. 447-69) and J. M. Nosworthy (*ibid.* 1945, xxvi. 158-71). Mr. John Crow kindly refers me to a passage in Thomas Fuller's *Pisgah-Sight of Palestine* (1650), p. 95, which may preserve another scrap of Marlowe's play not found in the mangled printed edition: "I seasonably remember how one being asked in the *Massacre of Paris*, whether he was a *Catholick* or an *Hugonite*, answered *he was a Physician.*"

1,250 lines of verse are all that have survived, and some of these are not garbled versions of Marlowe's lines but half remembered echoes from other plays with which the reporter has patched them up. The dialogue is stripped almost to the bare bones of the action.

The historical period covered is the murder of Coligny and the night of St. Bartholomew in 1572, the murder of Guise in 1588, the murder of Henry III and the accession of Henry of Navarre in 1589. Marlowe's play is then a chronicle play, presenting upon the stage the sensational news "de furoribus Gallicis" [2] which had been reported in England in many a pamphlet and ballad. The play was written before Henry IV had decided that Paris was worth a mass; hence he could be presented as the champion of the Protestant cause against the Machiavellian policies of the Guise faction, the weakness of Charles IX dominated by his mother Catherine de Medici, and his equally weak brother Henry III whose mind, like Edward II's,

> runs on his minions
> And all his heaven is to delight himself.

Perhaps we may most regret the reporter's ineptitude in the scene which represents the murder of the Duke of Guise. The historical evidence has survived in a form which is already dramatic, and not the less vivid in our minds for memories of the setting in the royal castle at Blois and of the rooms where the king and his guards waited for the murdered man. There is quality too in the words which history has recorded as passing between Henry III and his mother. His words to her after the murder "Je suis seul roi maintenant" are preserved in the play in a line which is too good to have come from a reporter: "I ne'er was king of France until this hour"; but the irony of the words—for that was exactly what Henry was not—is but dimly discerned in the text that has survived. And we look in vain for that enigmatic remark of the king as he spurned with his foot the body of the Guise: "Il paraît encore plus grand que vivant." It is one of those instinctive reflections which while they may come from the top layer of the mind yet illuminate at deeper levels the speaker and the situation. One might say that it was only waiting for a great context in order to become art: then, it might have been signed by Middleton or Webster.

We cannot doubt that it was the towering ambition of Guise that most attracted Marlowe to this theme. One soliloquy of his, and only one, has

---

[2] P. H. Kocher has noted that the main source of the first six scenes and of part of the eighth is an English translation of *De Furoribus Gallicis* (1573): *Publications of the Modern Language Association of America*, 1941, lvi. 349-68. He has not been successful in tracing a particular source for the later scenes: *Modern Language Quarterly*, 1947, viii. 151-73, 309-18.

survived, we may suppose, in something like the form that Marlowe gave it: significantly, it is nearly three times longer than any other speech in the play. Like the opening soliloquy in *Richard III* it is a proud confession of faith, the speech of a man "determinèd to prove a villain." In this speech Guise's character is fixed and determinate, as was Richard's. There can be no surprises except surprises of situation. It is the character of a man who uses religion as a stalking-horse, and the game which he shoots at is absolute power, the crown of France. As with Marlowe's other studies in ambition he has a mastering intellect, though over-reached in the end, and danger is the element in which he lives and thrives, "the chiefest way to happiness":

> What glory is there in a common good,
> That hangs for every peasant to achieve?
> That like I best, that flies beyond my reach.
> Set me to scale the high Pyramides,
> And thereon set the diadem of France;
> I'll either rend it with my nails to naught,
> Or mount the top with my aspiring wings,
> Although my downfall be the deepest hell.
> For this I wake, when others think I sleep,
> For this I wait, that scorns attendance else;
> For this, my quenchless thirst, whereon I build,
> Hath often pleaded kindred to the king;
> For this, this head, this heart, this hand, and sword,
> Contrives, imagines, and fully executes,
> Matters of import aimèd at by many,
> Yet understood by none.

If there was ambiguity in the presentation of Tamburlaine, there is none here. Poison, murder, and massacre are the steps by which Guise mounts the ladder of his ambition, but when the crown seems within his grasp he is outwitted by the man he had despised. In watching this play the orthodox could settle comfortably in their places to watch the downfall of a man who was at once a Frenchman, a Papist, an Atheist, and a King-queller.

The Massacre at Paris is exceptional among the plays of that date in being based on contemporary European history. It is a kind of plot which Shakespeare did not touch. In *Edward II* Marlowe is following the example which Shakespeare had already set: he goes to the English chronicles. Anyone who doubts whether Marlowe's gifts were really dramatic would do well to read Holinshed's account of the reign of Edward II and see with what art of selection, condensation, and adaptation Marlowe has shaped out of the chronicle history of a disagreeable reign an historical tragedy.[3] The title suggests a chronicle: "The troublesome reign and lamentable death of Edward the Second, King of England: with the tragical fall of proud Mortimer"; but although history, especially in Acts II and III, is not wholly assimilated into drama, the running-title "The Tragedy of Edward the Second" represents the play better. Marlowe did not read so widely in the histories as did Michael Drayton for the "Complaint" of Piers Gaveston written in the year of Marlowe's death, but he was not satisfied merely with Holinshed, and went elsewhere for many a detail: for example, the "fleering" song with which the Scots mocked the English disgrace at Bannockburn, with its refrains "With a heave and a ho," "With a rombelow." And he threw aside as unsuitable to his purposes much material connected with the wars with Scotland and Ireland and France, many a private war between baron and baron, and of course all those trivial disconnected details which the chronicles recorded. Moreover, historical dating and historical sequence he regarded as wholly within his control if it led to economy and coherence, above all if it led to the balance of dramatic power.

The balance of one character or motive with another is here essential, for this is his one play in which his purpose is to illuminate weakness, not strength. Weakness does not act but is acted upon, or if it acts its actions are frustrated and ineffective. Therefore Marlowe was forced by the nature of his theme to distribute the interest over a variety of characters as he never had occasion to do elsewhere, to exhibit not only the central figure of Edward in whom the play's intention is chiefly expressed but also the agents of power and corruption who act upon this figure. The stage is set for the conflict to follow in the four movements of the first scene. First, Gaveston just returned from banishment and eager to meet the King and to devise the sensuous pleasures which delight them both, a Gaveston who is not the mere self-seeker of the chronicles but as much infatuated with the King as the King with him, both men with a "ruling desire" which counts the world well lost for love and pleasure. Secondly, the King's quarrel with the lords bitterly jealous of the upstart Gaveston, a quarrel overheard by Gaveston, a movement in which we meet the King's chief enemies, Lancaster, both Mortimers, and Warwick. Thirdly, the reunion of Edward and Gaveston. We are used in Shakespeare to the image of sea or river overflowing the land, as a symbol of chaos, an in-

---

[3] The text of the earliest surviving edition of *Edward II* (1594) is unusually correct. There is, however, one curious confusion. In II. v, III. ii, and IV. iii, both in speech prefixes and in stage directions, "Mat.," "Matr.," or "Matre." often appears in error for "Arun." (Arundel). (The name "Matrevis" is nowhere given in full in these scenes.) See the Malone Society edition, p. xii. In the two places in which the error occurs in the text—"What lord *Matre.* dost thou come alone?" and "Tell me *Matre.* died he ere thou camst" (III. ii. 89 and 92)—"Arundel" cannot be substituted for "Matrevis" without destroying the metre. The error must, therefore, be the dramatist's; and if Dyce is right in attributing it to the doubling of parts by the same actor, Marlowe must be credited with an intimate knowledge of the company for which he was writing.

version of nature which is a token of evil in human nature; now the
image is from Edward himself and marks the absence of all sense of kingly
duty and moral scruple:

> I have my wish, in that I joy thy sight;
> And sooner shall the sea o'erwhelm my land,
> Than bear the ship that shall transport thee hence.

In a brief fourth movement Edward and Gaveston violently abuse the
Bishop of Coventry and add to the hostility of the lords the powerful
hostility of the Church. And so in the first scene, with great economy and
power, Marlowe has introduced all the leading characters which are the
necessary embodiments of his dramatic purpose except Queen Isabel: and
she appears in the second scene. Of these characters Gaveston is murdered
at the beginning of the third act; Lancaster is captured at the battle of
Boroughbridge at the end of the third act; Mortimer and Isabel alone
are as important in the last act as in the first; as the play proceeds their
share in the personal tragedy of the King becomes increasingly important.

The part played by one character is too important to omit even in the
briefest summary. Though of subsidiary importance the King's brother
Edmund Earl of Kent fulfils a function in this play to which I think there
is no parallel in Marlowe's other plays. Kent throws in his lot now with
the King now with the King's enemies in a vain attempt to trim the ship
of state. He is the one character in the play upon whom the affections can
rest, the one character—apart from the young Prince Edward—whose
concern for the King is wholly untouched by jealousy, hatred, lust, or self-
aggrandizement. This character is perhaps the only character in Marlowe's
plays who may be regarded as a point of reference.

The similarity between the theme of *Edward II* and that of *Richard II*,
written a few years later, is obvious: it must have been obvious to Shakespeare: he certainly knew Marlowe's play and he may have known it the
better from having acted in it. In both characters there is fundamental
weakness. It is not that there is a chink in their armour: they have no
armour at all. In both characters there is change, but the change is not so
much in them as in our feelings to them, as we see them passing from the
cruelty and selfishness of power to the helplessness and suffering of powerlessness. But the similarities between these two plays are superficial. It is
an altogether grimmer world into which Marlowe takes us, a world of
evil and corruption deeper and darker than that of *Richard II*. The turn-
ing-point of Edward's fortunes comes with the death of Gaveston. Tem-
porarily his fortunes recover with the victory at Boroughbridge, but the
beginning of his end is the escape of Mortimer to France, whither the
Queen and the young Edward have already been sent. Act IV shows
Edward's defeat and capture by the forces led by Mortimer and Isabel.

The critics have attacked Marlowe for inconsistency in his portrayal of Mortimer and Isabel, but is there more inconsistency than dramatic poetry may claim? There is change, certainly, rather than development, but which dramatist of this date attempted to show development? And how very few attempted to show it later! We must not ask of an Elizabethan play what we ask of a naturalistic play. The change in Mortimer's character and in Isabel's is to add pity and terror to Edward's end, to assist in the swing from detestation and contempt of Edward when abusing his power, to pity for Edward when he has fallen from high estate. Until the fourth act Mortimer is hardly distinguishable from the other proud and self-seeking lords: but as soon as Edward is defeated and the power falls into his own hands he becomes a Machiavel. "Fear'd am I more than lov'd," and one of the maxims attributed to Machiavelli[4] was that "it is better for a Prince to be feared than loved." Another maxim was that "A man is happy so long as Fortune agreeth unto his nature and humour," and it is Mortimer and Mortimer alone who calls upon Fortune. At the height of his power he boasts that he makes Fortune's wheel turn as he pleases, and quotes from Ovid the line *Major sum quam cui possit fortuna nocere.* And when Edward's murder is brought home to him, and he sees that his end is in sight, there is no moral compunction but mere acquiescence in the decree of an arbitrary fate.

> Base Fortune, now I see, that in thy wheel
> There is a point, to which when men aspire,
> They tumble headlong down: that point I touch'd,
> And, seeing there was no place to mount up higher,
> Why should I grieve at my declining fall?
> Farewell, fair queen; weep not for Mortimer,
> That scorns the world, and, as a traveller,
> Goes to discover countries yet unknown.

But it is the character of Edward's Queen Isabel that has proved the greatest stumbling-block to critics. Yet here again if we remember Marlowe's dramatic purpose and do not seek for realism, we shall find that he has not bungled a matter vital to the balance of his play, just as he made no mistake in departing from the chronicles which make no mention of an intrigue between Isabel and Mortimer before Edward's murder. Of this intrigue we hear much in the first two acts, but always from Edward and Gaveston. They are not to be believed, and the effect of these slanders on the King's neglected Queen is to light up his unhallowed passion for his favourite, his privado.

[4] See Simon Patricke's translation of Gentillet's *De Regno,* 1602, maxims ii. 10 and iii. 9.

> Like frantic Juno will I fill the earth
> With ghastly murmur of my sighs and cries;
> For never doted Jove on Ganymede
> So much as he on cursed Gaveston.

This the Queen speaks in soliloquy, and by the conventions of Elizabethan drama we are to suppose her speaking her inmost thoughts. Not until after repeated failures to win the affection of her husband, not until after her question "No farewell to poor Isabel thy queen?" has received the brutal reply "Yes, yes, for Mortimer, your lover's sake," does she betray the first hint of affection for Mortimer, again in soliloquy:

> So well hast thou deserv'd, sweet Mortimer,
> As Isabel could live with thee for ever.

But not yet has the moment arrived to swing the balance of pity towards Edward, and she continues:

> In vain I look for love at Edward's hand,
> Whose eyes are fix'd on none but Gaveston,
> Yet once more I'll importune him with prayers.

And if prayers fail, she will take refuge with her brother, the King of France. By this soliloquy we are prepared for her guilt, but she is not yet guilty. Marlowe keeps that in reserve until he needs it. And the first assurance of guilt is not given us until she and Mortimer have returned from France with their victorious army. Then this assurance *is* to be believed, for it is given us by Kent, whom I have called Marlowe's point of reference:

> Mortimer
> And Isabel do kiss, while they conspire:
> And yet she bears a face of love forsooth.
> Fie on that love that hatcheth death and hate.

Now Isabel plays she-Machiavel to Mortimer's Machiavel. Cruel as well as unfaithful, she has nothing to learn in the art of turning and dissembling. In public she is full of concern for the state of the country and the King's misfortunes, of thanks to "the God of kings" and "heaven's great architect"; in private, there is no villainy of Mortimer's which she does not aid and abet.

It adds to the horror that in the last two acts Edward is never brought face to face with his two tormentors. The fear of their cruelty preys upon his mind in prison, fear as much for his son as for himself, and as in many

an age besides Shakespeare's the cruelty of man and woman is expressed
in terms of beasts of prey:

> For he's a lamb, encompass'd by wolves,
> Which in a moment will abridge his life.

And again,

> Let not that Mortimer protect my son;
> More safety is there in a tiger's jaws,
> Than his embracements.

The revulsion of feeling from contempt to pity is now complete, and it
is in part the change in the characters of Mortimer and Isabel that has effected it.

> What, are you mov'd? pity you me?
> Then send for unrelenting Mortimer,
> And Isabel, whose eyes, being turn'd to steel,
> Will sooner sparkle fire than shed a tear.

At the end Edward is as terrified, as helpless, and as lonely as Faustus.
But he is not penitent. Neither is Shakespeare's Richard II. Like Lear
these two characters "did ever slenderly know themselves," and, unlike
Lear, they never come to know themselves. The chronicles present us with
a penitent Edward, but this was not to Marlowe's purpose. Edward's
thoughts are of Mortimer and Isabel, of his own sorrows, his "guiltless
life," his "innocent hands," and of the safety of his son:

> Commend me to my son, and bid him rule
> Better than I. Yet how have I transgress'd,
> Unless it be with too much clemency?

The humiliation and murder of Edward are narrated in full by the
chroniclers. The details are sordid, pitiless, horrible. And Marlowe leaves
out little. For one detail which he did not find in Holinshed, the washing
and shaving of the King in puddle water, he went to Stow. Compassion did
not come easily to Marlowe, and there is a cruelty in these last scenes
which we do not find in Shakespeare. In *Richard II* there is every sort of
alleviation. Richard is brought face to face with his accusers, and allowed
to indulge himself in scenes which make him at once the playboy and the
poet of the English kings. He takes affectionate farewell of his Queen—
how different an Isabel from Edward's. In place of Mortimer we have a
Bolingbroke. And at the end no passive submission, but death in coura-

geous action. Shakespeare's compassion is nowhere more evident than in his invention of the faithful groom of the stable and the talk with his master about "roan Barbary," when King and groom share a common humanity. In Marlowe there is no groom; instead, the invention of the murderer whom he christens, with a stroke of sardonic humour, Lightborn, the professional murderer who takes a pride in the fine handling of a man. Into his taut tight-lipped lines Marlowe packs the quintessence of all that Englishmen had heard or dreamt of Italianate villainy:

> You shall not need to give instructions;
> 'Tis not the first time I have killed a man.
> I learn'd in Naples how to poison flowers;
> To strangle with a lawn thrust through the throat;[5]
> To pierce the windpipe with a needle's point;
> Or whilst one is asleep, to take a quill
> And blow a little powder in his ears:
> Or open his mouth and pour quicksilver down.
> But yet I have a braver way than these.

The "braver way" is reported by the chronicles, but it was too strong even for the stomach of an Elizabethan audience, and the red-hot spit which Lightborn orders to be prepared is not called for. But the wail of the murdered man rang through the theatre, as it did, writes Holinshed,

through the castle and town of Berkeley, so that divers being awakened therewith (as they themselves confessed) prayed heartily to God to receive his soul, when they understood by his cry what the matter meant.

Charles Lamb said that this death scene moved pity and terror beyond any scene ancient and modern with which he was acquainted. But I wonder if there is not too much horror in the terror, if the scene is not so painful that it presses upon the nerves. In a short last scene Mortimer and Isabel meet their doom, and the young King Edward takes control. In the young Edward's words there is grief for his father and righteous anger with his murderer, but the words rather enforce the feeling that the dramatist does not deeply feel the sacredness of royalty, that the tragedy is in the main a personal tragedy without wider repercussions, and that in the supporting characters he has been exhibiting this and that variety of ambition, hatred, envy, lust, and the corruption of men and women in power or in search of power.

[5] Compare the experiences of Edward Webbe in Naples: "I was also constrained to drink salt water and quicklime, and then a fine lawn or calico thrust down my throat and pluck'd up again, ready to pluck my heart out of my belly." (*The rare and most wonderful things which Edw. Webbe an Englishman born hath seen*, 1590, sig. DI).

Marlowe's other heroes, except in *Dido* and *The Massacre at Paris,* are men of humble birth: this is his one full study of kingship. He is aware of the irony of kingship, and nowhere in this play is his verse finer and fuller than in the abdication scene. When Shakespeare came to write in *Richard II* of the "reluctant pangs of abdicating royalty" (the phrase is Lamb's), he remembered the scene, and well he might, for in imagery and in pathos it is nearer to Shakespeare than any other scene in Marlowe. But it stands almost alone in the play as a scene in which Marlowe's poetic power is fully released. When we have admitted that, we have admitted a weakness which no care for craftsmanship can redeem. Marlowe never returned to the theme of English history, as Shakespeare did again and again. He went on to write *Doctor Faustus* and there he fulfilled himself.

Edward II

by Wolfgang Clemen

In *Edward II* we encounter the same artistic problem as faced us in *The Jew of Malta*. For here is a play which on the one hand shows close structural affinities with the chronicle plays, in that it has a stirring plot with a rapid flow of incident and plenty of variety, while on the other hand it has points of contact with tragedy in its attempts to bring on to the stage heart-rending scenes filled with passionate utterances, deep pathos, and high tragic dignity.[1] Another striking thing about the play is that the kinds of situation which, at an earlier stage in the evolution of English drama, would have been turned into entirely static episodes or declamatory showpieces by a series of long and exaggeratedly rhetorical set speeches, here take the form of swiftly unfolding scenes of action containing a good deal of well-developed dialogue. Examples of this are the baiting of the King by the Barons (I. i. 74-133, I. iv. 8-93), the King's parting from Gaveston (I. iv. 106-69), his grief and mourning at Gaveston's departure (I. iv. 304 ff.), and his triumph at the defeat of the rebellious Barons (IV. iii. 1 ff.). The new dramatic technique employed in these and certain other episodes brings into prominence a whole variety of changing motive forces in the play; it enables us to apprehend all these episodes with great vividness as real actions carried out by the characters with and against one another. Moreover, we no longer find odd moments singled out from the course of events and raised to an artificial intensity by means of set declamations—mere pictures, so to speak, though given the illusion of life; instead, we seem ourselves to be participating in what is taking place.

In *Edward II* it is made quite clear that the characters not only carry the emotional burden of the play, but also sustain its plot; on the other hand, it is equally clear that the plot is not solely dependent on what

[1] Much has been written about the novel features of this play as a tragedy of character and a tragic history, and about its structure, its characterization, and its content. See, e.g., Ellis-Fermor, Levin, Poirier, Boas, Wilson, Briggs.

they do. Marlowe has struck a balance between a plot whose events are directed by its hero and one which develops independently of him and reacts upon him. It is true that the King sets certain events in motion, but he has also to maintain a passive role in the plot. This plot is broken up into a great many separate episodes, most of them quite short, but we can follow it as a close-knit, coherent and logical chain of cause and effect, for in all the episodes the person and character of the King are in some way involved. Thus Marlowe made an appreciable advance towards what is commonly described as "character-drama," but he was not equally successful all along the line. He was so intent on creating a fast-moving plot, especially in the earlier part of the play, that he did not leave himself enough room to develop the emotional significance of particular moments and to work out his situations in an unhurried way. The scenes follow one another much too quickly, and there are too many of them; they do not take root in our memory, as do the scenes in Shakespeare's histories from *Richard III* onwards, which by themselves form pictures with a symbolic impact and remain unforgettably in our minds as miniature plays in their own right. For all his skill in complicating the plot, the composition, especially in the first two-thirds of the play, is hurried and breathless, and nothing is carried through to its proper conclusion. For long stretches the language is entirely factual and its choice is determined by the practical consideration of keeping the plot moving; it supplies information, instruction, explanation, question and answer, and is all the time concerned solely with externalities. There are moments, indeed, when the emotional atmosphere begins to grow more intense, but the poetic power which is necessary to translate it into words almost at once fades away. We get no further than isolated outbursts of feeling which are too abruptly handled and do not impart their tone to the accompanying dialogue in the scene. Thus Marlowe's new dramatic technique conveyed too little of what the set speech had earlier given us too much of. He had not yet found for himself a language which, like that of Shakespearian tragedy, was capable of representing every kind of incident concretely, and which was at one and the same time succinct, emotionally satisfying, and forceful in expression. Even in *Edward II* he was still hovering uncertainly between two different levels of style; he could not reconcile his poet's command of language with his capabilities as a dramatist.[2]

This discrepancy is particularly noticeable in scenes in which some approach is made towards the expression of emotion but is not sufficiently followed up. An example of this occurs in Act I, Scene iv, where Edward falls into a monologue as he is grieving over Gaveston's departure, and will not pay any attention to the Queen and the other persons on the stage:

[2] Cf. Tucker Brooke, *The Works,* p. 309.

Re-enter the KING, *mourning.*

K. Edw. He's gone, and for his absence thus I mourn.
Did never sorrow go so near my heart
As doth the want of my sweet Gaveston;
And could my crown's revenue bring him back,
I would freely give it to his enemies,
And think I gain'd, having bought so dear a friend.
Q. Isab. Hark, how he harps upon his minion.
K. Edw. My heart is as an anvil unto sorrow,
Which beats upon it like the Cyclops' hammers,
And with the noise turns up my giddy brain,
And makes me frantic for my Gaveston.
Ah, had some bloodless Fury rose from hell,
And with my kingly sceptre struck me dead,
When I was forc'd to leave my Gaveston.
Lan. Diablo! What passions call you these?
Q. Isab. My gracious lord, I come to bring you news.
K. Edw. That you have parled with your Mortimer.
Q. Isab. That Gaveston, my lord, shall be repeal'd.

(I. iv. 304 ff.)

Here is a formal lament of the familiar type, but it is cut short, and we are immediately plunged into matter-of-fact dialogue. The earlier lament of the Queen when Edward repulses her is even more abruptly cut short (I. iv. 163 ff.), as is that of the younger Spencer when Edward is led away (IV. vi. 99 ff.).

Just the same kind of discrepancy may be observed in the soliloquies, especially those in the early part of the play. In these soliloquies the mythological imagery and classical parallels and the rhetorical exaggeration of the curses and protestations seem to be based on the stylistic pattern of the earlier classical tragedies, and they are curiously at variance with the very different language of their context.[3]

On one occasion, in the second half of the play, the Queen embarks on a speech of welcome to her friends on their return to England; this quickly gives place to mournful reflections on the state of affairs then prevailing, and then she goes on to appeal to the absent Edward. At this point the younger Mortimer interrupts her:

Nay, madam, if you be a warrior,
You must not grow so passionate in speeches.

(IV. iv. 15-16)

[3] Cf. Gaveston, I. i. 50-71; Queen, I. iv. 170-86; also the dialogue between the two Mortimers, I. iv. 385-418.

This interruption of Mortimer's seems to be symptomatic of what Marlowe himself did on more than one occasion when "passionate speeches" showed signs of breaking into his play. He was sensible that long-drawn set speeches in the manner of Tamburlaine would act as clogs on his new technique of rapid movement.[4] But apart from this consideration, he must have felt that for King Edward, whom he put into the play more as a passive than an active character, an entirely different style of speech must be adopted from Tamburlaine's passionate, highly eloquent declarations of his purposes, which stand as substitutes for action. The speech-technique especially of the later scenes enables us to see that active emotion has resolved itself into a tragic passivity, to correspond with which new forms of expression have had to be created.

It is not until the second half of the play that the set speech once more comes into its own as a legitimate feature of the dramatic architecture. Marlowe now deliberately employs this medium in order to make it clear that Edward's role is that of a martyr, and in order to awaken our sympathies for him in his suffering and to invest his figure with pathos, dignity and a measure of splendour. In the first half Edward's role is to a larger extent that of an active participant in the action; in this second part he comes to the fore much more as a sensitive and suffering soul, and not the least effective means of creating this impression is the entirely different language, much more intense than that of the first part, by which he is made to reveal himself. In about the middle of the play Edward's awakening to the necessity of resisting the Barons and the change in him from apathy to activity are indicated by means of a set speech containing the great vow of vengeance that he utters on his knees (III. ii. 128 ff.); so now, after the reversal of his fortunes, his new role as a passive sufferer is also inaugurated by means of speeches that are given special prominence. However, it is noteworthy that what would earlier have been a speech of self-revelation in the form of outright monologue is now addressed to another person and is accompanied by stage-business. As far as subject-matter is concerned, the words that Edward addresses to the Abbot are the same as those which princes who had fallen from prosperity into misfortune had been in the habit of repeating in English tragedy from the time of *Gorboduc* onwards. This time, however, it is not the sympathy of the audience that is indirectly being invited, as in earlier examples, but that of the Abbot; and since various of the other persons present are addressed in turn, the whole speech gives an effect of dramatic compression, and of belonging naturally to the dialogue sequence of which it forms a part:

> Father, thy face should harbour no deceit.
> O, hadst thou ever been a king, thy heart,

---

[4] See Briggs's note on IV. iv. 16, in his edn. of *Edward II*.

> Pierced deeply with sense of my distress,
> Could not but take compassion of my state.
> Stately and proud, in riches and in train,
> Whilom I was, powerful, and full of pomp:
> But what is he whom rue and empery
> Have not in life or death made miserable?
> Come, Spencer; come, Baldock, come, sit down by me;
> Make trial now of that philosophy,
> That in our famous nurseries of arts
> Thou suckedst from Plato and from Aristotle.
> Father, this life contemplative is heaven.
> O that I might this life in quiet lead.
> But we, alas, are chas'd; and you, my friends,
> Your lives and my dishonour they pursue.
> Yet, gentle monks, for treasure, gold nor fee,
> Do you betray us and our company.
>
>   (IV. vi. 8-25)

Whereas in this scene there are only comparatively short self-revelatory speeches of this kind (cf. 37 ff., 61 ff.), the central interest of the next scene, the scene which represents the abdication of the King, lies in two long set speeches, the longest in the whole play. The way in which Marlowe uses these two speeches brings out once more his powerful sense of drama; they add depth to the symbolic procedure of handing over the crown, and in them the figure of the King is endued with a genuine pathos very different from the impression he gave at the beginning of the play. Here Marlowe has contrived one of those great situations, packed with significance, which would be sure to call out the deepest sympathy and interest in the audience of his day. And at this moment he deliberately slows down the tempo, and makes of this episode a profoundly moving spectacle which, like the penultimate scene in the dungeon, is thrown into relief, by means of its concentration and the detail with which it is developed, against the rapidity of movement that marks the other scenes.

These abdication speeches, which have often been compared with the great abdication speech in Shakespeare's *Richard II* (IV. i),[5] show how Marlowe set about the task of creating a form of self-revelation which should reflect both past and present circumstances, and thereby make this episode the focal point of the plot; and also of bringing out the vehemence with which the King's passions are torn between conflicting impulses—an effect which is much more vividly produced here than in Shakespeare's play. Once again, as in *Doctor Faustus*, we see the attempt to portray a spiritual conflict through the medium of the set speech.

[5] Cf. Briggs, *op. cit.*, 182-3.

Moreover, the various elements that form the subject-matter, the review of the situation, the self-contemplation, the inner conflict, and the epigrammatic summing-up of the moral, all these things, together with the stage-business and the way in which the speaker interrupts his own reflections to address the bystanders, combine to produce a new form of set speech; and it is one which, even if some of its motifs remind us of the declamation and emotionalism of past days, is much more successful than the earlier type as dramatic self-expression, and is at the same time more closely in tune with the situation presented on the stage. Even now we have not completely got away from sententious maxims, such as

> But what are kings, when regiment is gone,
> But perfect shadows in a sunshine day?
>
> (V. i. 26-7)

However, passages of this nature, in their very versification emphasizing the independence of the single line, are very much in the minority. The speeches now display a greater homogeneity of structure and a subordination of the individual parts to the total effect, and this is reflected even in the verse structure, in contradistinction to that of *Tamburlaine*.[6] Just as he does in *Faustus*, Marlowe succeeds here in making the speeches express what is at that very moment going on in the speaker's mind, but this time he adds external action as well in the gestures of the King and the reactions of the other characters (e.g., V. i. 96-111). Thus we are now well on the way towards the dramatized and fully dramatic set speech which Shakespeare was to handle with such consummate mastery, and which he was to endow with new profundities of thought and feeling.

---

[6] Cf. Tucker Brooke, "Marlowe's Versification and Style," *SP*, XIX, pp. 186-205.

The Jew of Malta

by David M. Bevington

Much of the difficulty in interpreting *The Jew of Malta* stems from the same uneasy juxtaposition of moral structure and secular content already found in *Tamburlaine*. The protagonist, Barabas, is in part a lifelike Jewish merchant caught in a political feud on Malta, and in part an embodiment both of the morality Vice and of the unrepenting protagonist in homiletic "tragedy." In some early scenes of the play he is psychologically complex and briefly pitiable; and yet T. S. Eliot astutely interprets *The Jew* as a savage farce.[1] Spivack traces the farcical nature of Barabas to the stage tradition of the Vice: the way in which Barabas puts himself on show to the audience, the treachery to friend and foe alike, the theatrical laughing and weeping, the expert intrigue for its own sake.[2] The attempt to reconcile these strange opposites of plausibility and farce in Barabas' character leads to a series of moral uncertainties. H. S. Bennett calls *The Jew* "a challenge to our powers of assimilation,"[3] and most of its critics have pointed to the play's unevenness of tone and incongruity of effect.

Some critics and editors have attributed the lack of consistency in *The Jew* to a supposedly unreliable text, containing substantial revisions penned during the long years between the original production of 1589-1591 and the earliest printed version of 1633. Tucker Brooke, for example, believes it "probable that the extant text incorporates the results of at least two separate revisions; the first carried out before the revival in 1601, to which Henslowe alludes, the second that which must have been necessary before so old a work could be presented at Court and

"*The Jew of Malta*." From *From Mankind to Marlowe: Growth of Structure in the Popular Drama of Tudor England* by David M. Bevington. Copyright © 1962 by the President and Fellows of Harvard College. Reprinted by permission of the author and the Harvard University Press.

[1] T. S. Eliot, "Marlowe," *Selected Essays, 1917-1932* (New York, 1932), pp. 104-105; also available in *Elizabethan Essays* (London, 1934) and *The Sacred Wood*, 6th ed. (London, 1948).

[2] Spivack, *Allegory of Evil*, pp. 346-353. My discussion of *The Jew* inevitably owes much to Spivack's brief but incisive analysis of Barabas' position in the history of the Vice.

[3] H. S. Bennett, ed., *The Jew of Malta*, in the Methuen *Works of Marlowe* (London, 1931), p. 19.

at the Cock-pit." [4] These two assumptions are based only on a priori reasoning; Henslowe alludes merely to a performance in 1601, not to a revision. Nevertheless the argument has received widespread support, seemingly because scholars in search of classically "pure" tragedy have not wished to ascribe to Marlowe both the early scenes of tragic conflict and the later scenes of vicious and farcical degeneracy.

Recent studies have suggested, however, that the text of *The Jew* is not unreliable, and that the discrepancies between the 1633 quarto and the original performance are probably not fundamental. Margarete Thimme asserts with conviction that the text is all Marlowe's work.[5] H. S. Bennett, although believing that some drastic changes may have occurred, notes that there was "j cauderm [cauldron] for the Jewe" in the Admiral's inventory of 1598, and concludes that the final scene has not been vitally tampered with in any revision.[6] J. C. Maxwell finds by bibliographical analysis that the deficiencies in the 1633 text are far less the result of changes in manuscript than of an admittedly bad printing. The length of time between composition and publication, he argues, is not so serious as is commonly imagined, since the doctrine of "continuous copy" is an editorial fiction, and since "manuscripts, unlike apples, do not become corrupt simply by lying in a drawer." To class *The Jew* as a text with *The Massacre at Paris,* he concludes, "is to blur the clear distinction between memorial transmission (and, in this case, very poor memorial transmission) and careless printing from a manuscript that may have suffered some minor damage in revision and transcription." [7]

It is not far fetched to suppose that vice comedy may have formed a part of the earliest text of *The Jew,* since Greg has shown vice comedy to have been a part of the basic design of *Faustus.* An examination of structure in *The Jew* confirms the likelihood of basic similarity between the 1633 text and the first performance. The vicious and degenerate comedy in the later scenes is integral to the conception of the whole work as homiletic intrigue. In its original form the play probably contained a sequence of episodic plots corresponding in structure to the plotting phases of such homiletic tragedies as *The Longer Thou Livest* and *Enough Is as Good as a Feast.*

Symmetrical suppression and alternation, although not so sharply demarcated as in *Tamburlaine,* are the essential methods by which *The Jew* is put together. Barabas' partners and victims parade before us in linear sequence, usually in pairs. The two merchants appear only in the

---

[4] C. F. Tucker Brooke, ed., *The Works of Christopher Marlowe* (Oxford, 1910), pp. 231-232.

[5] Margarete Thimme, *Marlowes "Jew of Malta"* (Halle, 1921), pp. 8-17.

[6] Bennett, ed., *The Jew,* pp. 6-9. In the diction of the play, Bennett finds little evidence to support Fleay's view that Thomas Heywood contributed some scenes.

[7] J. C. Maxwell, "How Bad is the Text of 'The Jew of Malta'?" *MLR,* 48:435-438 (1953).

first scene, and like homiletic figures serve the limited function of high-lighting a characteristic in the protagonist, colossal wealth and mercenary ingenuity. Similarly, the three Jews function only in the first two scenes. Possibly they were originally two in number, for Barabas pointedly bids farewell to only two of them by name ("Farewell, Zaareth; farewell, Temainte"), and the third Jew speaks only one inconsequential line ("And very wisely said; it may be so") in his two appearances on stage. Once the Jews have served the purpose of evoking pity for Barabas, they are permanently suppressed. The Abbess and Nun in scene two are employed only once, as the dupes for Barabas' scheme to remove his hidden treasure from his confiscated house. Mathias and Lodowick, the first pair of victims to be slaughtered by Barabas, are introduced late in Act I and disappear in III, ii. They are superseded by the two Friars, who appear chiefly in the scenes following the murder of Mathias and Lodowick (III, iii-IV, iii), and then by the courtesan Bellamira and her accomplice Pilia-Borsa, who connive with Ithamore to blackmail Barabas after the suppression of the Friars (IV, iv-V, i). Marlowe's tendency to symmetrical pairing appears further in the combinations of Barabas and Ithamore, and of the foreign potentates Calymath and del Bosco. Thus the episodic nature of the plot is reflected in the series of groupings sur-rounding Barabas, as his villainous career moves forward by intrigue and duplicity.

The episodic succession must end in retribution, according to the moral formula, and in the final scenes of *The Jew* the action is dominated by political figures who engineer the retribution: the Turk Calymath, the Spaniard del Bosco, and Malta's governor Ferneze. They occupy the structural position of the judges in the homiletic drama such as Despair, God's Judgment, Correction, and Perseverance. Throughout the play, moreover, they have occupied the alternating and separate scenes of moral commentary, previously peopled by homiletic figures of moral purity whose virtuous conduct contrasted with the depravity of the vicious comedians. The political world of Malta provides this structural con-trast in the second scene, after Barabas' first solo appearance, and in the fourth scene (II, ii), after Barabas' success in removing his treasures from his house. The appearance of del Bosco (III, v) punctuates the interval between the slaughter of Mathias and Lodowick and the slaughter of the two Friars. The final grouping of the governors and princes in Act V corresponds structurally not only to the avengers in morality drama but to the procession of "reward" personalities whose triumphs offset the defeat and punishment of the protagonist. Of course there is something bizarre in considering Ferneze as a judge or "reward" figure, and it is the contrast between moral justification implicit in the homiletic structure of the play and Marlowe's accurate portrayal of *Realpolitik* that we shall consider in evaluating the play's ambiguity. It is important at present to emphasize the pervasiveness of the homiletic structure in the sequential progression of Barabas' victims and in the alternating and contrasting appearance of his enemies or judges.

A feasible casting for the speaking parts of *The Jew* requires at least seven experienced actors and three boys, and demonstrates the technical advantage of suppression and alternation in pairs: (1) Barabas (2) Machiavel, Ithamore (3) Ferneze (4) Calymath, first Friar (5) first Merchant, first Jew, Lodowick, second Friar (6) second Merchant, second Jew, Mathias, del Bosco (7) Pilia-Borsa, Messenger, Guard, Basso, Slave. The ranks of the boys would have to include two seasoned performers together with one or two beginners: (1) Abigail and Bellamira (2) Abbess and Katherine (3) Nun. It is quite possible that a few more adult actors were available, and that the doubling assignments need not have been this heavy. Even if the actors themselves did little alternating of roles, however, the structural heritage of alternation survives strongly.

No nondramatic source has been discovered for the plot and order of events in *The Jew,* and Bakeless conjectures that "probably none exists." [8] Ethel Seaton has shown that Philip Lonicerus' *Chronicorum Turcicorum tomi duo,* used by Marlowe in assembling materials for *Tamburlaine,* Part II, contains a reference to one Juan Miques or Michesius, a well-known Jewish man of affairs who may have served as a model for Barabas' character.[9] Miques also appears in Belleforest's *Cosmographie Universelle,* and other Jews named David Passi and Alvaro Mendez may similarly have contributed to Marlowe's conception of his hero.[10] With only these few general sources for *The Jew,* scholars have generally agreed that Marlowe (and possibly collaborators) must have improvised a great deal. "Out of a haze of surmise and unreliable report he saw clearly enough the main lines of his character. His reading and general knowledge of recent and current history gave him the rest." [11] As in the case of *Tamburlaine,* Part II, therefore, the structural ordering of events appears to have been the creation of the dramatist and his popular company. It is probably this fact which accounts for the linear arrangement of episodes, and the prominence of homiletic intrigue, in the sequence of the action.

Even if the structure of vice "tragedy" is clearly present in *The Jew,* this element can scarcely account for the play's greatness. As in *Tamburlaine,* Marlowe's genius cannot here be forced into the restrictive mold of the homiletic drama. Marlowe sees in Barabas far more than a maliciously evil Worldly Man. He reaches beyond the type to a particular person, and is seemingly less interested in moral example than in the

[8] Bakeless, *Tragicall History,* I, 334.

[9] Ethel Seaton, "Fresh Sources for Marlowe," *RES,* 5:385-401 (1929).

[10] Boas, *Marlowe,* pp. 131-132. Passi was first suggested by C. F. Tucker Brooke, "The Prototype of Marlowe's Jew of Malta," *London Times Literary Supplement* (June 8, 1922), p. 380.

[11] Bennett, ed., *The Jew,* p. 12.

intricate causality of human behavior. And yet however imperfectly Marlowe may fit into the homiletic formula, that formula does exist in his drama, and it exerts a profound if ambivalent effect. Paradoxically it is Marlowe's search for new themes that places such emphasis upon the older format, by exaggerating its incongruity in a drama of increasingly secular values. This incongruity can best be measured in a scene-by-scene analysis, describing on the one hand the elements of homiletic farce progressing to a "tragic" end for the unrepentant protagonist, and, on the other, the elements of a psychological treatise depicting a persecuted Maltese Jew. The study will necessarily focus upon the protagonist, and will have to examine the delineation of character insofar as Barabas appears to be a person of complex human emotions as well as a purely vicious type. Nevertheless the ultimate interest here lies in the conflict between the intricacy of character portrayal and inherited moral structure.

The prologue, spoken by Machiavel, is a conventional morality device heralding the appearance of the unregenerate protagonist. Machiavel himself poses as the personification of evil. This popular misconception of the Italian writer is in fact only a veneer, a topical label for the Father of Lies.[12] Marlowe prefers to clothe his personifications in historical garb, but the disguise does not conceal the fact that Machiavel's function, like that of Satan in *Conflict of Conscience,* is to serve as the progenitor of evil for his emissary in the world of men. Just as Satan promises to call forth his lieutenants Hypocrisy, Avarice, and Tyranny, Machiavel (who is significantly no longer a living person but a "soul" or spirit of malevolence) bids us prepare for his viceroy, the Jew:

> And let him not be entertain'd the worse
> Because he favours me.

Machiavel personifies in abstract and absolute form the vices that are to be found in Barabas: utter lack of conscience ("there is no sin but ignorance") and inordinate greed:

> [He] smiles to see how full his bags are cramm'd,
> Which money was not got without my means.

The tone of Machiavel's speech is one of diabolical amusement at his own villainy. We are to be entertained by a display of extraordinary cunning motivated solely by the love of evil for its own sake.

The first dramatic vision of Barabas confirms the image of evil. He is clever, miserly, devoid of conscience. His love for his daughter Abigail proves to be merely an extension of his self-absorbed greed. His narrow

[12] See Irving Ribner, "Marlowe and Machiavelli," *CL,* 6:348-356 (1954).

charity excludes even the three brethren of his race with whom he discusses the expected arrival of the Turkish fleet:

> Why, let 'em come, so they come not to war;
> Or let 'em war, so we be conquerors.—
> *Nay, let 'em combat, conquer, and kill all.*
> *So they spare me, my daughter, and my wealth.*   [*Aside.*
>
> [I, i, 148-151]

In fact he deliberately dupes the three Jews in his explanation of the Turkish visit, and quiets their fears only to ponder after their departure, "These silly men mistake the matter clean." It would be an error then to sympathize with Barabas as the representative victim of a downtrodden race, since his ill-will applies equally to Christian, Turk, and Jew. We can no more expect him to abjure his native evil than Worldly Man in *Enough Is as Good as a Feast,* who is guaranteed by his prolocutor to be stout in villainy and "in any wise wil not bow."

After this traditional exposition of the unredeemable worldling, the moral formula introduces a confrontation in the second scene between Barabas and his dramatic counterparts. At this point the ambiguity commences, for according to the moral pattern Barabas' enemies and future victims should represent the cause of virtue. Instead, because Marlowe's interest in his protagonist is too deep for simple denunciation, we are suddenly faced with the irony of finding Barabas the sympathetic victim of Christian treachery. Ferneze's method of taxation is patently despotic, and his refusal to allow Barabas to pay the tax after momentary reconsideration, in lieu of total forfeiture, is arbitrary. Barabas' defense becomes, by a curious inversion, the pleading of a wronged, sensitive, and helpless person:

> The man that dealeth righteously shall live:
> And which of you can charge me otherwise?
>
> . . . . .
>
> Ay, let me sorrow for this sudden chance;
> 'Tis in the trouble of my spirit I speak:
> Great injuries are not so soon forgot.
>
> [I, ii, 117-118, 207-209]

The second Jew, as he and his fellows depart, expresses a choric reaction to the preceding scene:

> On, then: but, trust me, 'tis a misery
> To see a man in such affliction.
>
> [I, ii, 212-213]

An Elizabethan audience, whatever its attitudes toward Jews in general, would have reacted with some indignation to Barabas' broadly human plight. The dramatist intended his audience to view his "villain," for the moment at least, with genuine sympathy.

When Barabas is left alone on stage, however, he reveals that his noble passion was in fact contrived as a means of deceiving others and winning sympathy from them. He laughs exultingly at his cleverness in duping them, and at the pity he has evoked:

> See the simplicity of these base slaves.
> Who, for the villains have no wit themselves,
> Think me to be a senseless lump of clay,
> That will with every water wash to dirt!
> No, Barabas is born to better chance,
> And fram'd of finer mould than common men,
>
> .   .   .   .   .
>
> For evils are apt to happen every day.
>
> [I, ii, 215-224]

He informs Abigail that she need not moan "for a little loss," since he has stored away more than has been confiscated. Even the news that he cannot gain access to his house to remove the treasure deters him for only a moment. He has a plan for every emergency.

Clearly Barabas' passionate reaction to the tax was all a pretense, intended to trick the audience as well as the three Jews. The revelation in soliloquy of this hypocrisy is an ironic undercutting of the apparent tragedy for a comic purpose. It shows Barabas as the "Vice," who mockingly and boastfully reveals his strategy to his audience after having cheated them into misplaced sympathy. His hate is not provoked by Ferneze's persecution; Barabas hated the world before, as a matter of policy.

At the same time, the injustice of Ferneze's decree remains a fact, and Barabas has been treated ignominiously. A second purpose of this second scene, then, is to provide an understandable motivation for the Jew's hate and his subsequent deeds of revenge. He is put in a position of having to fight back, so that his misanthropic behavior is made plausible:

> Daughter, I have it: thou perceiv'st the plight
> Wherein these Christians have oppressed me:
> Be rul'd by me, for in extremity
> We ought to make bar of no policy.
>
> [I, ii, 270-273]

The Vice has been secularized in the person of Barabas, a man with dangerous enemies. This aspect of Barabas shows something far more subtle and lifelike than the type of unrepentant Worldly Man. Even Abigail, a sympathetic character, perceives at first the justice of her father's retaliatory tactics. She reluctantly agrees to help in deceiving the nuns, so that Barabas may retrieve the money from his house. The Jew's plan to win back his own property from the Christians, even if by slightly devious means, is only to demand an eye for an eye. In one sense all of Barabas' later acts are acts of vengeance or self-defense, and stem from Ferneze's first pitiless deed. Hence the first two scenes are crucial in justifying Barabas' subsequent treachery. Nevertheless, the need for providing motivation should not obscure the purely Vice-like conception of Barabas' original character.

Critics have often contrasted the degeneracy of Barabas into pure villain in the last three acts of *The Jew* with his moral complexity as a person in the earlier scenes—a contrast usually accounted for by the theory of multiple authorship.[13] As we have seen, however, the Jew was actually a villain when he appeared in the first scene. His later career of viciousness is simply a return to his original nature rather than a new and puzzling development in character. Once Marlowe has established Barabas' motivation for revenge, he turns again to the pattern of vicious and comic intrigue. The structure becomes that of plotting and degeneracy in the homiletic drama, such as Worldly Man's succession of unfair triumphs over his innocent victims Tenant, Servant, and Hireling in *Enough Is as Good as a Feast*.

The shift to a structure of vice intrigue commences in Act II, iii, with the alliance of Barabas and Ithamore, the slave who is to assist the Jew's acts of "revenge."[14] Ithamore, too, is given a motivation for anti-Christian hatred. Barabas welcomes him as a comrade in hate:

> Why, this is something: make account of me
> As of thy fellow; we are villains both:
> Both circumcised; we hate Christians both.
>
> [II, iii, 214-216]

Yet their alliance for the purpose of revenging themselves upon Christian persecutors is patently a pretext. They not only "hate Christians both" but "are villains both"; the former is the ostensible motivation, the latter the basically vicious fact. Barabas' victims of the past have not all been Christians. He has turned his hatred upon invalids, orphans, and helpless persons without distinction of sect or nationality:

---

[13] See, for example, A. H. Bullen, ed., *The Works of Christopher Marlowe* (Boston, 1885), I, xl-xli; and Wilson, *Marlowe and Shakespeare,* pp. 64-66. See also Bennett, ed., *The Jew,* pp. 15-19.

[14] Spivack, *Allegory of Evil,* p. 349.

> As for myself, I walk abroad a nights
> And kill sick people groaning under walls:
> Sometimes I go about and poison wells.
>
> [II, iii, 175-177]

In battle he has delighted in playing the villain with both sides:

> And in the wars 'twixt France and Germany,
> Under pretence of helping Charles the Fifth,
> Slew friend and enemy with my stratagems.
>
> [II, iii, 188-190]

The description here does not correspond realistically with what we know of Barabas' life. He has been a merchant, not a warrior. In earlier speeches he has deliberately relinquished temporal power to Christian kings, asking only for peace that he may gain more wealth (I, i, 127-133). The present recital of vicious accomplishments is the record of a universalized genius of evil, not of the specific man. At the same time, Barabas does have particular and valid reasons for hating Christians, especially Ferneze.

Recognizing this dual aspect in the play's exposition, we may follow in successive scenes the resulting divergence of aim between a series of psychologically motivated revenges and a parade of triumphs by the Worldly Man over his innocent victims. Barabas' first deed of "vengeance" is directed against Mathias and Lodowick, two rivals for the love of Abigail. Barabas does not object to their love for his daughter; but Lodowick is the son of Malta's governor, and his blood must pay the price of Ferneze's unjust taxation. Barabas' hatred of Lodowick is therefore understandable:

> As sure as heaven rain'd manna for the Jews,
> So sure shall he and Don Mathias die:
> His father was my chiefest enemy.
>
> [II, iii, 249-251]

The reason for Mathias' death is far less clear, however. It is merely specious logic on the part of Barabas to include Mathias' name with Lodowick's in the speech just quoted. Mathias is guilty of no offense. Moreover, Abigail is genuinely in love with him. She consents, though much against her will, to aid in the plot against Lodowick without realizing that her father plans to destroy her lover as well. Her love for Mathias is not a moral problem for Barabas but an opportunity for intrigue. After both young men have been slain, Abigail broken-heartedly questions the necessity of Mathias' death:

> Admit thou lov'dst not Lodowick for his sire,
> Yet Don Mathias ne'er offended thee.

> [III, iii, 43-44]

What delights Barabas in the episode of Lodowick and Mathias is the cleverness of his act. He needs two victims in order to play one against the other. Mathias must die to complete a scheme of ingenious crime. Like Iago, another descendant of the Vice, Barabas operates through false rumor, the jealousies of love, setting friend against friend by means of evil suggestion.

Once Barabas has entered upon his career of revenge, each succeeding act is motivated in part by the need to suppress those who know too much or have revolted against him, or by the desire to further his revenge against Ferneze and the government. The structural result is a sequence of episodes involving a succession of victims, usually in pairs, who are suppressed with the forceful regularity of homiletic drama. Abigail learns the truth of Mathias' death, and turns nun in earnest. Consequently, she is a potential enemy to the Jew on two counts, of disloyalty and possession of dangerous knowledge:

> For she that varies from me in belief,
> Gives great presumption that she loves me not;
> Or, loving, doth dislike of something done.

> [III, iv, 10-12]

Her death must be the result, as another "vengeance" stemming from Barabas' original hatred for Ferneze. At the same time Barabas' primary concern in dispatching Abigail is less with the motive of his deed than with its execution. The Italian tradition of revenge, introduced by Machiavel, may serve in part as a literary source for Barabas' method in handling poisons, but the emphasis on artistry in evil is also the mark of the Vice and Worldly Man. Barabas gloats over his precious secret poison which cannot be detected upon the victim's body, and chuckles at the ironic appropriateness of a deadly porridge sent as alms to the nunnery.

The slaughter of the nuns leads to yet another situation in which Barabas has to protect himself by further violence. Friar Barnardine receives Abigail's dying confession of her father's villainy, and with Friar Jacomo he confronts Barabas with threatened exposure. Like Abigail, therefore, the Friars have become dangerous enemies to Barabas and must be dispatched with haste and skill:

> Now I have such a plot for both their lives,
> As never Jew nor Christian knew the like:
> One turn'd my daughter, therefore he shall die;

The other knows enough to have my life,
Therefore 'tis not requisite he should live.

[IV, i, 120-124]

This soliloquy emphasizes the two elements underlying Barabas' actions. The last three lines present the plausible motivation, although it is curious that the Jew speaks of only one Friar as possessing the knowledge of his crimes. Obviously Barabas realizes that both are partakers of the secret; "I fear they know we sent the poison'd broth," he whispers to Ithamore. The device of attributing a different motive to each of the two Friars is too rhetorical to be sincere. But it is in the two preceding lines that Barabas speaks as the Vice. This plot is to be a masterpiece, and the Jew prepares his audience to admire the beauty of its conception. The execution of his design is everything that he promises. He plays on the rapacity of the Friars, and pits them against each other (as he had done with Mathias and Lodowick) in the manner of the Vice by appealing to their ruling passion, greed.

The next episode, in which Ithamore becomes infatuated with the courtesan Bellamira and conspires with her and Pilia-Borsa to blackmail Barabas, is a business of comic intrigue. The scenes here are more burlesque than in the incident with the Friars: the tavern life and brothel humor, the quarrel over a whore, the grotesque "humors" of Pilia-Borsa's affected manner, and Barabas' ingenious disguise as a French musician in order to spy on the blackmailers. This vice comedy acts as a ludicrous and degenerate parody of the more serious bloody deeds of Barabas and Ithamore.

Even in this late episode, however, the motivation depends plausibly upon the train of events that has preceded this action. Barabas' need to do away with Ithamore and his new companions is identical with that which had brought Abigail and the Friars to their deaths, disloyalty to Barabas combined with knowledge that could expose him to the law:

Well, I must seek a means to rid 'em all,
And presently; for in his villany
He will tell all he knows, and I shall die for't.

[IV, v, 63-65]

At the same time, we know that Barabas had planned to rid himself of Ithamore sooner or later in any case. He deserves Ithamore's epithet of "bottle-nosed knave" (III, iii, 10) identifying him as a recognizable stage type.[15] It is his nature to hate everyone, even his fellows in vice, and the destruction of Ithamore stems ultimately from this simple hate.

Thematic unity in these scenes of worldly ambition follows that of the

---

[15] See Craik, *Tudor Interlude*, p. 51.

mid-century popular play. No hypothesis of later textual emendation is required to explain the connection between these successive episodes. In one sense, Barabas' acts depend upon one another as he seeks to revenge his wrongs or to cover up for his crimes. On the other hand, insofar as each evil deed is the result of Barabas' purely evil nature, there is no development of motivation at all. Each variation on the theme of vice casts additional light on the nature and operation of evil. The process does not logically unfold, but elaborates and intensifies by repeated example. The play moves steadily toward comic decline. Each succeeding incident becomes more ludicrous and more wildly improbable than the one before, as the reign of pure vice becomes increasingly separated from its original motive.

The structure of the final act follows the inevitable conclusion of all homiletic "tragedy," descending lower and lower into an insane depravity that can end only in punishment for the protagonist and restoration of order for those who remain. Barabas' frenzy in the manipulations of state affairs destroys even the pretense that he is driven by a desire for vengeance. When the Turks deliver Ferneze into his power, he is in a position to complete the personal "revenge" that has supposedly motivated all his previous acts of violence. Instead of doing so, he plots the destruction of his Turkish allies. The Vice traditionally knows no sides, and always prefers to pit one side against the other rather than seek aid against his supposed enemies. Barabas abandons the cause of revenge for one of intrigue for its own sake:

> Thus, loving neither, will I live with both.
>
> [V, ii, 111]

He boasts to the audience of his treachery in turning against the Turks, who would have helped him to destroy the uncircumcised Christians he professedly hates:

> Why, is not this
> A kingly kind of trade, to purchase towns
> By treachery, and sell 'em by deceit?
> Now tell me, worldlings, underneath the sun
> If greater falsehood ever has bin done?
>
> [V, v, 46-50][16]

Even when he is dying, having been trapped by Ferneze's counter-plot, the Jew boasts of his villainy and promises that he had intended the destruction of both sides:

---

[16] Quoted to much the same effect in Spivack, *Allegory of Evil*, p. 351.

> And, had I but escap'd this stratagem,
> I would have brought confusion on you all,
> Damn'd Christians, dogs, and Turkish infidels!

[V, v, 84-86]

Barabas' farewell is that of the evil genius in the moral play who aims at the annihilation of everything decent "underneath the sun."

Barabas' punishment appears to answer for his sins. The formula of the moral play demands providential justice to end the worldly success of vice, and we ought to be satisfied with Barabas' fate. His death is not accidental, like that of Cambises or Tamburlaine. A boiling cauldron is sufficient atonement even for a lifetime of atrocities. The Jew was evil, and he answered for it; the lesson seems clear and edifying. The difficulty, however, lies in the instrument of that justice. Ferneze lacks the personal virtue to act as agent of God's righteous anger; and yet the moral framework of the play puts him in a position of doing just this. In fact, Ferneze speaks of himself in this role:

> So, march away; and let due praise be given
> Neither to Fate nor Fortune, but to Heaven.

[V, v, 123-124]

Almost in the same breath, Ferneze perpetrates his own last act of duplicity by refusing to free Calymath, whom the Jew's treason has delivered into his hands. The play ends where it began, without the establishment of a moral order on Malta but merely with the restoration of the expediency that has always been Ferneze's method of governing. His appeal to divine justice is a mockery.

This curious dilemma has come about through the transference of a secular story into the structure of moral drama. In order to rationalize the native viciousness of Barabas it is necessary to provide him with enemies and persecutors; and since he is a Jew on the island of Malta, the Christians must play the part of villainy in those crucial first scenes when for a short time our sympathy focuses on Barabas. These Christians on Malta are Roman Catholics, and Catholics frequently appeared on the Elizabethan stage as villains. Nevertheless, the portrayal of them as evil results in moral confusion in the ensuing scenes of the play, since they cannot justly provide a virtuous foil for Barabas' villainy. For example, the two Friars are presented as greedy and unscrupulous in their desire for gold. They are also lecherous, and have mistresses within the walls of the convent. To dupe such unworthy members of a much feared church in Marlowe's day must have merited applause rather than condemnation. The anti-Papist jokes, often on Barabas' lips, surely evoked appreciation from his original audience:

And yet I know the prayers of those nuns
And holy friars, having money for their pains,
Are wondrous;—*and indeed do no man good.*   [*Aside.*
                                              [II, iii, 80-82]

The same problem of moral ambiguity occurs in *Faustus* when the protagonist snubs the Prince of Rome and his superstitious Friars. In *The
Jew,* the function of such anti-Catholicism is to provide motivation for
Barabas' acts as a Maltese Jew; but because Barabas is also a villain,
such factors work against the moral function of the plot, which suggests
that all of his acts are wicked and are to be punished.

If the conflict is evident in Barabas' religious enemies and victims, it
is even more apparent in his political antagonists. Quite early in the
action Ferneze is singled out as the man who must bring the Jew to
justice. As Barabas grows more violent and evil, Ferneze comes inevitably
to represent his moral opposite. The governor is prompted to revenge
by the death of his son and Don Mathias:

Upon which altar I will offer up
My daily sacrifice of sighs and tears,
And with my prayers pierce impartial heavens,
Till they [reveal] the causers of our smarts,
Which forc'd their hands divide united hearts.

                                              [III, ii, 31-35]

Ferneze repeatedly refers to himself as the executor of divine law in
hunting down Barabas. When the supposedly dead body of the Jew is
thrown over the walls of the city, Ferneze remarks:

Wonder not at it, sir; the heavens are just.

                                              [V, i, 55]

It is in the context of moral drama that such a conclusion is to be expected. The structure of the play demands a relationship between cause
and effect in Barabas' career. The difficulty is that in rationalizing Barabas' original plight, Marlowe has created villains out of those very persons who must later become the agents of retribution.

Ultimately, Marlowe's world of chronicle is morally neutral. Ferneze,
Calymath, and del Bosco are no better and no worse than Barabas;
Ferneze's final victory is merely a fact. The contest for Malta is a struggle
for balance of power between leaders who are inspired by a lust for
dominion and wealth:

> *Ferneze* . . . What wind drives you thus into Malta road?
> *Basso.* The wind that bloweth all the world besides,
>   Desire of gold.
>
> [III, v, 2-4]

Abigail sees that the material world does not always proceed according to God's plan, and therefore makes a second and entirely devout conversion to the life of a nun:

> But I perceive there is no love on earth,
> Pity in Jews, nor piety in Turks.
>
> [III, iii, 50-51]

Such injustices are never denied or amended, and they fit uneasily into a dramatic plan inherited from a religious tradition. Once again, as in *Tamburlaine,* we find in the combination of secular material and moral structure a key to the play's characteristic ambiguity.

Marlowe's Atheist Lecture

by *Paul H. Kocher*

In a paper which he laid before the Privy Council at some time shortly before Marlowe was stabbed to death on May 30, 1593, Richard Baines specified a number of blasphemies which he said the dramatist had uttered. Though most scholars today incline to believe the charges true, the circumstances surrounding them remain dark. It will therefore be of some value to show by an examination of the Baines document itself that the whole or the greater part of it is nothing more or less than a record of Marlowe's share in a single conversation at which Baines himself or some informant of his must have been present.

I

A look at the document will show that if a few relatively minor transpositions are made in the order of the statements attributed to Marlowe, they reveal a progress and transition of ideas which strongly suggest that the course of a single discussion is being traced. The thoughts follow one another with a naturalness of association which seems to preclude their having been either merely fabricated by Baines or even collected by him from Marlowe's actual talk on a number of scattered occasions. Transpositions are necessary where Baines, setting down the trend of the conversation from memory, remembers a statement after he has passed on from the topic to which it clearly belongs.

I here reproduce in full the Baines document,[1] indicating before the various statements the order in which I believe Marlowe made them:

A note Containing the opinion of on Christopher Marly Concerning his damnable [opini] Judgment of Religion, and scorn of Gods word.

"Marlowe's Atheist Lecture," by Paul H. Kocher. From *The Journal of English and Germanic Philology*, XXXIX (1940), 98-106. Copyright 1940 by the University of Illinois. Reprinted by permission of the author, the University of Illinois Press, and Russell and Russell, Inc. (the present publishers of Paul H. Kocher's *Christopher Marlowe: A Study of his Thought, Learning and Character*, in which the above article has been incorporated).

[1] Reprinted in C. F. Tucker Brooke, *The Life of Marlowe* (London: Methuen & Co. Ltd., 1930), Appendix IX, pp. 98-100. Words in brackets were scored through in the original.

1a   That the Indians and many Authors of antiquity haue assuredly writen
of aboue 16 thousand yeares agone wheras [Moyses] Adam is [said] proued
to haue lived within 6 thowsand yeares.

            He affirmeth that Moyses was but a Jugler & that one Heriots being
1b   Sir W Raleighs man Can do more then he.

            That Moyses made the Jewes to travell xl yeares in the wildernes,
1d   (which Jorney might haue bin done in lesse then one yeare) ere they Came
to the promised land to thintent that those who were privy to most of his
subtilties might perish and so an everlasting superstition Remain in the
hartes of the people.

1e   That the first beginning of Religioun was only to keep men in awe.

1c   That it was an easy matter for Moyses being brought up in all the artes
of the Egiptians to abuse the Jewes being a rude & grosse people.

2a   That Christ was a bastard and his mother dishonest.

2c   That he was the sonne of a Carpenter, and that if the Jewes among
whome he was borne did Crucify him theie best knew him and whence he
Came.

2d   That Crist deserved better to dy then Barrabas and that the Jewes made
a good Choise, though Barrabas was both a thief and a murtherer.

3a   That if there be any god or any good Religion, then it is in the papistes
because the service of god is performed with more Cerimonies, as Eleva-
tion of the mass, organs, singing men, Shaven Crownes & cta. That all
protestantes are Hypocritical asses.

3c   That if he were put to write a new Religion, he would vndertake both
a more Exellent and Admirable methode and that all the new testament is
filthily written.

2e   That the woman of Samaria & her sister were whores & that Crist knew
them dishonestly.

2f   That St John the Evangelist was bedfellow to Christ and leaned alwaies
in his bosome, that he vsed him as the sinners of Sodoma.

2g   That all they that loue not Tobacco & Boies were fooles.

3d   That all the apostles were fishermen and base fellowes neyther of wit
nor worth, that Paull only had wit but he was a timerous fellow in bidding
men to be subiect to magistrates against his Conscience.

3e   That he had as good Right to Coine as the Queen of England, and that
he was aquainted with one Poole a prisoner in Newgate who hath greate
skill in mixture of mettals and hauing learned some thinges of him he
ment through help of a Cunninge stamp maker to Coin ffrench Crownes
pistoletes and English shillinges.

3b   That if Christ would haue instituted the sacrament with more Cere-
moniall Reverence it would haue bin had in more admiration, that it
would haue bin much better being administred in a Tobacco pipe.

2b   That the Angell Gabriell was baud to the holy ghost, because he
brought the salutation to Mary.

4a   That on Ric Cholmley [hath Cholmley] hath Confessed that he was per-
swaded by Marloe's Reasons to become an Atheist.

            These thinges, with many other shall by good & honest witnes be aproved
to be his opinions and Comon Speeches and that this Marlow doth not
only hould them himself, but almost into every Company he Cometh he

perswades men to Atheism willing them not to be afeard of bugbeares and hobgoblins, and vtterly scorning both god and his ministers as I Richard Baines will Justify & approue both by mine oth and the testimony of many honest men, and almost al men with whome he hath Conversed any time will testify the same, and as I think all men in Cristianity ought to indevor that the mouth of / so dangerous a member may be stopped,

4b   he saith likewise that he hath quoted a number of Contrarieties oute of the Scripture which he hath giuen to some great men who in Convenient time shalbe named. When these thinges shalbe Called in question the witnes shalbe produced.

                                                          Richard Baines

It will be observed that the accusations fall under four main topics: (1) attacks on the theological version of early history with respect to the Old Testament figures, Adam and Moses; (2) scoffs at Christ as to the immaculate conception, his divinity, and his sexual looseness; (3) criticism of the "methode" of the Christian religion; (4) statements of Marlowe's efforts to secure converts to atheism. This fourth division is shaky, and perhaps no attempt should be made to set up such a topic, since it seems to consist of the left-overs of Baines' recollection. The other three topics, however (with some reservations as to topic 3), not only are well compacted within themselves but can be seen to flow readily into one another. That this is so will be more convincingly demonstrated if an interpretation and paraphrase of the whole is given. We may express its spirit and tendency, without claiming an impossible accuracy in details, somewhat in this fashion:

The theological explanation of early history, Marlowe may be thought to declare, is false. It teaches (1a) that mankind began with Adam less than 6000 years ago, whereas we know that there are accounts of a history much earlier. It is also false (1b) in holding Moses to be a true performer of miracles.[2] He merely performed juggling tricks which Harriot can better today. By them (1c) he was easily able to hoodwink the Jews, who were an unsophisticated people. In order to conceal these deceits and perpetuate superstition (1d) he secured the death of his confederates by multiplying the hardships of the journey in the wilderness. Therein he

---

[2] Whether or not Marlowe stated it explicitly in the actual conversation the underlying connection in his mind between the two first assertions is pretty clearly the thought of Harriot. Marlowe, who is known to have been friendly with the mathematician, almost certainly either derived the first assertion from Harriot or at least discussed it with him. See Nash's allusion in *Pierce Penniless* (1592): "I heare that there be Mathematicians abroad that will prove men before Adam." (F. S. Boas, *Marlowe and his Circle*, Oxford, 1929, p. 70). And Harriot's notes show that he was engaged in calculating the chronology of Genesis (J. Bakeless, *Christopher Marlowe*, New York: Morrow & Co. 1937, p. 202). The idea of Harriot, present in Marlowe's mind when he makes the first assertion, produces or helps to produce his second assertion as to Moses' jugglery, in which Harriot is expressly named.

was a typical founder of religion. Religions are begun by unscrupulous men as a device to attain power (1e).

Christ is another pretender and false leader. If the theological account of his conception through the Holy Ghost is to be credited, his mother was an adulteress (2a), he himself was a bastard, and the Angel Gabriel was a bawd (2b). But of course the account is trumped up. Christ was in fact a man like any other, and his claim of divine sonship was merely a humbug (2c). The Jews, who knew him all his life, were in the best position to realize his true origin and were justified in crucifying him (2c). He deserved death because his deception of the people was worse than murder or thievery (2d) and because he was in addition sexually impure. Did he not fornicate with the woman of Samaria and her sister (2e) and have unnatural relations with St. John the Evangelist (2f)? However, he can scarcely be blamed for the latter, since all sensible men do the like (2g)—and smoke tobacco.

The fact of the matter is that, considering the frauds of prophets and Messiahs, no organized religion is worthy of credence; and indeed we may go further and ask whether any God at all can be believed in.[3] But certain established religions are wiser than others in the method of their appeal. Catholicism is superior in this respect to Protestantism because it has insight enough to know that men's religious feelings are best aroused by the use of elaborate ceremonial (3a). Protestants censure Catholics for employing a ritual but are hypocrites since they themselves use a different, though inferior, one (3a).[4] Christ was foolish in not seeing this psychological principle and building his religion more firmly by surrounding the sacrament of holy communion with more impressive ceremonies (3b). Why not administer it in a tobacco pipe, for example (3b)? Moreover the presentation of Christianity has been bungled in other ways; the abominable style of the New Testament is an instance (3c). Christ made another error of strategy in choosing ignorant, worthless fishermen as his apostles to spread his doctrines (3d). Paul was the only man of brains among them but he was a coward, as is shown by his violation of his conscience in bidding men obey the law of the state (3d).[5]

[3] This bridge of ideas can only be conjectural. Between sections 2 and 3 there is a lacuna which, although not impassable, requires some structure of speculation. It should also be admitted that unity and consecutiveness are more difficult to see in the allegations which I have grouped as topic 3 than in the earlier allegations. Baines' memory seems to grow more jumbled as he proceeds.

[4] Baines' inclusion of the statement of Protestant hypocrisy in the paragraph dealing with ceremonies tends to indicate that Marlowe attacked Protestants in that particular rather than in general.

[5] Presumably Marlowe is referring to *Romans*, XIII where Paul directs Christians to submit to their temporal rulers. Neither there nor elsewhere, however, so far as I know, is there evidence that the apostle acted against his conscience in so doing. Marlowe probably has somehow in mind the problem, frequently mooted in the Renaissance as in all times, whether a Christian must obey human laws which contravene God's laws. The orthodox view is that he must not.

Many laws unjustly encroach upon the rights of the individual and should not be obeyed. The present English law against coining is just such a law, and I for one do not intend to obey it (3e).

Everything makes it plain that Christianity is a bugaboo from whose tyranny men must be freed. I have succeeded in converting Cholmley to my views (4a) and have written a pamphlet, which I have given to certain great men, pointing out the self-contradictions in the Bible (4b).

Too much should not be claimed for this attempt to rebuild the conversation, of course. It is completely tentative and is intended rather to suggest the running of a general current of continuity through the whole than to maintain the correctness of any one of the proposed interpretations and links of thought. In the nature of the case, we must expect some gaps in Baines' record of the talk. We cannot suppose that in every detail he reported what he heard completely or intelligently or fairly. Nor should we forget that others present undoubtedly took part in the discussion, voicing ideas, not set down by Baines, which gave direction to what Marlowe said. It is enough if we are able to show in Marlowe's remarks a degree of continuity which points to the singleness of the occasion.

To the objection that the Baines document represents no more than the rolling snowball of malicious rumor against Marlowe the present theory can give no conclusive answer. It can, however, comment that surely this is a most remarkably compact, remarkably cohesive sort of snowball and that it bears prints which look suspiciously like those of Marlowe's fingers. For the rest, it must rely on the persuasiveness of its affirmative argument.

II

If Marlowe made these remarks at one time, are they simply the chance delivery of a chance occasion? Very possibly not. Some of them, and perhaps the general scheme of the whole, may be traceable to a lost, unpublished, "atheisticall" tract written by Marlowe himself.

There are several references to the existence of one or more such tracts. In 1640 Simon Aldrich, a Cambridge scholar and fellow in the years 1593 to 1607 and a man of critical and cultured mind—in short, a most creditable witness—told the Kentish poet Henry Oxinden "that Marlo who wrot Hero & Leander was an Atheist & had writ a booke against the Scripture, how it was all one man's making, & would have printed it but could not be suffered." [6] Then there is the well-known

---

[6] Mark Eccles, "Marlowe in Kentish Tradition," *N&Q*, CLXIX, 20-23; 39-41; 58-61 (1935) at p. 41.

declaration assigned to Richard Cholmley "that Marlowe told him that he hath read the atheist lecture to Sir Walter Raleigh and others." The most probable meaning of "read the atheist lecture" is that Marlowe did literally read a manuscript, perhaps the identical one mentioned by Aldrich, to Raleigh's circle. The whole context of Cholmley's assertion indicates[7] that Marlowe presented to Raleigh's group a formal argument; and the most likely occasion for a presentation of that kind would be the author's reading of a work newly written, not yet published.

Most interesting of all, however, is what Thomas Beard writes only four years after Marlowe's death. Marlowe, he says,

> . . . fell (not without iust desert) to that outrage and extremitie, that hee denied God and his sonne Christ and not only in word blasphemed the trinitie, but also (as it is credibly reported) wrote bookes against it, affirming our Sauiour to be but a deceiuer, and Moses to be but a coniurer and seducer of the people, and the holy Bible to be but vaine and idle stories, and all religion but a deuice of pollicie.[8]

Beard makes a specific distinction between what the dramatist said and what he wrote. Then under the latter heading are listed four blasphemous opinions, of which three appear in almost exactly the same form in the Baines document and the fourth is implicit there. Not one iota of evidence exists to show that Beard either knew Baines or had access to the Baines document, which was filed with the papers of the Privy Council and was no doubt treated as a secret of state. Whence, then, the remarkable similarity between the two sets of allegations? The most plausible explanation is that when Marlowe engaged in the discussion which Baines heard he was either reading directly from the book (or books) Beard mentions or else drawing some of his ideas from it in the course of conversation. The latter alternative is the more acceptable because a number of the statements reported by Baines (like those about coining and "Tobacco & Boies") are apart from the main subject of religion and are of a kind which Marlowe would hardly put into a book anyway.

---

[7] The full text reads: "That he saith and verily believeth that one Marlowe is able to show more sound reasons for atheism than any divine in England is able to give to prove divinity, and that Marloe told him he hath read the atheist lecture to Sir Walter Raleigh and others." Reprinted by Tucker Brooke, *op. cit.*, p. 65. It would not be surprising if this "atheist lecture" included the list of contradictory Biblical texts which Baines refers to in his last paragraph: ". . . he saith likewise that he hath quoted a number of Contrarieties oute of the Scripture which he hath giuen to some great men who in Convenient time shalbe named." The verb "giuen" implies a manuscript (left with some of the audience after being read), and the "great men" are not likely to be any but Raleigh and his associates since these are the only prominent men, interested in advanced religious speculation, thought to have been close enough to Marlowe to warrant his taking the risk of communicating dangerous papers to them.

[8] From *The Theatre of Gods Iudgements*, Ch. xxv. Reprinted by Tucker Brooke, *op. cit.*, Appendix xv, pp. 112-113.

If this hypothesis is correct, we can get from an examination of the more seriously intentioned items in the Baines list a notion, distorted perhaps but nevertheless illuminating, of the real nature of the book which Marlowe wrote. It was a work attacking Christian dogma on rationalistic and historical grounds. It was primarily concerned not to disprove the existence of God, although that may possibly have been Marlowe's ultimate objective, but to discredit the authority of Scripture. Here the choice of Moses and Christ as the chief subjects of attack is highly significant. Renaissance religion considered Moses, giver of the Law, and Christ, redeemer of men condemned by the rigor of the Law, the two main underpropping columns of Christianity. If these could be destroyed the whole edifice must crumble. Marlowe strikes not by denying that such men as Moses and Christ ever lived but by stripping them of divine authority and explaining them as ambitious men seeking power under the pretext of religion.

Something may also be said of Marlowe's motives in entering into the discussion which Baines heard. He probably did not merely happen into it; he talked with the serious purpose—serious despite the occasional entry of sardonic humor—of making converts. There are numerous rumors that Marlowe regarded himself as a prophet of the new irreligion and entered into active propaganda for it. Baines says in his last paragraph concerning Marlowe's opinions that ". . . this Marlow doth not only hould them himself, but almost into every Company he Cometh he perswades men to Atheism willing them not to be afeard of bugbeares and hobgoblins . . . and almost al men with whome he hath Conversed any time will testify the same." The playwright Kyd avers "it was his custom when I knewe him first as I heare saie he contynewd it in table talk or otherwise to iest at the devine scriptures gybe at praiers, & stryve in argument to frustrate & confute what hath byn spoke or wrytt by prophets and such holie men . . . all which he wold . . . sodenlie take slight occasion to slyp out . . ." [9] Cholmley confessed himself to have been brought to atheism by Marlowe. Thomas Fineux was another of his proselytes, for Aldrich told Oxinden that Fineux "learnd all Marlo by heart & divers other bookes: Marlo made him an Atheist." [10] Finally, Marlowe was in contact with Raleigh's circle, which the Jesuit Robert Parsons describes as using positive efforts to secure disciples:

Of Sir Walter Rawley's schoole of Atheism by the waye, & of the Conjurer that is M[aster] thereof, and of the diligence used to get yong gentlemen of this schoole, where in both Moyses, & our Sauior, the olde, and the new Testament are iested at, and the schollers taughte amonge other things to spell God backwarde.[11]

[9] From Kyd's unsigned note to Puckering. Reprinted by Tucker Brooke, *op. cit.*, Appendix XII, pp. 107-8.
[10] Eccles, *op. cit.*, p. 40.   [11] Cited by Boas, *op. cit.*, p. 70.

Parsons thus tells us that Moses and Christ are the targets of the Raleigh school,[12] and that it is eager to enlist new members; Baines and Beard tell us of the concentration of Marlowe's strictures upon Moses and Christ, and there is good evidence that Marlowe is an energetic apostle of "atheism." It is hard to avoid the conclusion that Marlowe was an active member of the Raleigh group or at least had a community of belief and program with it.

Without too wild a use of the imagination, then, we may think of Marlowe as coming one day not long before his death into a company in which Baines is present. As the talk proceeds, the dramatist "suddenly takes slight occasion to slip out" a remark upon the subject uppermost in his thought. A discussion ensues. Marlowe, as a self-assertive man bent on convincing his hearers, is the positive and guiding force in the discussion. The ideas occur to him in somewhat the same words and in the same general order in which he has set them down in the tract he recently wrote. Comments by his audience lead to incidental digressions. Far from being convinced by the argument, Baines is alarmed and shortly afterwards makes from memory a report of what he has heard. The method which best assists his memory is that of following the conversation from its beginning as well as he can. His recollection serves him clearly at the start but grows more sketchy as he proceeds to what I have numbered as topic 3. Inevitably, he sometimes forgets, sometimes misrepresents what Marlowe said. In the main, however, he turns out a record which is of extraordinary value as showing both Marlowe's manner in conversation and the basic structure of his lost anti-Christian treatise.

We cannot say whether Marlowe wrote only one such treatise, as might be inferred from Aldrich, or several, as Beard avers. The former seems on the whole the more likely. But even if he produced several, the dominant homogeneity of subject-matter in the Baines charges tends to show that they stem from only one. Whether as manuscript or manuscripts, Marlowe's unpublished writing seems to have circulated with some freedom: it was heard of by Beard, heard of or seen by Aldrich, perhaps shown to Cholmley and Fineux, and listened to by Raleigh and others from Marlowe's own lips.

---

[12] Of interest in this connection is Anthony à Wood's later declaration of Harriot (Bakeless, *loc. cit.*) that ". . . . he had strange thoughts of the Scriptures. . . . He made a Philosophical theology wherein he cast off the Old Testament, so that consequently the New would have no foundation." This is not far from what Marlowe seems to have been trying to do. Harriot was of course the "Conjurer" spoken of by Parsons.

Marlowe's Humor

by Clifford Leech

"I haue (purposely) omitted and left out some fond and friuolous Iestures, disgressing (and in my poore opinion) far vnmeet for the matter, which I thought, might seeme more tedious vnto the wise, than any ways els to be regarded, though (happly) they haue bene of some vaine conceited fondlings greatly gaped at, what times they were shewed vpon the stage in their graced deformities: neuertheles now, to be mixtured in print with such matter of worth, it wuld prooue a great disgrace to so honorable & stately a historie." [1] These statements appear in the address "To the Gentlemen Readers: and others that take pleasure in reading Histories" prefixed to *Tamburlaine* by Richard Jones the printer in 1590. The late Una Ellis-Fermor, in her edition of the play (1930), drew attention to the two possible meanings of the words—that Marlowe had originally included more comic matter than now appears in the text, and that actors' "gags" had found their way into the copy in Jones's hands. But she evidently found greater probability in the latter interpretation (p. 67), and further considered that a number of passages in the extant text were gags that had escaped Jones's vigilance.[2] One of the recurrent features of Marlowe criticism has been the tendency first to deplore and then to deny his authorship of comic passages in the plays. And recently the disbelief in Marlowe's capacity for humor has made an especially vigorous appearance in C. S. Lewis's discussion of *Hero and Leander* in his *English Literature in the Sixteenth Century* (1954). Here we are told that, in such an undertaking as this poem, Marlowe had to be careful that his necessary realism of treatment did not awaken our disgust or incredulity; and Lewis adds: "Nor our sense of humour: laughter at the wrong moment is as fatal in this kind as in tragedy" (p. 487).

Against such views one may weigh T. S. Eliot's well-known assertion that Marlowe's "most powerful and mature tone" was that of a "savage

"Marlowe's Humor" by Clifford Leech. From *Essays on Shakespeare and Elizabethan Drama in Honor of Hardin Craig.* Copyright © 1962 by the Curators of the University of Missouri. Reprinted by permission of the University of Missouri Press.
[1] Quotations from Marlowe are from *The Works of Christopher Marlowe,* ed. C. F. Tucker Brooke (1910).
[2] *Tamburlaine the Great,* ed. Una Ellis-Fermor (1930), notes on Part 1: 2.4.28-35, 3.3.215-27; on Part 2: 1.3.61-3, 3.1.74-5, 3.5.100-2, 3.5.136-7, 3.5.156-7.

comic humour," a humor akin to that of *Volpone* (*Selected Essays,* 1932, p. 123). Since Eliot's essay was published, it has become commonplace to echo this sentiment in relation to *The Jew of Malta,* but there has been less regard for its applicability to Marlowe's writing as a whole. In the present essay I wish to draw attention to the pervasively comic tone in *Dido Queen of Carthage,* in *The Massacre at Paris,* and in *Hero and Leander.* Ultimately there will come, perhaps, a recognition of the important part played by savage humor in *Tamburlaine* and in *Doctor Faustus:* they are tragic plays, but the tragedy is of the sort in which humor is at home, insisting on the bizarre and the puny coexistent with the splendid within the mind and behavior of each man, however single. That is not to say, of course, that the comic scenes in our extant *Faustus* come straight from Marlowe's pen: indeed, that is less than likely. But it is to suggest that Marlowe's vision of the world, as presented in these plays, included the comic. More easily than Shakespeare, he could laugh at his hero while sharing that hero's aspiration and anguish. In *Edward II* the situation is more complex, but Marlowe has not left humor out of account.

Nothing will be implied here concerning the dates of composition of the writings considered. *Dido* and *Hero and Leander* may have been worked at during Marlowe's Cambridge years, though the maturity of the style makes that difficult to credit; they may, on the other hand, date from the end of his short career. What I think may be suggested is that in Marlowe's writing as a whole, without any necessary relation to dates of composition, we can see varying ways in which humor may be woven into the fabric. In *Faustus* and *Tamburlaine,* as already asserted, it is part of a predominantly tragic response to the world, complicating but not destroying the tragic attitude. In *The Jew of Malta* and *The Massacre at Paris* the humor is more assertive, equally savage but no longer finding its place alongside a sense of a man's greatness: what is presented is a wry picture of a world of little men, dreaming of greatness and playing out their atrocities but—whether in Barabas or the Guise—exposing their puniness even in the moments of highest ambition. In *Edward II,* as notably appeared in the 1958 production by the Marlowe Society (acted in Cambridge, Stratford-upon-Avon, and London), we have a play of subdued tragedy, subdued comedy. The titular hero blunders and suffers, as do Mortimer and Isabella and Gaveston. We sympathize with them, we are shocked by the ends they meet, but Marlowe has kept all of them throughout at the mercy of circumstance, and lingers with pity over each error as it is made. And, as the dreams are modest here, so too is the occasion for laughter. Nevertheless, a fund of humor is available at need —in the baiting of a bishop by Edward and Gaveston, in Edward's infatuation, in the climbing antics of Young Spencer and Baldock, in Warwick's cruel jibe at the condemned Gaveston, in Lightborn's petty joy in his executioner's skill. But in *Dido* and in *Hero and Leander* the relationship between the comic and the serious is different from that in any of these. Although both stories end in death, the dominant tone is that of a gentle and delighting humor: the affairs of men and gods are seen as a spectacle engagingly absurd.

In the essay referred to, Eliot has drawn attention to the comic element in the style of *Dido,* a style "which secures its emphasis by always hesitating on the edge of caricature at the right moment" (p. 124). My concern is rather with the play's incidents and plan of composition. Throughout we are made aware of action on two planes, the human and the divine. In the beginning we see Jupiter dandling Ganymede, and Mercury and Venus also appear in the first scene. At the end of Act 1 Venus speaks to her son Aeneas, and their encounter and their relationship exemplify a recurrent interweaving of the two levels of being. Venus and Juno and Mercury all intervene in the human action. Cupid masquerades as Ascanius during a substantial portion of the play. Moreover, there are parallel relationships on the two levels: the divine boys Ganymede and Cupid are set against the human boy Ascanius; Venus and Dido are both mothers, Venus in actuality to Cupid and to Aeneas, Dido in fancy to Ascanius and to Cupid in Ascanius's shape; the rivals Venus and Juno (rivals for the apple and for Jupiter's love) are matched by the rivals Dido and Anna (for Iarbus's love). Because the mortals are ever at the gods' bidding, their stature cannot be great: it is Cupid in his disguise who causes Dido to love Aeneas; it is Mercury who gives to Aeneas the command to leave Carthage: in neither case is there the possibility of resistance or even much reluctance, for Aeneas, browbeaten as he is by Dido's reproaches, has only a fitful wish to stay with her. But not only are the mortals puny: the gods, interrelated with the mortals and echoing their patterns of conduct, are trivial too. The opening of the play, showing Jupiter's infatuation with Ganymede, at once establishes the play's attitude.

Virgil was Marlowe's primary source, and in places he followed the *Aeneid* with, in Tucker Brooke's words, "schoolboy slavishness" (*Works,* p. 390). Yet there are extraordinary differences between the ways in which the two poets present the hero. The founder of the Roman fortunes is, in Marlowe's hands, not very much of a hero. In the tale to Dido of Troy's destruction, he recounts how he failed to rescue three women in his escape from Troy:

> O there I lost my wife: and had not we
> Fought manfully, I had not told this tale:
> Yet manhood would not serue, of force we fled,
> And as we went vnto our ships, thou knowest
> We sawe *Cassandra* sprauling in the streetes,
> Whom *Aiax* rauisht in *Dianas* Fane,
> Her cheekes swolne with sighes, her haire all rent,
> Whom I tooke vp to beare vnto our ships:
> But suddenly the Grecians followed vs,

And I alas, was forst to let her lye.
Then got we to our ships, and being abourd,
Polixena cryed out, *Æneas* stay,
The Greekes pursue me, stay and take me in.
Moued with her voyce, I lept into the sea,
Thinking to beare her on my backe abourd:
For all our ships were launcht into the deepe,
And as I swomme, she standing on the shoare,
Was by the cruell Mirmidons surprizd,
And after by that *Pirrhus* sacrifizde.

(565-83)

It is Iarbus who asks, "How got *Æneas* to the fleete againe?" (586), and Achates who replies, "As for *Æneas* he swomme quickly backe" (591). The dramatic convenience of this is evident, for it establishes the hero as a man ready to part company with a woman when necessity arises. But it is important to note that here Marlowe has written independently of his source. In the *Aeneid,* when Creusa is missing, Aeneas goes back for her and searches in the heart of the burning city, abandoning the quest only when so commanded by her ghost; Cassandra is referred to merely as glimpsed during the fighting; and Polyxena does not appear in this context.

In his relations with Dido, Aeneas is no more impressive than in his own account of his conduct in Troy. In 3.2, in the cave, he is a little absurd in his slowness to catch Dido's drift. When he accepts her love, he vows most solemnly to be faithful:

With this my hand I giue to you my heart,
And vow by all the Gods of Hospitalitie,
By heauen and earth, and my faire brothers bowe,
By *Paphos, Capys,* and the purple Sea,
From whence my radiant mother did descend,
And by this Sword that saued me from the Greekes,
Neuer to leaue these newe vpreared walles,
Whiles *Dido* liues and rules in *Iunos* towne,
Neuer to like or loue any but her.

(1038-46)

Yet just over a hundred lines later he is saying, "*Carthage,* my friendly host, adue" (1151), because Mercury has appeared to him in a dream. He considers whether or not to engage in a farewell encounter with Dido, but decides it will be safer to forgo it. When Anna insists on his seeing the queen, he lies:

> *Dido.* Is this thy loue to me?
> *Æneas.* O princely *Dido,* giue me leaue to speake,
> I went to take my farewell of *Achates.*
>
> (1222-4)

He is quickly made ridiculous when Dido replies that Achates may certainly go at once, and he has to invent the excuse that the weather is just
now unfavorable, a subterfuge that Dido easily exposes. Then, to demonstrate nis fidelity, he asks:

> Hath not the Carthage Queene mine onely sonne?
> Thinkes *Dido* I will goe and leaue him here?
>
> (1235-6)

Both Aeneas and Dido believe that Ascanius is with Dido (though actually
it is Cupid in Ascanius's shape): unless there is an oversight here, Marlowe is implying that up to this point Aeneas has forgotten, or has been
prepared to abandon, his son in his attempt to steal away.

Although Aeneas especially suffers from Marlowe's handling, Dido is
not treated altogether gently. She has not much reticence or dignity as
love comes on her, and she is as lavish with gifts as an insecure lover can
be. When Aeneas asks if her citizens will not repine at her making him
"their soueraigne Lord," she replies:

> Those that dislike what *Dido* giues in charge
> Commaund my guard to slay for their offence:
> Shall vulgar pesants storme at what I doe?
> The ground is mine that giues them sustenance,
> The ayre wherein they breathe, the water, fire,
> All that they haue, their lands, their goods, their liues,
> And I the Goddesse of all these, commaund
> *Æneas* ride as Carthaginian King.
>
> (1277-84)

The arrogance is a dim echo of Tamburlaine's, and the implicit criticism
is stronger because this "Goddesse of all these" has already shown herself a
mere woman indeed. Later she is ready to give up her throne if she may
live privately with Aeneas, saying to Anna:

> Now bring him backe, and thou shalt be a Queene,
> And I will liue a priuate life with him.
>
> (1605-6)

So the King in *Edward II* was prepared to abandon England to his nobles if Gaveston could be his:

> Make seuerall kingdomes of this monarchie,
> And share it equally amongst you all,
> So I may haue some nooke or corner left,
> To frolike with my deerest *Gaueston.*

(365-8)

Marlowe allows his Dido a stately ending, with Latin words to utter as she enters the fire. But there is a subdued casualness in the way the story is brought to its terminal point, the rapidly consecutive suicides of Dido and Iarbus and Anna—Dido for love of Aeneas, Iarbus for love of Dido, Anna for love of Iarbus—hinting at the comic.

In everything that has been noticed so far, the humor has shown itself indirectly, invoking the discreet smile, the detached shrug. There is direct comedy, however, in 4.5, where a Nurse has charge of Cupid in Ascanius's shape. She is taking him into the country, so that Dido may hold him as a pledge of Aeneas's fidelity. It is ironic that the pledge is Love himself, and that Love's mother has little heed for a mortal's love, being concerned only with her son Aeneas's fortunes. Moreover, the Nurse is infected by Cupid as Dido was: despite her eighty years, she begins to think of a husband. We have seen how the gods are made petty through their mirroring of human conduct, but now Dido's infection is mirrored in the Nurse's. For a moment there are three levels of action—of the gods, of High People, and of Low People—and each is comically affected by the interrelation.

Marlowe may have been hurried in the composition of this play; he may have collaborated with Nashe, whose name appears with his on the title-page; in any event, it is not a fully achieved piece of writing. *The Massacre at Paris,* however, is much less than that in the "bad" text that has survived. Here we have a play of only 1263 lines with a dramatic action covering a substantial stretch of time. The story of the massacre is over by line 540, and the whole sequence of events runs from Navarre's marriage to his accession as Henry IV. Superficially it is an anti-Guise play, but of all the characters only Ramus (for the brief moment of his appearance and murder) and Navarre are neutrally handled. Anjou, when he has become Henry III, gets favorable treatment in being presented as the ally of Navarre and the friend and admirer of Elizabeth, but his earlier conduct has been repellent. He is the murderer of Ramus. He exults in the Guise's death and in showing his dead body to the Guise's son:

> Ah this sweet sight is phisick to my soule,
> Goe fetch his sonne for to beholde his death.

(1032-3)

Then he orders the deaths of Dumain and Cardinal Guise, and boasts to the Queen Mother of what he has done. This brutality is very different from the slaughter of the Damascus virgins or the many other barbarities of Tamburlaine. Anjou, like the Guise, can aspire, but his methods are those of common cunning and his musings on greatness are shoddy. Early in the play two Lords of Poland offer him their country's crown, and he accepts it on the understanding that it can be abandoned if the French crown becomes available. He is flattered by this Polish invitation, especially as it means he will have the Czar and the Turk as immediate foes:

> For Poland is as I haue been enformde,
> A martiall people, worthy such a King,
> As hath sufficient counsaile in himselfe,
> To lighten doubts and frustrate subtile foes:
> And such a King whom practise long hath taught,
> To please himselfe with mannage of the warres,
> The greatest warres within our Christian bounds,
> I meane our warres against the Muscouites:
> And on the other side against the Turke,
> Rich Princes both, and mighty Emperours.
>
> (459-68)

The reigning Czar was Ivan, and Süleyman the Magnificent had a few years before been in command of the Turkish fortunes. Anjou in such company is an unimpressive champion of Christendom, one incapable of recognizing the grander manifestations of the aspiring mind.

The small brutalities of Anjou and the Guise have not the overt absurdity of Barabas's boast:

> As for my selfe, I walke abroad a nights
> And kill sicke people groaning under walls:
> Sometimes I goe about and poyson wells;
>
> (939-41)

but the element of grim humor is evident enough. On occasion, however, Marlowe's method is more direct, as it was with the introduction of the Nurse in *Dido*. Fitting the more savage tone and pattern of event in *The Massacre*, the humor is here of a more aggressive sort. After the death of the Admiral, two unnamed figures debate in prose on how to effect the disposal of his body: if they burn him, they think, the fire will be infected and then the air; if they throw him into the river, the water will be tainted, then the fishes, then themselves; so hanging, they decide, is best. Later the Soldier who has come, on the Guise's order, to shoot Mugeroun, lover of the Guise's Duchess and minion of Anjou, has a prose passage in which Mugeroun's relations with the Duchess are presented in a rapid sequence of gross images: the passage occurs in a slightly extended form in Collier's version of the scene, allegedly dependent on a manuscript leaf of the play. Moments such as these in *The Massacre* and *Dido* show Marlowe underlining the comic element which is indeed securely inherent in the writing as a whole. In *Tamburlaine* we can see the sudden relaxations into comic prose, often in the midst of a blank verse scene, as perhaps overemphatic pointers to the proper interpretation of the play. Although in all other respects *Dido* and *The Massacre* are slighter and far less organized than *Tamburlaine*, the directly comic moments are in them more shrewdly managed. Dido's Nurse, the Guise's hangmen and hired assassin, are presented in isolation, and we are ready to see the play's implications becoming explicit in their utterance. In *Tamburlaine* the shifts from implicit to explicit are too sudden for us to be at ease with them, except in the incident (in Part II, 4.1) where Calyphas loiters in his tent and provides a close analogue to the directly humorous moments of these other plays.

Hero and Leander has the quieter humor of *Dido*, but is far more expert in its control. As in the play, so here the worlds of gods and men are intertwined. Hero is "*Venus* Nun," Neptune would have Leander for his minion. There is an immediate irony in the notion that a priestess of the love-goddess should be vowed to chastity, and this is reinforced by the pictures of divine riot displayed on the crystal pavement of Venus's temple:

> There might you see the gods in sundrie shapes,
> Committing headdie ryots, incest, rapes:
> For know, that vnderneath this radiant floure
> Was *Danaes* statue in a brazen tower,
> *Ioue* slylie stealing from his sisters bed,
> To dallie with *Idalian Ganimed,*
> And for his loue *Europa* bellowing loud,
> And tumbling with the Rainbow in a cloud:
> Blood-quaffing *Mars* heauing the yron net,
> Which limping *Vulcan* and his *Cyclops* set.
>
> (1. 143-52)

There is comic reticence in the withholding of Venus's name in the last couplet here, but indeed the comedy comes through in every line. Rarely have the gods been treated with such concentrated fun: "headdie" with the casual catalogue of line 144, "slylie stealing" and "sisters" in line 147, the swift change from "dallie" in line 148 to "bellowing" in line 149 and "tumbling" in line 150, the ludicrous "Blood-quaffing" for Mars and the richly associative "heauing" in line 151, together might almost justify a charge that Marlowe was overdoing the comedy, were it not that the poem (as Marlowe left it) is so consistent in tone that we are made at ease in a world of extravagance. The slyness with which the poet refrains from inserting Venus's name here is anticipated fifty lines earlier, when we are told:

> The men of wealthie *Sestos,* euerie yeare,
> (For his sake whom their goddesse held so deare,
> Rose-cheekt *Adonis*) kept a solemne feast.

> (1. 91-3)

The formality of "held so deare" and "solemne feast" is mocked by "Rose-cheekt," and the poem's intertwining of gods and mortals at once appears in that the first encounter of Hero and Leander takes place at a time when the memory of Adonis is being honored. In the long passage at the end of the first sestiad, where it is explained why Cupid could not win the favor of the Destinies for Hero and Leander, this intertwining is presented more elaborately. The enmity of the Fates, we are told, arose from the love of Mercury for "a countrie mayd": she resisted his vigorous wooing until, thirsting after immortality ("All women are ambitious naturallie"), she demanded a cup of nectar as the price of her favors. Mercury stole the nectar from Hebe ("*Hebe Ioues* cup fill'd") and gave it to the girl. Jove came to know of the theft ("as what is hid from *Ioue?*") and "waxt more furious Than for the fire filcht by *Prometheus.*" So Mercury was banished from heaven, and Cupid, in pity for him, persuaded "the Adamantine Destinies" to dote on Mercury. From them, to effect his revenge, Mercury secured the restoration of Saturn and the banishing of Jove to hell. So for a time the golden age returned:

> Murder, rape, warre, lust and trecherie,
> Were with *Ioue* clos'd in *Stigian* Emprie.

> (1. 457-8)

But Mercury soon neglected the love of the Destinies, and they in revenge restored Jove to power. Mercury's punishment was

> That he and *Pouertie* should alwaies kis.
> And to this day is euerie scholler poore,
> Grosse gold from them runs headlong to the boore.
> Likewise the angrie sisters thus deluded,
> To venge themselues on *Hermes,* haue concluded
> That *Midas* brood shall sit in Honors chaire,
> To which the *Muses* sonnes are only heire:
> And fruitfull wits that in aspiring are,
> Shall discontent run into regions farre;

And few great lords in vertuous deeds shall ioy,
But be surpris'd with euerie garish toy;
And still inrich the loftie seruile clowne,
Who with incroching guile keepes learning downe.
Then muse not *Cupids* sute no better sped,
Seeing in their loues the Fates were iniured.

(1. 470-84)

This ending, appropriate enough for a University Wit, might seem over-sententious without the familiar tone of the final couplet and its cunning juxtaposition of "loues" and "Fates." The unexpected extension of the satire to the condition of human society brings the parallel between gods and men before us in a new way. Previously the small loves and angers of the gods had been exposed: even Prometheus does not escape when the word "filcht" is used of his gift of fire to men, and the mock-reverence of "as what is hid from *Joue?*" follows quickly on the casual mention of the filling of Jove's cup.

In this ending of the first sestiad, it is "a countrie mayd" whose resistance to Mercury causes revolution and counter-revolution on Olympus, disorders human society, and sets the Fates against all lovers, including Hero and Leander. Moreover, the account of Mercury's rough wooing and the girl's resistance is an anticipation of Leander's approaches to Hero in the second sestiad. Fleetingly we may be reminded of the association of Dido and the Nurse in their common subjection to Cupid. In this poem, however, the lovers are handled with a frank delight. Sensual and comely, with a tripping or a swimming or a panting motion, they move delicately through the verse. They are taken no more seriously than Dido and Aeneas, but their existence gives us far more pleasure. At their first meeting love is immediate, Leander feeling "Loues arrow" and Hero's gentle heart being struck by the fire that blazed from Leander's countenance. It is a speed the poet approves: "Who euer lov'd, that lov'd not at first sight?" But if love is immediate, mutual comprehension is not. Leander kneels, but Hero does not guess that she is the object of his devotion:

He kneel'd, but vnto her deuoutly praid;
Chast *Hero* to her selfe thus softly said:
Were I the saint hee worships, I would heare him,
And as shee spake those words, came somewhat nere him.

(1. 177-80)

One of Marlowe's recurrent devices in this poem is the use of dissyllabic rhyme, which he manages in such a way as to achieve a familiar tone and a sense of human hesitation. Here the effect is reinforced by the pause after "words" and the modest suggestiveness of "somewhat." In the ensuing eighteen lines there are three more examples of dissyllabic rhyme, and the last of them, at the end of the verse-paragraph, has a broad, oddly Byronic effect:

> At last, like to a bold sharpe Sophister,
> With chearefull hope thus he accosted her.

> (1. 197-8)

Here "bold sharpe" unexpectedly presents Leander in a fresh light, as he waxes in a young man's sudden confidence, "Sophister" being a Cambridge term for a second- or third-year undergraduate. This broadness can be found at times in the poem's descriptive imagery, as in:

> Who builds a pallace and rams vp the gate,
> Shall see it ruinous and desolate.
> Ah simple *Hero,* learne thy selfe to cherish,
> Lone women like to emptie houses perish. . . .

> (1. 239-42)

—an image echoed perhaps at the beginning of the second sestiad:

> And therefore to her tower he got by stealth.
> Wide open stood the doore, hee need not clime.

> (2. 18-19)

The comedy does indeed grow more vigorous as the love affair develops. The near-approach to consummation at the second meeting, Leander's second crossing of the strait and Neptune's wooing of him, the shivering of the cold and wet Leander as he begs for the warmth of Hero's bed, the ensuing contest that fully engages the poet's wit, the coming of daylight to the lovers—all these things help to achieve a comedy that is never out of control, never ill-tempered, never mean or ungenerous. There is, indeed, an almost moving touch—almost, because we must never feel that our sympathies are completely engaged—in the account of Hero's embarrassment in the morning. And Marlowe, fittingly enough, does not resist a comparison between Leander and Dis:

> Whence his admiring eyes more pleasure tooke
> Than *Dis,* on heapes of gold fixing his looke.

> (2. 325-6)

The poet has some affection for his small human figures, but rather less for the gods.

"*Desunt nonnulla*" we read at the end of Marlowe's share in the poem,

and perhaps the task of finishing defeated him. A scourge of God could
be shown at the moment of death, but the story of Leander's drowning
might have been difficult to treat in the manner of the poem. Dido could
enter the fire, but she is not alive as the lovers in the poem are, and she
has not been treated with the same affection as they. The thing could
have been done, but perhaps the tone of voice would have been awkwardly
changed. Indeed the last lines of the second sestiad have a harshness that is
new and not easy to accommodate to what we have previously known:

> By this *Apollos* golden harpe began
> To sound foorth musicke to the *Ocean,*
> Which watchful *Hesperus* no sooner heard,
> But he the day bright-bearing Car prepar'd,
> And ran before, as Harbenger of light,
> And with his flaring beames mockt ougly night,
> Till she o'recome with anguish, shame, and rage,
> Dang'd downe to hell her loathsome carriage.
>
> (2. 327-34)

The inert catalogue of the penultimate line, with the heavy alliteration
that follows, seems to lack the full assurance of the rest of the poem, and
perhaps Marlowe felt it.

The humor in *The Jew of Malta* and in *Faustus* presents, of course,
larger problems than are touched on here. The object of the present exercise has been to urge fuller recognition of the variety of Marlowe's
humor, and its high degree of integration with the fabric of his writing.
Above all, I have tried to present *Hero and Leander* as a major comic
poem.

Chronology of Important Dates

1564	Born at Canterbury, son of a shoemaker. Baptized at St. George's Church, February 26.
1579	14 January: Entered the King's School, Canterbury, as a scholar.
1580	December: Entered Corpus Christi College, Cambridge. Shortly afterwards elected to a scholarship founded by Archbishop Parker.
1584	Graduated B.A. Marlowe's continuing to hold his scholarship after this date seems to imply that he was assumed to be preparing for holy orders.
1587	Graduated M.A., after the University had received a letter from the Privy Council declaring that Marlowe had been "emploied . . . in matters touching the benefitt of his Countrie," and denying the rumor that he planned to go to Rheims "and there to remaine" (*i.e.,* as a seminarist). *Historia von D. Iohañ Fausten* published at Frankfurt.
c. 1587	*Tamburlaine,* Parts I and II, acted by the Lord Admiral's Men.
1588	Robert Greene's prefatory epistle to his *Perimedes the Blacksmith* refers to the stage "daring God out of heaven with that Atheist *Tamburlan,*" and to "such mad and scoffing poets, that have propheticall spirits as bred of *Merlins* race."
1589	Arrested for being concerned in a fight in which William Bradley was killed by Thomas Watson (presumably the poet): the jury found that Watson acted in self-defense: Marlowe released after less than two weeks.
1590	*Tamburlaine,* Parts I and II, published in one volume, without author's name.
1592	*The Historie of the damnable life, and deserued death of Doctor Iohn Faustus* published (English version of the 1587 *Historia*).

Bound over to keep the peace toward the Constable and Sub-constable of Holywell Street, Shoreditch.

Greene's *Groats-worth of Wit bought with a Million of Repentance,* a tract written on his death bed, addressing a "famous gracer of Tragedians," urges him to abandon atheism and "Machiuilian pollicie." This tract was edited by Henry Chettle, who in the introduction to his *Kind-Harts Dreame* later in 1592 expresses regret for the attack on Shakespeare in the tract but indicates that he has no wish to be acquainted with another "play-maker" who had taken offense.

1593

12 May: Thomas Kyd, author of *The Spanish Tragedy,* arrested and tortured on suspicion of treasonable activities. His room searched, and papers found "denying the deity of Jhesus Christe."

18 May: Warrant issued by Privy Council for Marlowe's arrest. Two days later, arrested at Sir Thomas Walsingham's house near Chislehurst, Kent, and required to give daily attendance on their lordships "vntill he shalbe lycensed to the contrary."

30 May: Marlowe spent the day at an inn at Deptford Strand, near London, in the company of Ingram Frizer, Robert Poley, and Nicholas Skeres. Poley was a double-spy; Skeres had probably been concerned with him in the Babington Plot (1586); Poley and Frizer, like Marlowe, had relations with Sir Thomas Walsingham. According to the story told at an inquest on June 1, after supper Marlowe and Frizer quarrelled about the reckoning, and Frizer stabbed Marlowe in self-defense. Frizer was pardoned on June 18. Marlowe was buried at St. Nicholas' Church, Deptford, on June 1.

Probably soon after Marlowe's death, Kyd wrote to Sir John Puckering, the Lord Keeper, saying that the blasphemous papers found in his room belonged to Marlowe, who shared the room with him two years before.

On June 2 (?) Richard Baines, an informer, submitted allegations that Marlowe had spoken treasonably, blasphemously, and in praise of homosexuality.

1594

Edward II published with Marlowe's name on title-page.

Dido Queen of Carthage published with the names of Marlowe and Nashe on title-page.

1598

Hero and Leander published. Later in the same year a second edition, including Chapman's continuation and the division into "Sestiads."

Before 1599   *All Ouids Elegies: 3 Bookes. By C.M.* published without date, allegedly at Middleburgh in Holland.

1600   *Lucans First Booke translated Line by Line* published.

1601 (?)   *The Massacre at Paris* published.

1604   *Doctor Faustus* published ("A-text").

1616   *Doctor Faustus* published ("B-text").

1633   *The Jew of Malta* published after revival at Cockpit and Court.

Notes on the Editor and Authors

CLIFFORD LEECH, editor of this volume. Chairman of the Department of English at University College, Toronto. Author of *Shakespeare's Tragedies and Other Studies in Seventeenth Century Drama* (1950), *John Ford and the Drama of his Time* (1957), *The John Fletcher Plays* (1962), *O'Neill* (1963), *Webster: The Duchess of Malfi* (1963). General Editor of the Revels Plays (1958-   ).

ROY W. BATTENHOUSE. Professor of English at the University of Indiana. Editor of *A Companion to the Study of St. Augustine* (1955).

DAVID M. BEVINGTON. Assistant Professor of English at the University of Virginia.

MURIEL C. BRADBROOK. Fellow of Girton College, Cambridge. Author of *Elizabethan Stage Conditions* (1932), *The School of Night* (1936), *Ibsen, the Norwegian* (1946), *Shakespeare and Elizabethan Poetry* (1951), *The Growth and Structure of Elizabethan Comedy* (1955), *The Rise of the Common Player* (1962).

J. P. BROCKBANK. Professor of English at the University of York.

WOLFGANG CLEMEN. Professor of English at the University of Munich. Author of *Shakespeares Bilder* (1936; expanded English version, *The Development of Shakespeare's Imagery*, 1951), *Kommentar zu Shakespeares Richard III* (1957), *Chaucer's Early Poetry* (1964).

T. S. ELIOT, O.M. Nobel Prize-winner (1948).

UNA ELLIS-FERMOR (1894-1958). Professor of English, University of London, 1947-58. Editor of *Tamburlaine* for the Case Marlowe (1930). Author of *Christopher Marlowe* (1927), *Jacobean Drama* (1936), *The Irish Dramatic Movement* (1939), *Shakespeare the Dramatist* (1961). General Editor of the New Arden Shakespeare (1951-58).

W. W. GREG (1875-1959), kt. President, Malone Society (General Editor, 1906-39). Author of *Pastoral Poetry and Pastoral Drama* (1906), *Two Elizabethan Stage Abridgements* (1923), *Dramatic Documents from the Elizabethan Playhouses* (1931), *A Bibliography of the English Printed Drama to the Restoration* (1939-59), *The Editorial Problem in Shakespeare* (1942), *The Shakespeare First Folio* (1955). Editor of *Henslowe's Diary* (1904-08), *Marlowe's Doctor Faustus 1604-1616: Parallel Texts* (1950), Jonson's *Masque of Gipsies* (1952).

PAUL H. KOCHER. Professor of English at Stanford University. Author of *Science and Religion in Elizabethan England* (1953).

HARRY LEVIN. Professor of English and Comparative Literature at Harvard University. Author of *James Joyce: A Critical Introduction* (1941), *Contexts of Criticism* (1957), *The Power of Blackness: Hawthorne, Poe, Melville* (1958), *The Question of Hamlet* (1960), *The Gates of Horn* (1963). Editor of *The Portable James Joyce* (1947), *Coriolanus* in the Pelican Shakespeare (1956).

ETHEL SEATON. Honorary Fellow of St. Hugh's College, Oxford. Author of *Literary Relations of England and Scandinavia in the Seventeenth Century* (1935), *Sir Richard Roos* (1961). Editor of Abraham Fraunce's *The Arcadian Rhetoricke* (1950).

EUGENE M. WAITH. Professor of English at Yale University. Author of *The Pattern of Tragicomedy in Beaumont and Fletcher* (1952). Editor of *Bartholomew Fair* in the Yale Ben Jonson (1963). He is the editor of the volume on *Shakespeare: The Histories* in the Twentieth Century Views series.

F. P. WILSON (1889-1963). Merton Professor of English Literature in the University of Oxford, 1947-57. General Editor, Malone Society, 1948-60. Author of *Elizabethan and Jacobean* (1943), *Seventeenth Century Prose* (1959). Editor, with Bonamy Dobrée, of *The Oxford History of English Literature* (1945-63).

Selected Bibliography

EDITIONS

The Works of Christopher Marlowe, ed. C. F. Tucker Brooke (Oxford, 1910).

The Works and Life of Christopher Marlowe, gen. ed. R. H. Case, 6 vols. (London, 1930-33): Life and *Dido*, ed. C. F. Tucker Brooke, 1930; *Tamburlaine*, ed. U. M. Ellis-Fermor, 1930; *The Jew of Malta* and *The Massacre at Paris*, ed. H. S. Bennett, 1931; *Poems*, ed. L. C. Martin, 1931; *Doctor Faustus*, ed. F. S. Boas, 1932; *Edward II*, ed. H. B. Charlton and R. D. Waller, 1933 (revised F. N. Lees, 1955).

Edward II, ed. W. D. Briggs (London, 1914).

Marlowe's Doctor Faustus 1604-1616: Parallel Texts, ed. W. W. Greg (Oxford, 1950).

The Tragical History of the Life and Death of Doctor Faustus: A Conjectural Reconstruction, ed. W. W. Greg (Oxford, 1950).

Doctor Faustus, ed. John D. Jump (London, 1962) [Revels Plays].

Revels Plays editions of *Tamburlaine, Edward II, The Jew of Malta, Dido*, and *The Massacre of Paris* are in preparation.

BIOGRAPHY

J. L. Hotson, *The Death of Christopher Marlowe* (London, 1925).

C. F. Tucker Brooke, *Life of Marlowe* included in the Case Marlowe noted above (London, 1930).

M. Eccles, *Christopher Marlowe in London* (Cambridge, Mass., 1942).

F. S. Boas, *Christopher Marlowe: A Biographical and Critical Study* (Oxford, 1940).

J. Bakeless, *The Tragical History of Christopher Marlowe*, 2 vols. (Cambridge, Mass., 1942).

CRITICISM, &C.

In addition to works excerpted from in this volume and those mentioned in the introduction, the following should be noted:

U. M. Ellis-Fermor, *Christopher Marlowe* (London, 1927).

P. Henderson, *And Morning in His Eyes* (London, 1936).

M. M. Mahood, *Poetry and Humanism* (New Haven, 1950).

M. Poirier, *Marlowe* (London, 1951).

N. Brooke, "Marlowe as Provocative Agent in Shakespeare's Early Plays," *Shakespeare Survey* 14 (1961), pp. 34-44.

J. B. Steane, *Marlowe: A Critical Study* (Cambridge, 1964). *Tulane Drama Review* (Marlowe Issue), VIII, 4 (Summer 1964).

C. Crawford, *The Marlowe Concordance*, 5 vols. (Louvain, 1911-32) [Bang's *Materialen zur Kunde des älteren englischen Dramas*, vols. XXXIV, N.S. II, V, VI, VII].

S. A. Tannenbaum, *Marlowe: A Concise Bibliography* (New York, 1937; Supplement, New York, 1947).

TWENTIETH CENTURY VIEWS

British Authors

JANE AUSTEN, edited by Ian Watt (S-TC-26)
THE BEOWULF POET, edited by Donald K. Fry (S-TC-82)
BLAKE, edited by Northrop Frye (S-TC-58)
BYRON, edited by Paul West (S-TC-31)
COLERIDGE, edited by Kathleen Coburn (S-TC-70)
CONRAD, edited by Marvin Mudrick S-TC-53)
DICKENS, edited by Martin Price (S-TC-72)
JOHN DONNE, edited by Helen Gardner (S-TC-19)
DRYDEN, edited by Bernard N. Schilling (S-TC-32)
T. S. ELIOT, edited by Hugh Kenner (S-TC-2)
FIELDING, edited by Ronald Paulson (S-TC-9)
FORSTER, edited by Malcolm Bradbury (S-TC-59)
HARDY, edited by Albert Guérard (S-TC-25)
HOPKINS, edited by Geoffrey H. Hartman (S-TC-57)
A. E. HOUSMAN, edited by Christopher Ricks (S-TC-83)
SAMUEL JOHNSON, edited by Donald J. Greene (S-TC-48)
BEN JONSON, edited by Jonas A. Barish (S-TC-22)
KEATS, edited by Walter Jackson Bate (S-TC-43)
D. H. LAWRENCE, edited by Mark Spilka (S-TC-24)
MARLOWE, edited by Clifford Leech (S-TC-44)
ANDREW MARVELL, edited by George deF. Lord (S-TC-81)
MILTON, edited by Louis L. Martz (S-TC-60)
MODERN BRITISH DRAMATISTS, edited by John Russell Brown (S-TC-74)
OSCAR WILDE, edited by Richard Ellmann (S-TC-87)
RESTORATION DRAMATISTS, edited by Earl Miner (S-TC-64)
SAMUEL RICHARDSON, edited by John Carroll (S-TC-85)
SHAKESPEARE: THE COMEDIES, edited by Kenneth Muir (S-TC-47)
SHAKESPEARE: THE HISTORIES, edited by Eugene M. Waith (S-TC-45)
SHAKESPEARE: THE TRAGEDIES, edited by Alfred Harbage (S-TC-40)
G. B. SHAW, edited by R. J. Kaufmann (S-TC-50)
SHELLEY, edited by George M. Ridenour (S-TC-49)
SPENSER, edited by Harry Berger, Jr. (S-TC-80)
LAURENCE STERNE, edited by John Traugott (S-TC-77)
SWIFT, edited by Ernest Tuveson (S-TC-35)
THACKERAY, edited by Alexander Welsh (S-TC-75)
DYLAN THOMAS, edited by Charles B. Cox (S-TC-56)
YEATS, edited by John Unterecker (S-TC-23)

TWENTIETH CENTURY VIEWS

European Authors